LIMITING GOVERNMENT

LIMITING GOVERNMENT

An Introduction to Constitutionalism

András Sajó

Foreword by
Stephen Holmes

CEU PRESS

Central European University Press

First published in Hungarian as *Az önkorlátozó hatalom* in 1995 by
Közgazdasági és Jogi Könyvkiadó, MTA Állam- és Jogtudományi Intézet, Budapest

English edition 1999 by
Central European University Press
Október 6. utca 12
H-1051 Budapest
Hungary

400 West 59th Street
New York, NY 10019
USA

Distributed by
Plymbridge Distributors Ltd., Estover Road, Plymouth PL6 7PZ, United Kingdom

ISBN 963-9116-25-4 Cloth
ISBN 963-9116-24-6 Paperback

Library of Congress Cataloging in Publication Data
A CIP catalog record for this book is available upon request

Printed in Hungary by Akaprint

TABLE OF CONTENTS

Foreword by Stephen Holmes *ix*

Introduction *xiii*

Chapter 1 **The Constitution as Fear and Acceptance** *1*

1.1. Fear's Creatures *1*
1.2. Types of Fear *5*
  1.2.1. Fear of corporatism *5*
  1.2.2. Hungarian fears *6*
  1.2.3. Identity *6*
1.3. Ulysses Binds Himself to the Mast 7
1.4. Definitional Dangers *9*
  1.4.1. The concept of constitutionalism *9*
  1.4.2. The concept of the constitution *14*
1.5. Constituent Power *17*
1.6. What Precedes a Constitution? Order and Acceptance *23*
  1.6.1. Demands for security *23*
  1.6.2. The homogeneity of society *24*
  1.6.3. Citizenship: acceptance and inclusion *25*
  1.6.4. The guarantee of coexistence 27
1.7. The Content of a Constitution: Neutrality or Common Objectives? *29*
1.8. The Legal Nature of a Constitution *39*
  1.8.1. The supremacy of the constitution: protecting the constitution by making amendment difficult *39*
  1.8.2. Amending the constitution *39*
  1.8.3. Binding nature and direct applicability *43*

Chapter 2 **The Taming of Democracy** *49*

2.1. Diluted People's Sovereignty and Weak Democracy *49*
2.2. Majority Rule *55*
2.3. The Constitutional Limits to Democracy *57*
2.4. Referendum and Destabilization *64*

Chapter 3 **Dangerous Liaisons: Checks and Balances and the Separation of Powers** *69*
3.1. The Balancing Act *69*
3.2. Separation and Dependence in Creation and Termination 77
3.2.1. Creation 77
3.2.2. Personal dependencies *87*
3.3. Separate Operations and Joint Decisions *89*
3.4. Additional Counterbalancing Factors *94*
3.4.1. The role of the judiciary in the balancing of powers *94*
3.4.2. The federal (vertical or lateral) separation of powers *95*
3.5. When Does the Counterweight Become Excessive Weight? *97*
3.6. Separation and Freedom *99*

Chapter 4 **Parliamentarism and the Legislative Branch** *103*
4.1. The Transformations of Parliament *103*
4.1.1. The evolution of parliamentarism and its transformation into a representative system *103*
4.1.2. The cooling off of popular sovereignty in parliamentary systems: the free mandate *107*
4.1.3. Parliament: A club for the finest gentlemen *112*
4.1.4. A critique of classical parliamentarism. Party rule and corporatist assemblies *116*
4.2. The Structure and Operation of Parliament *121*
4.2.1. Parliament as an institution *121*
4.2.2. The conditions of free debate and decisionmaking *129*
4.2.3. Parliament's self-determination *134*
4.2.4. Collective participants *140*
4.3. Unicameral versus Bicameral Systems *149*
4.4. The Legislative Process *155*
4.4.1. Primary legislation *155*
4.4.2. Delegation of the legislative function *161*

Chapter 5 **The Executive Power** *173*
5.1. The Discrete Charm of Efficiency *173*
5.2. Who or What is the Head of the Executive? *175*
5.2.1. Kings and presidents *175*
5.2.2. Governments and prime ministers *180*
5.3. The Prerogatives of the Executive Power *183*
5.3.1. The prerogatives in opposition to parliament *183*
5.3.2. Protecting the government: the vote of no-confidence made difficult *185*
5.3.3. The executive submits bills and "fills in the gaps" of missing legislation *189*
5.3.4. The budget *190*
5.4. The Myth of Responsibility *194*
5.5. The Internal Division of the Executive Power *198*

Chapter 6 **The Rule-of-Law State and Its Executors** *205*
6.1. Rule by Law and the Rule-of-Law State *205*
6.2. The Administration of Justice *218*

Chapter 7 **Constitutional Adjudication** *225*
7.1. Who Guards the Guardians? *225*
7.1.1. Madison loses a case in court and gains authority *225*
7.1.2. The victory of judicial review *232*
7.1.3. Interpreting and rewriting the constitution *238*

Chapter 8 **Fundamental Rights** *245*
8.1. Freedom and Human Rights *245*
8.2. Defining Fundamental Rights *255*
8.2.1. Should the legislature be authorized to define fundamental rights? *255*
8.2.2. Which fundamental rights should be protected by the constitution? *259*
8.3. What Do Fundamental Rights Imply? *271*
8.3.1. State power bound *271*
8.3.2. The effect of fundamental rights on nongovernmental relationships *272*
8.4. When Fundamental Rights May Be Restricted: Reconciling the State with Freedom in Constitutionalism *277*
8.4.1. Limiting fundamental rights *277*
8.4.2. The limits to limiting rights *280*
8.5. What Purpose Do Fundamental Rights Serve If Abused? *283*
8.6. How Precise Should the Definition Be? *286*

Since rigidity is brittle and flexibility is resilient, rigidly constrictive constitutions–in the real world of unexpected and dangerous political crises–may be invitations to unconstitutional rule.

A democratic constitution will necessarily impose limits upon office holders, who, even when elected, cannot always be trusted to act in the interests of the people as a whole. But how, Sajó asks, can a "democratic" constitution legitimately place limits on the people themselves? One answer, though debatable, is this: an enlightened community will be aware of its own proclivity to make mistakes and will want to organize collective decision making to improve chances for self-correction and to minimize the damage done by its own impulsive or uninformed choices.

This insight helps explain why a democratic community - which has no illusions about the superior wisdom or virtue of its political "elite"– can support a constitutional order that places restrictions upon the will of the people. The legitimacy of a constitution lies in its consequences not in its source. The public will support a constitution not because it was framed by "immortal" ancestors, to whom blind deference is owed, but because it makes decent governance possible. A consequentialist theory of legitimacy suggests that constitutionalism is concerned not solely with the organization of the state but more comprehensively with the organization of state-society relations. For James Madison and Alexander Hamilton, the principal institution of limited government was periodic elections, what they called "dependency on the people." Sajó makes the same point when he emphasizes the origins of constitutionalism in the capacity of the British Parliament to discipline the king by threatening to withhold taxes. What this suggests is that an effective constitution will not only limit government but will also help ensure that the political system enjoys sufficient support to solve collective problems. The need to mobilize support from all important social forces may also help explain why a mix of property rights and welfare rights characterizes all modern liberal regimes. This uniform combination of latitudes and entitlements suggests that the ancient "mixed regime" is still alive, having simply abandoned the countervailing branches of government (Tribunes and Senate) for the all-inclusive house of rights.

As Sajó argues, the separation of powers refers not to the establishment of watertight compartments, divided on functional lines, but to "partial agency." In a separation-of-powers system, each branch of government partakes of the powers of–has partial agency in–the other branches. Judicial review and executive veto are classic examples–the judiciary and the executive sharing in legislative power. Joint power of appointment is another case, whereby two organizationally independent agencies can be constitutionally compelled to cooperate in making binding decisions. One purpose of this functional overlap or blurring of domains is to help each branch defend its turf against the predictable encroachments of the coequal branches. Power can be checked only by power. Hence, boundaries cannot be maintained by drawing lines, however artistically, but only by creating "a power to bite back" when attacked.

This approach leads constitutional theory to focus on political, rather than legal, limits on the abuse of power, on elections and opposition parties, for instance, rather than on courts. Sajó's discussion of legislative committees of inquiry and oversight–which work poorly so long as the executive controls career opportunities for members of the parliamentary majority–also touches on this important point. In a well-functioning separation-of-powers system, standing parliamentary committees can serve not only to keep the ministries accountable but also as recruitment and training grounds for future leaders of the executive branch. In addition, they can serve what some optimists see as probably the highest and most important function of a liberal constitution, to give power to intelligence. But this, as Professor Sajó might say, is perhaps more of a hope than an expectation.

INTRODUCTION

Contemporary political societies operate in the name of democracy. We live under the spell of equality. Even the communist regimes claimed to be people's democracies, "the only genuine form of democracy." Democracy satisfies everyone's wish to be treated as equal. One may believe that she is more or better than her compatriots, but she will, and has to, accept the assumption of equality. Otherwise, she may loose too much. Her own equality might be challenged. Without assuming the equality of every member of society, every member's equal human dignity, there might be an endless, all-destructive politics of exclusion. This is dramatically demonstrated where there is ethnic cleansing. Political democracy, as we know it, is also a convenient assumption for those who are in fact not equal but more powerful than others. Through the use of democratic processes they, in fact, will keep and perhaps improve their positions. The democratic forms of politics and the legislation created through sporadic elections based on equal vote satisfy the needs of the powers that be. Democracy allows political victors to take their booty without depriving others of the chance of a better arrangement in the future. Put less cynically, democracy allows all the citizens of a state to change public affairs for the better, in a civilized process–at least in principle.

The new governments emerging from the leftover trash of the defeated fascist regimes and Soviet totalitarianism were envisioned and legitimated as democracies. Unfortunately but inevitably, democracy proved a cheap and easy-to-satisfy legitimation for the new regimes. In many of them, the democratically elected governments acted quite often as if their being freely elected justified their unlimited and unscrupulous abuse of government power. The recent history of the lack of discretion among the democratically elected powers in Eastern Europe makes it imperative to discuss and learn those manners, institutions, and principles that efficiently limit all governments, democratically created and controlled or not. Democracy itself might be an element of limiting power, but as it is exercised, it is often only the tool of the tyranny of a majority (or that of a vocal minority claiming to act for some democratic majority).

Constitutionalism is the set of principles, manners, and institutional arrangements that were used traditionally to limit government. But taken so much for granted, it is seldom discussed in any systematic manner, at least these days. This is not surprising. Constitutionalism is closely linked to traditional nineteenth century liberalism, which always escaped textbook definitions and resisted positive description. At first glance both liberalism and constitutionalism exist primarily as a negation. However, at those unique times of creating new political, social, or national structures, the importance and the problematic nature of fundamental choices become clear. After having not even hoped for such change for forty years, I have had the good or bad luck to live through such a change. The constitutional foundation began in 1989, when communism collapsed in Eastern Europe. It was at the moment of foundation that constitutionalism became directly relevant. It was at this moment that old, half-forgotten precepts required consideration beyond mere reconsideration. It was also in this process that one had to learn how easy formal democracies might and will become corrupt in the absence of a constitutional culture. Preaching that democracy justifies all sorts of political action is misleading and offers cheap excuses. One has to understand that it is not true that democratic decisions are acceptable in all circumstances. Constitutionalism is intended to serve as a limit to democracy running amok. Constitutionalism is a kind of monomaniac. It asks all the time: Is this governmental arrangement, is this decision of the power holders, preventing freedom? Is it preventing the curtailment of liberty?

In 1992, Stanley Katz and Irena Grudzinska-Gross, then of the American Council of Learned Societies, suggested that I write a book for the East European public to offer the somewhat missing constitutional perspective to the constitution-making debate. Hungarian and Russian versions of an introductory book were prepared. However, it seemed to me that the issue was equally relevant in more established democracies. But there was no introductory textbook on constitutionalism for students of law, political science, history, or government. There was very little that the general public might use in this area. No book registered in the catalogue of the Library of Congress, written in the past years had "constitutionalism" in its title. There was an intellectual vacuum to be filled. As a devoted follower of Pascal, I fear empty spaces, especially where the intellectual empty space allows for the undermining freedom. The space had to be filled with all the key principles that I find constitutive of constitutionalism. I begin with constitutional precommitments dictated by founding fears of society making. Constitutions–written and conventional–are discussed as creatures of a founding fear. The function of constitutions is to tame democracy and popular and state sovereignty. But constitutionalism, and the constitution serving it, is more than simply a promise. It requires a set of institutional arrangements, and there is more than one governmental structure that satisfies the centralization of power in one person or body. Various forms of separation of powers and checks and balances are discussed, with a review of the legislative and executive branches in their changing internal and interdepartmental relations, challenging each other. Separation of powers was already understood as the precondition to constitutionalism in the French Declaration of 1789. But modern constitutionalism has additional components: the rule of law and constitutional adjudication are these additions. Finally, the book discusses the role of fundamental (individual) rights in maintaining liberty.

The present version of this book keeps many of the original Hungarian and other East European examples, as they show fundamental constitutional conflicts in a most dramatic way and in a contemporary context. Therefore, they have relevance beyond the provincial. Of course, the bulk of this book deals with the classical solutions and founding moments as they emerged in U.S., British, and Continental constitutional history.

I am grateful to the American Council of Learned Societies, the Collegium Budapest, the Reuben Clark School of Law (Brigham Young University, Provo), the Institute of Law of the Hungarian Academy of

Sciences, the Central European University, and the Open Society Institute for their support. Dwight Semler took the trouble of turning a rough translation into accessible English. Zsuzsa Kovács, Kinga Pétervári, and Renáta Uitz provided generous editorial assistance. Those friends who supported me in this venture are aware of my grateful indebtedness, therefore, I am not dedicating this book to them. Instead, I dedicate this book to those who deserve this little treatise: those in power in Eastern Europe and elsewhere, whose arrogance and ignorance compelled me to write.

Chapter 1

THE CONSTITUTION AS FEAR AND ACCEPTANCE

> What kind of trouble could befall a person
> who can govern his country with ceremonies?
> What use would ceremonies be to the person
> who cannot govern his country with them?
> *Confucius*

1.1. FEAR'S CREATURES

Public opinion in postcommunist countries is full of the cobwebs of "constitutional" delusions from the past, ranging from the teachings of the Holy Crown in Hungary to the Jacobin-communist people's sovereignty. For their muddled thinking, the "constitutional theorists" of today, former correspondence students at Marxist-Leninist night schools, are blameless. So, too, are the university professors who cannot distinguish between the division and the separation of the branches of power. There is no one to blame for the confusion–only history. Unlucky Hungarian history, unfortunate Rumanian history, and for that matter, any other history in East and East Central Europe are responsible for all sorts of constitutional ideas. History nestled all sorts of political ideas into people's minds, except that of classical constitutionalism.

Communist ideas about constitutions hold that a constitution should provide a vision, a program. It should describe in attractive but abstract terms what "future" society will become. The promises encapsulated in a communist constitution will then be realized by that wise gathering of industrious "toilers" called to the parliament, or the soviet (council). Legislation will provide social engineering, following scientific laws of socioeconomic development. We saw–though we might have forgotten since the collapse of communism–that this kind of constitution, with its hallucinatory visions of the future, is wholly incapable of fulfilling any real institutional role and cannot protect society from the power of the state. This seductive theory of building a future placed society at the mercy of the state, with the Communist party dominating the machinery of government.

Constitutions–since the basic laws of the Greek city states (*polis*) until today–concern the relationship of the state's fundamental organs and its institutions. If during the process of creating this basic arrangement the principles of constitutionalism are kept in mind, these relations establish a system of limits that allow the freedom of the citizenry to prevail. Constitutions are about power; a constitution impregnated with the ideas of constitutionalism is about limited power.

> [T]he constitution...is the nexus of fundamental institutions prescribing the scope and rightful succession to ruling positions and the authority to use force. Or in a phrase crude enough to miss the saving holiness, "who gets what, when and how" [Laswell]. The constitution is the autobiography of the power relationship, concrete and spiritual, in any human group, and like all autobiographies, it includes some fancies which are not lived up to, and excludes some vices which are lived only too well.[1]

The autobiography of power is a biography written at its birth. That biography is the constitution. It is a biography of a life that has not yet been lived and that is written as dictated by the moment's necessity at its creation. It follows the practical demands of its making and adoption, and it is not enlightened by the wisdom of the Fates. The state, for its part, must live up to this biography. The most industrious readers are the judges who, to the extent they believe in it, seek to compel the state to live according to its preordained life.

Constitutions that serve constitutionalism are not born to foster illusions and promises of revolutionary utopias. Nor do they prescribe a future society's creation. It is not a bright future that such constitutions convey. Instead, they reflect the fears originating in, and related to, the previous political regime. If a constitution has a vision, it should concern a different exercise of power than the past one, which is to be avoided.

When drafting the U.S. Constitution, in 1787, the Founding Fathers had a near paranoid desire to avoid both a monarchy and a popular democracy. Even the paranoid have real enemies.

[1] Herman Finer, *Theory and Practice of Modern Government* (1949; Westport: Greenwood Press, 1970), 12.

In 1787, a rumor spread among the states that some in Philadelphia wanted to restore the monarchy. Nothing leaked out of the discussion hall while the talks were going on; but those present emphasized in their letters addressed to the public that, although they could not foresee the outcome of the negotiations, one thing they did know was what they did *not* want, namely, the restoration of royal oppression.

Fear of Nazi rule and the memorable horror of ungovernability under the Weimar Republic haunted the writers of the German Constitution after World War II. In 1958, Charles de Gaulle wanted never to replicate the parliamentary paralysis of the Fourth French Republic. Fear and self-assertion by denial were present at the moment of great constitutional foundations.

The acknowledgment that fear drives the minds and pens of constitution makers, the admission of human frailty, is not very attractive. Admitting fear, and with it, the dangers of government is not the desired intellectual heritage of those wishing to present the working classes or, for that matter, any citizenry with a constitution they would claim as their own. But isn't it fear that motivates those who deny that fear motivates and that motivates all those engaged in constitutional considerations? Or is it ignorance? Naturally it is a hard sell to make negative ideas acceptable and accepted. But there are more complex reasons for admitting fear. The primordial fear that triggers constitution making concerns the fundamental uncertainty surrounding the whole social order, the possibility that the strife which prompted the creation of the constitution in the first place may be renewed. It is an ancient superstition that one best not continually mention the ghosts of evil. On the other hand, the image of a constitution as the means for creating a rational order, and as an achievement of state engineering, is built on the enlightment tradition, which promises to override irrational inclinations like fear. The modernity of enlightenment is built on the rational suppression of fears, but true rationalism is not oppression but the recognition and comprehension of those fears.

The constitutions of the transition from communism, beginning with the 1989 Hungarian and Polish amendments, also reflected unique fears. Although fear is the only good advisor when writing a constitution, the solutions chosen in 1989–90 could not rid themselves of the earlier cocksure models prevailing under communism. A division of the branches of power is not alien to these transition constitutions which expressly reject the monopolization of power. Yet the Hungarian Constitution (and the Bulgarian one, likewise) made the one-chamber parliament as one distinguished branch of power, the trustee of power, stemming from the people's sovereignty. The Hungarian Parliament has supremacy just like the all-powerful British Parliament but without its two-hundred years of self-limitation and the mild control of the House of Lords. *Nota bene*, British parliamentary supremacy was paid for when its obstinacy resulted in the loss of the American Colonies. British parliamentarism has evolved into a democratic cabinet dictatorship, and most of the nonpresidential democracies in Eastern Europe (Hungary, Slovakia, the Czech Republic, and Bulgaria [at least until the street demonstrations of 1996–97]) are moving rapidly in this direction.

Where a parliament may do anything (bar the restrictions touching upon the essence of human rights), in the end it turns out to be too weak. In postcommunist states, public opinion still expects initiative to originate from the government, as the executive is believed to be "professional." This tradition, inherited from the previous regime, fits in well with the management of party machinery, and it is convenient for the members of the various parliaments too. Given the conditions, namely, lack of time, money, and expertise, and due to the good services of self-proclaimed experts who make up for these deficiencies, the MPs think it natural that initiative should be handed over to government officials. This is also required by party discipline, which in modern mass democracies represents one of the most important limits of traditional constitutionalism. (It does not necessarily follow that the multiparty dictatorship must violate constitutionalism.) In a constitutional system like that in Hungary, where there is nothing to counterbalance the power of the majority except the Constitutional Court and where majoritarianism is mistakenly identified as democracy, the evolution of a cabinet dictatorship is inevitable. In such a system it depends only on the circumstances whether the leadership is found in one person, albeit democratically supervised. If this one person has only as much empathy as Margaret Thatcher had toward democracy or ethnic minorities, then, in Hungary, Poland, and the Czech or Slovak republics constitutionalism will have more difficulty surviving this "lack of empathy" than would England cushioned by its tolerant traditions.

1.2. TYPES OF FEAR

1.2.1. Fear of Corporatism

Speaking of fear in the context of constitutionalism, the writing of a new constitution itself can be a threat. Could it be we let the genie out of the bottle by amendment? For many, a new constitution is threatening because a constitution from "those people" (the current framers) is unacceptable. In most postcommunist countries, constitutions were drafted with the participation of communists or former communists. If long-standing communists are in power, word around town would have it that no constitution could come from "them." The expressions used, "from those people," or "them," is significant. The real danger, however, is that "those people," whoever "they" might be at any given moment, cannot withstand corporatist and bureaucratic pressures. It is a "captivating" stupidity that democracy requires us, the people, to entrust decision-making to the state bureaucracy and other experts. What people accept here as expertise is often only self-interest. And since the experts kindly make expert decisions, they could handle execution and implementation, too, couldn't they?

The central point of this rather obvious misrepresentation is that it is assumed that the public's welfare is served when physicians (the "experts on health") decide how health-care funds should be used. Perhaps, as some "democrats" assert, patients could also "participate," because that would make the process more democratic. Likewise, theater managers would decide what form of subsidies theaters should receive. In this most-expert world everyone has his appropriate role: the taxpayer pays and the audience watches or looks on astounded. This "expert" particularism is what people's sovereignty, with its vision of the *general* will and with the democratic institutions representing this general will, should be destined to prevent, that is, to prevent the interest of the expert shoemakers from being scrutinized when the quality of shoes is evaluated. It is *my* foot that is aching, these are *my* shoes that are soaked through, and all these pains just because of the shoemaker's "expert opinion," which serves his convenience! Corporatism is the dictatorship of shoemakers. The expert is the member of that guild who benefits from the arrangements that are based on "expert advice."

1.2.2. Hungarian Fears

With or without writing a constitution the young Hungarian Republic has to face three menacing dangers. The first is that the overburdened welfare state will go bankrupt. This bankruptcy will manifest itself in an increasingly overextended, hence increasingly powerless, executive. The dinosaur state will collapse; it will die in the midst of anarchic convulsions, burying the unfathomable side of society. It will pass away, not because of its burdens but because its honest, sclerotic spine, which was once created for a nimble lizard, could not endure such weight. The second danger is Carl Schmitt's antiparliamentarism–converted to populist small change. Hail the dictator representing national unity! Hail simple solutions! The third is the neocorporatist order of expert shoemakers: "nobody should interfere in matters that are not his or her concern." A humble version of this in constitution making is institutional "corporatism," the system in which the leaders of the existing state institutions ensconce their own interests in the new constitution with the help of a transparent ploy, namely, that they are the experts who know best how to manage its institutions.

If this is what constitution making can become, it is little wonder that bright, and not so bright, minds are less concerned with the problems and fears that a new constitution should solve than with the threats accompanying codification itself. But if this is what suits Hungarian society–or, let us be blunt, the elites in power–then constitution making serves the purpose of (and, therefore, is the means of) pouring the murky water of the above concoction into the country's tumbler. Constitution making, then, is a bet with God but not Pascal's God.

1.2.3. Identity

Of what is the constituent power that desires a constitutional order afraid? The constitution offers identity, while identification is perhaps impossible. We are the people, but whom can we exclude from among us? And to voice the more dangerous possibility, when can *we* be excluded? Do we have to be equal? Hooray! But are "they," too, equal with us? How can we avoid this? How can we avoid the daily civil war? On what is the constitution *silent*? Upon what concealment is our collective identity built? Fear of ourselves is the fear that is the most difficult to confess. What will happen if we gain power? "Power corrupts and absolute power corrupts absolutely," so says Lord Acton. This is also true about our own power. "People have one serious enemy, their own government," as Saint-Just noted in the debate on the French Constitution of 1791. In view of Saint-Just's performance as a statesman, we have to recognize that he was right.

And what happens if we fail to gain power? All the power that we accumulated will be used by our foes; perhaps against us! We (friends and foes) are better off if the power of the state, and every power that could become absolute, is restricted. It must be limited so that it observes its own rules and so that these rules are acceptable, in theory, to everyone else. It is in this restricted device that a constitution, written according to the dictates of constitutionalism, will prove valuable, providing more than mere legal norms encapsulating a given state organization. (It is possible, in this sense, to have a constitutional government without a written constitution.) There are states that, even acting in full accordance with their written constitutions, cannot exclude the possibility that an organized tyranny will emerge. There are countries that have constitutions of sorts, but they are worth no more than an umbrella left at home during the rain.

1.3. ULYSSES BINDS HIMSELF TO THE MAST

Cunning aids in defeating fear. To borrow Jon Elster's Homeric metaphor, the constitution maker, like the resourceful Ulysses, ties himself to the mast because he wants to listen–has to listen–to the sirens, but he knows he is incapable of resisting the temptation their song presents if he does not tie himself to the mast.

> There are particular moments in public affairs, when the people stimulated by some irregular passion, or some illicit advantage, or misled by the artful misrepresentations of interested men, may call for measures which they themselves will afterwards be the most ready to lament and condemn. In these critical moments...[it may be] salutary...to suspend the blow mediated by the people against themselves, until reason, justice and truth, can regain their authority over the public mind.[2]

[2] *The Federalist Papers* No. 73: Hamilton (New York: Mentor Book, 1961), 443.

The ideas pertaining to various constitutions and constitutionalism differ, depending on when and where we, a people of Ulysses, expect to hear the siren song, and constitutionalism depends on how we tie ourselves to the mast. Keep in mind that democracy is built into constitutionalism, consequently, the song of the siren comes from us; the desire for authority will be our wish (or at least the wish of the current majority).

The first objective of constitutional self-limitation is to increase resistance against the dictates of the actual moment. If our ship sails past the sirens and someone wants to swim back, that is an entirely different matter. One cannot live forever tied to a mast. If one wants to experiment, so be it. At worst, the person will drown, but it was his own decision.

> What is understood by a republican government in the United States is the slow and quiet action of society upon itself [*tranquil rule* of the majority]...It is a conciliatory government, under which resolutions are allowed time to ripen, and in which they are deliberately discussed, and are executed only when mature...But the power of the majority itself is not unlimited. Above it in the moral world are humanity, justice, and reason; and in the political world, vested rights. The majority recognizes these two barriers; and if it now and then oversteps them, it is because, like individuals, it has passions and, like them, it is prone to do what is wrong, while it discerns what is right.[3]

In the name of such tranquil rule, Tocqueville rejected the invention of the "modern age," namely, that of the Jacobins and utilitarians: the absolute power of the majority. He held that the power of the majority cannot be unlimited because in the moral world, humanity, reason, and justice stand above the majority, while in the political world inalienable rights prevail. Tocqueville warns us about making rash decisions that the accidental winners of democratic election lotteries, conscious of their mission, and those who simply wish to become rich as a result of an election victory are prone to make. Tocqueville lived in the first half of the nineteenth century. Modern democracy must handle states that are larger and socially more complex than those existing then. Now states face social problems that are more dynamic and require more nimble

[3] Alexis de Tocqueville, *Democracy in America* (New York: Vintage Books, 1945), 433–434.

answers than were those known to Tocqueville. In the age of electronic markets, a stock exchange can collapse in ten minutes, taking with it national economies and the world economy. It stands to reason that constitutional decision-making mechanisms should satisfy the new demands of efficiency, too.[4]

1.4. DEFINITIONAL DANGERS

1.4.1. THE CONCEPT OF CONSTITUTIONALISM

Constitutionalism is the restriction of state power in the preservation of public peace. It seeks to cool current passions without forfeiting government efficiency. This definition is obviously inadequate, but the imperfection is comforting. Everything that is conservative resists the oppression of definition. Using a slightly counterintuitive logic, one could say that, as constitutionalism cannot be molded into a given shape by giving it exhaustive conditions, it is clearly a rather conservative concept or value.

At the beginning of the nineteenth century, when people began referring to this concept, constitutionalism was an intellectual trend that could be relatively well defined; but it is clear that it did not have, nor will it have, an unambiguous schoolbook definition. A constitution and the workings of a government on the basis of this kind of constitution could qualify in all points for precepts of other constitutions that operate within the framework of constitutionalism. Yet the whole thing simply does not "come together." Constitutionalism is a matter of taste, and taste oscillates around a hard core. Constitutionalism is not merely a legal prescription or prudence elevated to the rank of prescription. Law cannot be a substitute for morality, tradition, or everyday common sense. As great thinkers from Montesquieu to Tocqueville emphasized, constitutionalism has operational elements besides law. "Like the navigator, he may direct the vessel which bears him, but he can neither

[4] Unfortunately, part of constitutional protection is only subsequent and corrective and not preventive. If judicial review of a law comes two years after its enactment, then the violation of the constitution might be beyond repair.

change its structure, nor raise the winds, nor lull the waters that swell beneath him..."[5]

It can be called the genius of the people, or the nation's intellect, or justice, or a reasonable tradition, without which the written constitution is just a mere collection of words. But it would be a mistake to conclude from what has been said thus far that the legal side of constitutionalism is irrelevant and that law does not count where the spirit of the age makes itself felt. The spirit of the age may need formal support, and the legal factor is especially important where the "spirit of the age" has not yet taken shape, where there is simply no constitutional practice nor justice. The question is this: How do we "construct *enduring* forms of political order? The fate of revolutionary liberalism will depend on many things besides constitutional creativity; culture, economics, and geopolitics will make a tremendous difference. Nonetheless, the creative role of constitutionalism is easy to underestimate."[6] Law and constitutionalism, written into law, cannot replace the cement of society, but they are important additives. Sometimes it is the state's role to integrate society, and in such cases these additives become particularly important.

British constitutionalism survives without a written constitution. There, judges cannot review statutes, the majority of civil liberties and rights are not guaranteed by severe protective laws, and Parliament can reshape the political system whenever it desires. Without idealizing the British system, the withdrawal of constitutional freedom in England is out of the question, just as it is in those countries where constitutionalism is protected by a fortress of legal provisions. The vast majority of the public are of the opinion that constitutionalism cannot be restricted or abolished. Neither the Crown nor Parliament would do anything of the sort nor would the ministers or the intelligence services. Those in power probably share this view. Even if freedom is restricted on odd occasion, the logic of the institutions manages to make politicians see that they have been remiss: it is either the time to forgo something or for correction. The exercise of power is *built on trust*, contagious trust. Those in power know what kind of fair play is expected of them, and they act accordingly. They may abuse power, have luxury

[5] Tocqueville, 171.

[6] Bruce Ackerman, *The Future of Liberal Revolution* (New Haven: Yale University Press, 1992), 3 (emphasis added).

cars and expensive girlfriends, or help a school friend obtain a lucrative government commission, but they do not threaten freedom.[7] They step down, according to the rules of the game, if they must. This political system, built on the trust and belief in the observance of conventions, cannot operate elsewhere, for it would be too dangerous. Where else could a parliamentary spirit prevail which is founded on the fact that ministers and MPs are a community, indeed, that they belonged to one social community and all take their share of good and bad? This is why members of the government feel that it is a necessity to answer all questions, and this is why they strive to answer them on merit, even if this is done in the strictest schoolyard style. The reason why a simple statement from a minister is (mostly) considered satisfactory is because it was made (so it is believed) after a careful and unbiased study of all the necessary criteria.

It is not for us to judge whether the British live in self-deception; theirs is an efficient myth that has passed the test of civilization as a result of historic evolution. But in other countries it is simply impossible to operate on such assumptions. With the experiences of an authoritarian system of government behind our backs, as is the case of postcommunism, or in the shadow of an authoritarian system, the basic guiding principle is suspicion. The assumption of postcommunist citizens is that those in power will be corrupted by it not because in all cases corrupt people come to power, but because this is the way things work. We cannot risk making any contrary assumptions. No matter how expensive the constitutional order or how alien and partly unsuccessful legal regulation of the political sphere is, one *has to be suspicious* of the state and of those who exercise power. The fact that those currently in power are above most suspicion, indeed, that they are "on our side" and "we on theirs" (so we believe), the institutional guarantees of recurrent free elections provide little solace. Politicians may go but only be replaced by others. Or they stay–but for too long. This is why Jefferson said:

[7] It may well be that this kind of freedom is a bit old-fashioned and is based on authority; but on the whole, the yardstick is cut by honest and often tolerant officials. For other nations this often seems rather insufficient, at least if one is to go by the decisions passed by the European Court of Human Rights in Strasbourg, which found it unacceptable, among other things, that prisoners in the UK were subject to the decisions of wardens in matters of discipline and probation, without access to a court of justice. It was not the treatment that was unacceptable but the absence of judicial review.

> [Do not] be deluded by the integrity of their own purposes and conclude that these unlimited powers will never be abused, because [they] themselves are not disposed to abuse them. They should look forward to a time, and not a distant one, when corruption in this, as in the country from which we derive our origin, will have seized the head of government...Human nature is the same on every side of the Atlantic.[8]

We recognize constitutionalism, or rather its violation, primarily by experience. We learn from experience that the absence of certain conditions and given practices, after a time or under great hardships, leads to the restriction of freedom and oppression. It is generally not one sign that calls attention to this but a host of signs.

Constitutionalism is a storehouse of experiences, of unsuccessful and despotic governments included, but it is not a collection of recipes. It cannot give concrete prescriptions for a constitution and the governmental practices woven around it, but it can trigger outraged loathing. Our attitude toward constitutionalism is similar to that of Augustine's attitude toward God. The would-be saint bishop said that he could not define God, but he knew what sacrilege was. There is no satisfactory definition of constitutionalism, but one does not only *feel* when it has been violated, one *can prove it.* What brings about this almost instinctive antipathy toward certain acts of government differs from country to country and from age to age. The doctrine of constitutionalism was the answer given to oppression during and after the French Revolution, and it was related to concrete forms of abuse and usurpation. Constitutional ideas and constitutionalism in all ages refer to abuses of power because they exist in the collective memory. The constitutional text, where it exists, can help us to recognize these abuses. It is relatively easy to recognize interpretations that deviate from the possible meaning of the text and practices that violate it. Frederick Schauer likens the interpretation of the text of a constitution to the frame of a picture. From the interpretation it is possible to establish what went outside the frame, even though the canvas gives us no guidance as to what to put within it.[9]

[8] Thomas Jefferson, *Notes on the State of Virginia*, ed. William Penden (Chapel Hill: University of North Carolina Press, 1954), 121.

[9] Frederick Schauer, "An Essay on Constitutional Language," *UCLA Law Review* 29 (1982): 797, 828.

Constitutions are written out of fear of an earlier despotic power, though, having been written, they begin a life of their own. From then on, new crises will add to the original fear, and answers to the old and new consensus constitute what will be considered constitutional. Today, the French consider a system constitutional where the executive power has a distinguished role, because they remember the impotence of parliamentarism and have forgotten the executive authority's idleness and excesses, against which, in 1789, their ancestors originally strove to strengthen legislative power.

Constitutions that have emerged after tyranny and one-party dictatorship are full of apprehension concerning one-party systems and the monopolization of power. Freedom is seen as the institutional negation of the oppression recently endured. Often it is only the reverse of these institutions of oppression that is included in the constitution. In Hungary, and in some other former communist regimes, Parliament had a ghost-like existence, so, after 1989, it was turned into the supreme organ of legislation, whose powers can hardly be delegated.[10]

All means of government touched by the oppressors is seen as suspicious. Constitutionalism, following the advice of suspicion, looks upon everything that gave strength to the former regime with commendable ill will, nearly forgetting that the oppression's technical basis was, in reality, its unique combination and arrangement of the tools of governing. The antiterrorist legislation of 1986 in France institutionalized a series of solutions, the constitutionalism of which is suspect (separate courts, the punishment of terrorist *intentions*, the easing of the conditions under which suspects could be arrested)–though none of this became widespread practice. But in a fledgling constitutional state, all isolated lapses, all exceptions, raise the possibility of returning to oppression, and the granting of exceptions runs the immediate danger of becoming accepted practice.

[10] In Hungary, a funny twist of history or the immortality of office led to the continuity of a strange legal technicality. Parliamentary supremacy was favored by state socialism too, as the communists realized that Parliament could be the most docile tool in the hands of the hidden power. The Act on Legislation of 1987 stipulated the exclusivity of legislation in a number of issues. In 1987, however, the Presidential Council of the People's Republic could still stand in for Parliament at any time. It was this supremacy and exclusivity of socialist legislation that the republic inherited.

A second example will serve to demonstrate how the immediate past, which shaped in a negative way the emerging constitutional order, may rule out the institutional arrangements that are legitimate in other countries that did not share or have already forgotten their decisive historical experience. During state socialism, parliament's authority was delegated to a presidential council (presidium); thus there was no formal possibility for political accountability. Consequently, there is something fishy about delegation in posttotalitarian eras. Hitler exercised power under the law of authorization, so delegation must be at fault. Similarly, for one hundred and fifty years Americans resisted the delegation of legislation, but today the delegation of power is not considered an issue for the overwhelming majority of experts. The French have simply constitutionalized the system by creating original executive legislation, while the Italians consider interim executive legislation acceptable under formal parliamentary review.

The experiences of oppression are inherited from generation to generation. No matter how much it annoys honest Germans, Nazism's denial is still the point of departure for the constitutional order.[11] But even well-defined constitutional fears subside and change with time. For those living in peace and democracy, constitutionalism may become a comforting knowledge taken for granted; the routine of a constitutional state is the source of renewed self-confidence and practical compliance.

1.4.2. The Concept of the Constitution

Lawrence Sterne's immortal *Tristram Shandy* begins with the conception of a hero who barely manages to grow any further in the course of the novel, though we know that our hero exists and things will happen to him. A constitution is what it becomes during its life; but if we wish to define it, we must recognize that its creation is of utmost importance, and what happened before its adoption is at least as crucial as its later vicissitudes.

There are constitutions that are not made–they just exist, like the British, Israeli, and New Zealand unwritten constitutions. Similarly, the

[11] A *Bundestag* (lower house) president, who was well known for his democratic commitment, had to resign for making a remark that could be misunderstood as accepting a fascist idea.

Hungarian Kingdom of the Austro-Hungarian monarchy was without a written constitution, and yet it qualified as a constitutional state in its time. On the other hand, constitutions like the American one can actually be viewed through an exhibition glass, if one is lucky enough to find the right glass case during a school outing. It goes without saying that the U.S. Constitution is much more than its beautifully written script on yellow parchment. The constitution–more so, constitutionalism–cannot be bound to its written condition, though the majority of modern states have written constitutions.

The elements of a written constitution link up in a way with that which might be advantageous from the point of view of constitutionalism (for example, the restriction of power). In certain basic points, because of appropriate prescriptions, a written constitution is more difficult to amend. If the constitution is a written legal document, it is suited to judicial-legal application, making it possible for its attributes to be specially enforced.[12]

Most of the great historical constitutions were created in order to crown and close political or social revolutions, indicating what the given victors deemed important and preventing people from thinking about repeatedly changing the social and political order. Other constitutions were created to ward off revolutions and to restore certain prerevolutionary conditions.

The U.S. Constitution was a pragmatic instrument: it had to correct the functional mistakes of the Articles of Confederation. Yet it had an element of the state- and social-order foundation that Hannah Arendt considered of "enormous, overriding importance," as "the actual content of the constitution was by no means the safeguard of civil liberties but the establishment of an entirely new system of power."[13] At the same time, it closed the revolution; it preserved the achievements of the revolt

[12] According to the advocates of the unwritten constitution, a charter is too rigid, while the constitution that manifests itself in traditions enables a more flexible approach. That the judges have nothing to apply is more of an advantage because it upholds the separation of the branches of power, inasmuch as it excludes the possibility of judges making laws and governing at the same time.

[13] Hannah Arendt, *On Revolution* (New York: Viking Press, 1963), 146. In Arendt's view, the problem of the Founding Fathers was not how to limit government but how to create a power that would prevent the collapse of the existing social order of the newly independent states.

against the British, while prohibiting the "extremist republican-democratic" order institutionalized in Pennsylvania in the revolutionary spirit of 1787.

Constitutions as foundations are created so that a nation in a new condition can declare to its own citizenry, as well as to the rest of the world, that it exists. The newborn baby cries out; consequently it lives. Other constitutions are written in order to delude the public; the "great" Stalinist Constitution of 1936 was created to beguile the world. The world, or parts of it, wanted to be deceived, and it was, for a while, deceived indeed. In many countries, constitutions referring to all sorts of rights have been proclaimed. Perhaps the intentions were good, but what was promised was unfeasible from the very outset. To be sure, there is no shortage of promises, especially if they are made to gain international acceptance.

Various and conflicting political needs appear in one constitution. The German Basic Law was initiated as a system imposed by the Allied powers because they needed a future ally with independent statehood. The Germans then wrote a constitution that was antirevolutionary; it rejected inhumanity and the achievements of Hitler's revolution, but it was pragmatic-corrective, too, inasmuch as it remedied the Weimar Constitution. The postsocialist constitutions rejected the former communist forms of government, but they did not dare be fully counterrevolutionary. They refrained from returning to precommunist structures, and they refrained from denying socialist welfare rights. Further, except in matters of citizenship (Russians in the Baltic states) and communist secret police agents in the former East Germany and the Czech Republic, no serious measures were taken against the supporters of the former communist regimes. A large portion of the populations had vested interests in the discarded orders. On the other hand, a large number of the postcommunist constitutions served as proclamations of new nation-statehoods.

1.5. CONSTITUENT POWER

All the above is mere political history of the origins of constitutions. To be sure, the actual creation process also leaves its mark on what has been created. If one is born with the aid of forceps, the surgical marks remain. Owing to the mother's alcoholism or syphilis, the infant may need to undergo a long period of treatment, generally with lasting impact.

Who has the right to create or put forward a constitution? And in whose name? To whom does the constituent power pertain? Or, taking a different track, whose constitution will be adopted? According to classical constitutionalism, reaching back beyond Rousseau's social-contract theories, the constitution is differentiated from an ordinary statute by the fact that it has the backing and agreement of a *whole people*, and it is actually, or at least in theory, an acceptable arrangement for all the people constituting a society.[14] According to a far more restricted and slightly metaphysical definition, the constitutional compact is primarily a governmental arrangement that enables a society to satisfy certain general requirements, among those being "equality," "the guarantee of subsistence-level existence," and freedom. In this instance it is not necessary to have the actual approval of all the citizens. It is enough to prove that the original arrangement of the regime is not

[14] In ordinary legislation the general popular will *may* be enforced via the representative system, but in practice this will is indirect, and, due to the majority decision, it is usually the expression of a group interest, or an incidental part interest, even though the points of view of other groups are taken into consideration in the utmost degree. The constitution, however, as Bolingbroke has pointed out, meets with everyone's approval. In practice such a constitution does not exist, and the theory was actually popular when no constitution had to be created but could be considered as granted. It was possible to declare of this constitution that it was backed by general consensus or consent. The problems began when efforts were made to legitimate the actual constitution in a truly democratic manner.

A further problem with the general consensus concerns the date of the actual agreement. Should such agreement exist at the moment of acceptance or continuously throughout the time the constitution is in force? It is possible to defend the latter viewpoint too, without seriously violating legal security, provided it is presumed that the constitution is generally accepted and that this presumption can be rebutted only by a popular referendum amending the constitution. Whenever a radically new interpretation is given to the norms of the constitution via constitutional review, this is also frequently perceived as an expression of a new social consensus.

to anyone's serious disadvantage. In the creation of actual constitutions, both approaches did play a role.

The birth of revolutionary constitutions is "irregular." Those who create constitutions in revolutionary times often do so without official authorization. It is rare, even in nonrevolutionary situations, that a completely new constitution is written according to the prescriptions of the old one, that is, a new one is legitimately created under the old one's authority. The drafting of the U.S. Constitution was an irregularity; it was written by a group of men who were authorized to complete a different task. The delegates from Philadelphia were sent by the Continental Congress to prepare the reform of the Articles of Confederation, and this is what they were given authorization to do from the member states delegating them. In a procedure that violated the prescriptions of the Articles of Confederation, the delegates decided in secret to formulate a new constitution that was never officially adopted by the delegating Congress but that, through its unconstitutional consent, did not obstruct the document's prescribed, democratic ratification procedure. (The democratically elected representative bodies of the member states of the future Union and the special state-ratification congresses decided on its ratification.)[15]

Whatever may be the authorization and mandate of the framers of a constitution, the people's will can legitimize their work subsequently.[16] Such popular legitimatization of new constitutions is the consolidating referendum. In 1958, under pressure from the army, de Gaulle was given a mandate to form a government. He accepted on the condition that his government be allowed to write a new constitution that would then be put to a referendum. The procedure was not in conformity with the amendment procedures of the Constitution of 1946. De Gaulle was given the mandate on July 1, with the condition that he respect certain

[15] The U.S. Constitution was enacted in the name of all the people, the only problem being that 95 percent of the inhabitants of the United States were barred from participating in the ratification process.

[16] This was the viewpoint adopted, among others, by the French Constitutional Council when de Gaulle had the Constitution, written under his personal influence, amended by irregularly putting up the issue of direct presidential election for referendum. The referendum affirmed de Gaulle's proposal, and the Constitutional Council found this sufficient proof of constitutionality.

principles. On September 28, 80 percent of the voters–two-thirds of the voting population–voted in favor.

In the age of popular sovereignty, the absence of formal legitimacy, that is, the illegitimate origins of the constitution, does not cause any significant problems. For legitimacy purposes it is enough to declare that whatever happened was done in the name of the people and, subsequently, to bring proof of this when the people in some form or other–usually by referendum–confirm the constitution.

It can happen that state sovereignty is restricted, and in such cases the constitution can serve the purpose of making sovereignty complete. Legitimacy comes from the authority exercising sovereignty, by prescribing certain procedures and giving ultimate approval to the procedure. The German Basic Law was created in this manner. It was first initiated by the authorities of the Allied forces, while approval had to come from the institutions authorized by the military occupants, after they themselves found the Basic Law acceptable. The document adopted by the parliamentary assembly was approved by the democratically elected parliaments of the individual member states; so democratic legitimization was present. Similarly, the constitutions of a number of former colonies, such as Ceylon (Sri Lanka), were formulated under restricted sovereignty, which later on became a source of doubt and had delegitimizing effects.

The classical and, in theory, most satisfactory solution is when a *constituent assembly*, elected specifically for this purpose, formulates, and perhaps adopts, the constitution. This practice originates from the Massachusetts Constitution of 1780. A constituent assembly was convened in France, in 1945, in order to formulate the constitution of the Fourth Republic. As a result of its election, the constituent body received its legitimacy directly from the people. Occasionally a special constituent assembly is authorized to amend the very constitution that mandates the formation of the constituent assembly for this purpose, or it allows the assembly to formulate a proposition for its amendment that is put to a referendum.

The ideas of a constituent assembly do not necessarily coincide with the popular will. It might not attract the nation's will at the ratifying referendum, though it is an open question whether the majority in a referendum is in fact the best expression of sovereignty. During the constitution making process in France, in 1945–46, the framers sought to win the strongest possible public confirmation. Hence the Constituent Assembly prepared only a draft on which a referendum was taken; the proposition was rejected. The proposition of a second assembly received a relative majority, *de facto* nearly two-thirds of the French population did not support it because 31 percent abstained. Still, the new constitution was the legitimate expression of national sovereignty. But was this what the nation really wanted? After the collapse of the constitutional order in 1958, the French public decidedly turned against their sovereign product. Granted, there is no functioning constitution that can satisfy the entirety of a nation. But even though no single party can manage to win the backing of the majority of the population for one text, people can still live in a democracy under a constitution that seems forced upon them.

Sometimes special rules of incompatibility are adopted for the members of the constituent assembly. Moreover, in theory a constituent assembly cannot deliberate on current legislative issues.[17] Another condition, in principle, is that the framers cannot be members of the parliament that is elected under the new constitution for at least one election cycle. This condition seeks to prevent framers from formulating rules in view of their would-be positions. This rule was applied in France, in 1791. The consequences were tragic as most of the qualified, moderate reformers were members of the National Assembly, and in the first Convention, second-rate people, including second-rate provincial lawyers, who could turn radical all too easily (Robespierre's team), were chosen to replace them.[18]

In view of the historical experiences and the contradictory theoretical requirements, to what extent should the constitution-making process be democratic? Since democratic processes expose drafting to everyday

[17] The French National Assembly of 1789 did not fulfil the theoretical requirements of a constitutional body. The assembly was not elected for constituent purposes, and it was the assembly's own idea to delegate a constitution-making mandate to itself.

In the postcommunist constitution-making process, a constituent assembly operated in Bulgaria, but the bulk of its time was taken up with legislation.

[18] This practical objection to non-reeligibility is invalid if the constitutional assembly is convened with this rule in mind; consequently the majority of politicians are free to stay away. If a constitutional assembly has relatively few members, there might be enough first-rate politicians left to fill the legislature thereafter.

politics, to what extent does the need for democracy count if it endangers the success of the process?

The combination of an immaculately conceived constituent assembly with popular democracy's requirements is rare. The text that both society accepts and that offers a workable framework for efficient government is often formulated at secret meetings of a small number of elites (for instance, the United States, 1787; Germany, 1918 and 1948; France, 1958; Spain, 1978; Hungary, 1989 and 1990; and Russia, 1993).[19]

The objection that later became commonplace came immediately to the fore when the first elite, national constitution, that of the United States, was ratified: the constitution reflected the values and objectives of an aristocratic elite. Patrick Henry, the self-proclaimed "guardian" of the "people's rights," had every right to ask at the ratifying convention in Virginia: "What right had they to say, *We, the people*?...Who authorized them to speak the language of, *We, the people*, instead of *We, the states*?...The people gave them no power to use their name."[20]

In all likelihood the American framing process was not the only one in which the objections to the absence of democracy proved somewhat parochial. With the acceptance of the constitution it was not the democratic, small-minded, sparring, and local considerations that determined history. Constitutions generally–and especially the ones that have made history–always rose above everyday common beliefs and misconceptions of the masses. No matter how much the majority insists on its misconceptions, which are thrown out of the constitution, the parochialism, bigotry, and conservatism of the democratic majority are characteristically not the voice of the people. Rather, it is the voice of the mediocre politician who is a slave to election and reelection and who thinks he cannot advocate any values that the voters will not celebrate as their own on election day.

Perhaps this opposition coming from parochialism is the reason why, in the constitutions that made history, the drafters resisted detailing rights. The fundamental question in a constitution is the structure it defines for the state. And even the citizen who is in favor of traditional

[19] The Hungarian drafting was so secret that there was not even a chance to polish the text. The uninitiated participants insisted on the text that they themselves concocted.

[20] Page Smith, *The Constitution: A Documentary and Narrative History* (New York: William Morrow, 1978), 248.

values (nonvalues) and who follows his party's or parish's guidance in the referendum accepts that a government restricting oppression is better than a despotic one, especially if the voter was not among the beneficiaries of the despotic regime.

There is nothing to hide or be ashamed of if attempts are made to isolate the constitution to a certain degree from the will of the majority, even if the majority has been democratically confirmed. Modern constitutional ratification is usually a compromise among party elites; it is a unique elite product that is painted with a democratic glaze. But the constitution of a modern constitutional and democratic state derives its power from the sovereignty of the people, provided that the constitution is not against the people, provided it leaves open the means for the people (the individual voter) to determine their own everyday affairs, and provided it gives them the opportunity to block the acceptance of the constitution or amend it if they strongly disagree with it.

It is never ever written, but there is no politician who would not admit to another in the secluded corridors of parliament that the public does not know what they are voting for or against in a referendum. Where public opinion is free and unencumbered from distortions, a government that deprives its people of their right to vote and the guarantee of their personal safety, for instance, by making one-man rule possible, will not pass muster in a referendum. Hitler's oppressive rule was accepted in a referendum not only because an economic crisis and the aroused instincts of the masses ensured broad support but also because, by the time of the elections, public opinion was taken over by terror, exclusion, and mass psychosis.

A draft constitution's chances are bad, too, when the constitution-making process is *unauthentic*. Authenticity does not come from making the drafting process open but from the personal credibility of those involved in the preparation of the draft, from the fact that the codifiers are individuals who are not influenced by socially acceptable personal interests and whose personal integrity is respected. In this respect, too, it is not a good thing if those who are directly engaged in constitution drafting are well-known politicians, because by and large they do not possess these features.

A constitution that is accepted by a referendum is not of a "higher order" than the one adopted by a constitutional assembly. Both can be exposed to the small-mindedness of party politics and institutions, especially after revolutionary or nation-founding enthusiasm wears off.[21] In the name of national sovereignty both majority and minority parties are able to infuse parochialism into the people's will, hence squandering the opportunity to codify a social compact that will be acceptable for generations.

1.6. WHAT PRECEDES A CONSTITUTION? ORDER AND ACCEPTANCE

1.6.1. Demands for Security

What exists before creation? What is the deeper social function that requires of the revolutionary, the counterrevolutionary, the nationalist, and perhaps even the dictator too, to agree upon or accept a fundamental order? To what does this "fundamental order" refer? It is a fundamental order resulting from government; it is about the relationship between the state and the people, which in given cases, may also include the relationship among the citizens as mediated by the state. (For the content of this horrific legal definition, see the section on state-provided services.)

It is only worth discussing the protection of the citizen from the power of the state, and similarly of its share in state-provided benefits, if we know what the state is for. For what serves such a dangerous form of social organization?

When we imagine a state, we think also that its existence is preceded by anarchy and disorder; life and existence are uncertain. Disorder not only precedes the state, but it can even crop up at any time in the life of a modern politically governed society. The country may be attacked. People may be made slaves. We can be attacked on the street. Thieves may sit on the board of the bank where one's hard-earned money is deposited. This dodgy fear motivates people even when their constitution seems to encapsulate the feeling and idea that their protector, the state, is their own creation. Constitutional texts constitute the archaeo-

[21] See, for instance, the result of the referendum of 1994 in Switzerland, when entry into the European Union was rejected.

logy of popular fears; and history shows that behind the suspicion that the protective state will cheat, there is a more fundamental fear, a fear of a life without the state. There is an underlying fear of the state of nature "...which is worst of all, continual fear, and danger of violent death; And the life of man, solitary, poor, nasty, and short."[22]

Constitutions are full of enabling provisions considered necessary for the preservation of law and order as well as public peace. People are more inclined to accept a restriction of rights (at least other people's rights), to refrain from democratic participation, in return for avoiding disorder. Public peace and safety are considerations that leave people ready to endure government power that is exercised illegally and even oppressively in order to do away with an existing chaos. Among other things, this explains why the majority in Germany accepted Hitler's power with little resistance.

In communities where there is adequate social cohesion, there is no real need for government, as relationships are governed by existing traditions, beliefs, and the order of other nongovernmental normative expectations. When does government's time then come? When the regulations ensuring order have to be formulated artificially, especially when the means by which this condition is achieved are general, central regulations, i.e., the laws that are enforced through force.

1.6.2. The Homogeneity of Society

The cohesive power of the state–the law and the force warranting it–is far from limitless. To be able to live in a political society a minimum of collective identity is required, which cannot exist without homogeneity, a kind of community spirit or collective consciousness. A minimum of homogeneity among people is necessary to avoid continuous strife and to tolerate one another. That minimum is what certain Indians thought about the "palefaces" who happened to cross their lands: they considered whites like uninteresting stones not worth kicking.

According to Rousseau, apart from homogeneity, in order for a "general will" to exist, some sort of continuity is also needed. Furthermore, people should remain close to home or at least within their com-

[22] Thomas Hobbes, *Leviathan* (Cambridge: Cambridge University Press, 1991), 89.

munity.[23] If the chances of extricating oneself from the community are considerable, then society is susceptible to destabilization, relationships become incidental, and interdependence ceases.

1.6.3. Citizenship: Acceptance and Inclusion

The constitution is built on a *dual assumption*, referring to a prior or underlying order. Both assumptions are vague and have several meanings (or the meaning is uncertain). According to the first one, the state guarantees peace to its citizens, that is, *peace* for those to whom we want to give peace because they are identified with us. *Homogeneity* is the second assumption, the uncertainty of which comes from the fact that we can never know *what it is that we have to identify ourselves with*, what we have to live up to in order to be accepted in the political community, who has the right to define identity, and what kind of a peace it is for which we have to give up a significant part of ourselves.[24] At this point

[23] The modern world is characterized by increased mobility. This presents a serious challenge to constitutional order, inasmuch as it brings together cultures and identities that, due to the shortness of time, do not have a chance to adapt to one another, consequently, they may become incompatible. The French constitutional order finds it difficult to come to terms with its Muslim minority. In a similar way, the secular French state and its Constitution found Catholicism in secular affairs an odd diversity that was difficult to handle.

At the same time, mobility compels governments, at least in those countries where mobility is considered "natural," to express the exigencies of world citizens. The world citizen expects a minimum of personal safety, not only at home but from the authorities of all states. Westerners' tentative trips to the Soviet Union were exciting because one could not take for granted that this principle would apply in the case of a communist country.

The European Union (and the European Human Rights Convention) satisfies the expectations of "world" citizenship. In the Union, citizens of the member states have at their place of residence the right to vote for the European Parliament and, in the majority of cases, in local elections. Even the social benefits provided at the place of residence are to be equally allocated among the citizens of the member states, regardless of their citizenship.

[24] The Nazis deprived people of nationality on the basis of irrational arguments, declaring them to be enemies at the same time. Stalin did the same with certain ethnic groups (Germans, Tartars, and Caucasian groups), but the Soviet system required its citizens to identify politically, too, in order to be left in peace, though one could never

we have to make reference to another hidden presupposition of the state and of constitutionalism. To whom does the need for homogeneity refer? To our people–us. And what happens to the person who does not qualify, who is "different?" That person will not become a citizen and the rights will not apply to him. Citizenship is the foremost issue, the definition on which the constitution is founded. But this issue is often answered later, after having established the constitutional order of the government.[25]

In nineteenth-century Europe, the legal status of an individual residing in a given state was not a serious issue: a resident was a citizen or at least a subject.[26] The medieval continental concept of the people (*populus*) was political. Similarly, such political understanding served to exclude compatriots with no property or education from exercising political rights. The granting of citizenship has its origins in the requirement for homogeneity. Lord Chancellor Eldon, referring to this need for homogeneity, opposed the recognition of equal rights for Catholics. In his view the British Constitution was not based upon the principle of equal rights to all men indiscriminately, but of equal rights to all men conforming to, and complying with that constitution required for its security.[27]

How true indeed is Arendt's remark that citizenship–the belonging to a state–is the most important human right. The person who is excluded is deprived of social peace. He who has no citizenship is devoid of the right to protection and unassailability. Nazism laid bare the consequences of exclusion. A fear of such deprivations and the radical changes of Germany's territory in 1945 (the millions of refugees) led to the German Basic Law, which goes into some detail determining in the con-

---

be quite sure whether one loved the country and the wise leader enough, that is, whether one exhibited adequate identification.

[25] According to the Belgian Constitution of 1831, the acquisition and loss of citizenship is determined by law.

[26] In the United States, immigrants, slaves, and Indians "caused" a more difficult practical problem. The early American approach excluded from the nation those groups that the political class considered different, primarily on racial grounds.

[27] Joseph Charles Heim, "The Demise of the Confessional State and the Rise of the Idea of a Legitimate Minority," *Majorities and Minorities* eds. John W. Chapman and Alan Wertheimer, Nomos 32 (New York: New York University Press, 1990), 11, 18–19.

stitution who can be considered German and prohibiting that anyone be divested of their German citizenship.[28]

1.6.4. The Guarantee of Coexistence

Constitutions presuppose and promote homogeneity, even at the price of exclusion, but societies are never fully homogeneous. The constitution either suppresses (or to use a more refrained term, denies) differences in the interest of homogeneity, or alternatively, it guarantees that differences will be maintained within certain limits if the limits are observed.

In the name of homogeneity everyone has a chance to become a good French or Romanian citizen and to be equal in this status. Identification with the neutral yet national constitution or with one another, within the framework of a national constitution, are the constitutional options of existence. According to the 1791 French principle, which became the leading principle for the nation-state, anyone on the basis of the prescriptions of the constitution can become a good French citizen and *French* citizen only. In 1791, the only thing the French state required from the newly emancipated Jews in exchange for equality was that they *swear* allegiance to the nation. When orthodox Jews were reluctant to pronounce the name of "God Almighty" during the swearing-in ceremony, the patriots granting them freedom were astonished and outraged. Granting citizenship generously means that all citizens have to accept the uniform national identity of the "receiving" majority. One had to be a Frenchman and Frenchman only in exchange for citizenship. Another instance of this principle is the example of Breton children. In the second half of the nineteenth century, Bretons were viciously caned whenever they spoke Breton in school (the only language they knew) instead of working diligently to show their gratitude for being so graciously accepted into the French Republic.

Americans were less demanding most of the time. The government is neutral toward most national identities. Paradoxically, the state is held together by the fact that the state cannot take sides with any funda-

[28] According to the prescriptions of the law, citizenship may be lost but only if the person does not become stateless.

mental social or cultural difference.[29] Such accommodationist constitutions allow for the compatibility of diverse identities and indicate only the extreme limits of acceptable differences. For instance, several constitutions declare that some nationalities, perhaps named in the constitution, may use their own language (Art. 23 of the Canadian Charter of Rights and Freedoms (1982)), or that (nearly) all major languages in use are official (India), or, to give a different example, that all denominations are free to exercise their religion within the confines of their own church. The state remains neutral, which could mean either that it does not do anything, as when the state and church are separate in accordance with the U.S. Constitution, or that the government provides its services by taking into account the special features of each fundamental group (that is, it provides education, official documents, and the like in all languages).

The constitutional acceptance of human differences or, for that matter, the guarantee that individuals can differ indicates that living in a constitutional order means not only that the citizen is given protection against government power. Constitutionalism means further that citizens and their fundamental elementary communities are protected from the *rule of the majority*, or the strongest.[30] Providing protection against the majority is especially important if the state in question is democratic and if, possibly, the constitution institutionalizes representative government, which, from the point of view of the protection of citizens and in order to let their political will prevail, would otherwise be desirable.

Rules for the protection of minorities can be quite neutral, but sometimes detailed agreements between given parties (that is, ethnic

[29] It is another matter whether this passivity or neutrality allows for dominance of one or another culture. In the United States, differences of opinion concerning "English only" come to the fore nearly every twenty years, usually following a new wave of refugees and immigrants.

[30] The Fiji and Malaysian constitutions provide guarantees against the economic dominance of a minority, or of a non-native ethnicity, recognizing in exchange the equal civil rights of the minority. (The alternative would be the suppression of privileges at the cost of civil war.) The recurring massacres in Rwanda and Burundi in the past decades illustrate the importance of the issue. South Africa and Zimbabwe are border-line cases. In Zimbabwe, the white minority has been given certain guarantees, but recently the protection of their property rights has become uncertain.

groups, member states, and the like) are necessary. The example of the separation of the state and church (cited above) is a typical neutral solution, while detailed agreements usually appear in federal systems. The Flemish–Walloon problem was settled by the gradual regionalization of Belgium's constitutional order, namely, by transferring the decision-making rights of the Belgian Parliament to the Flemish, Walloon, and Brussels communities' assemblies.

It is certain that the constitution which encapsulates individual and group differences as subordination of one to the other is disadvantageous to social stability. It is also detrimental to both the oppressors and the oppressed, though clearly to a very different degree. "The easing of the conflict of interests and the harmonization of interests–at the fastest possible pace permitted by security–needs constant attention."[31]

1.7. THE CONTENT OF A CONSTITUTION: NEUTRALITY OR COMMON OBJECTIVES?

> Within any modern state, citizens are structurally related to state authority in three basic ways. Citizens are collectively the sovereign *creators* of state authority, they are potentially *threatened* by state-organized force and coercion, and they are *dependent upon the services and provisions organized by the state*.[32]

Since the end of the eighteenth century, constitutions have been prepared to provide a solution for the second problem (the threat by the state). But in order to be able to protect oneself from the state–at least within certain limits–it was necessary to define in the constitution how the will of the state is determined by the citizen's community. The state does not function in vacuum. Citizens are threatened not only by the insecurity and almightiness of government but by the tyranny of the majority or by small groups that refuse to recognize the rights of others.

[31] Bentham quoted in Frederick Rosen, "Majorities and Minorities: A Classical Utilitarian View," *Majorities and Minorities*, 26.

[32] Claus Offe, "Democracy Against the Welfare State? Structural Foundations of Neoconservative Political Opportunities" *Responsibility, Rights and Welfare: The Theory of the Welfare State*, ed. J. Donald Moon (Boulder: Westview Press, 1988), 189.

In the struggle for power among groups, without constitutional precaution no attention would be paid to public welfare.

Madison considered the tyranny of factions as equal in importance to the tyranny of the state:

> By faction I understand a number of citizens, whether amounting to a majority or minority of the whole, who are united and actuated by some common impulse of passion, or of interests, adverse to the rights of other citizens, or to the permanent and aggregate interests of the community.
>
> ...
>
> Extend the sphere and you take in a greater variety of parties and interests; you make it less probable that a majority of the whole will have a common motive to invade the rights of other citizens; or if such common motive exists, it will be more difficult for all who feel it to discover their own strength.[33]

The regulations of the state must be formulated in a manner that the state protects its citizens from groups while not becoming a tool in their hands. Putting aside the inequitable distribution of property, as it was, the religious denominations presented the greatest threat to the division of society. The First Amendment to the U.S. Constitution, asserting antifactionalism, completely separated the state from the church, despite the fact that the political elite as well as the majority of citizens considered religion a moral obligation.[34]

In the vast territory of the United States, the different groups could also be separated geographically. Madison's republican constitutionalism is based on advantageous geographic fragmentation. True, in the several representative bodies the members could set up voting coalitions on an incidental basis (logrolling), which resulted in occasional antiminority (and just as frequently prominority) groupings. In Europe, Madison's idea could only prevail to a lesser degree. On the one hand, the different social, religious, and ethnic groups were forced to live "much closer" to one another, and on the other hand, in the political representation of social groups, the factions could not maintain their isolation. Modern

[33] *The Federalist Papers* No. 10: Madison 78.

[34] In 1789, seven member states had established state churches. The separation provision (the nonestablishment clause) served political neutrality at the federal level. The separationist approach as articulated by Jefferson and Madison expected that states would allow for all denominations to have their own schools and that no Christian denomination should finance another through taxation.

party organizations and election systems enable factions to link up permanently and organize themselves into parties. An incidental association based on a shared interest can become a permanent structure. The parliamentary voting system is ideal for enabling the formation of antiminority coalitions because of series voting. If party *A* is indifferent to *x* minority issue, but for *B* it is important that the minority be injured in issue *x*, consequently, *B* will be willing to vote with *A* in issues *y* and *z* in exchange for a supporting vote in issue *x*.

According to the Madisonian view, the bipartisan, clear-majority-producing system does not favor constitutionalism as a minority-protection program. The one-block majority can be merciless with the minority on all points, and if there are two parties in the legislative body, these groups can also leave those not having any representation out in the cold. It might be justified to restrict the formation of a two-party or two-pole system by constitutionally prohibiting the exclusion of small parties. The prevailing trend, which accommodates nongovernability and efficiency concerns, moves in the opposite direction; thresholds are constitutionalized, prohibiting the representation of smaller constituencies in parliament. But governmental efficiency can be ensured through different, alternative devices.[35]

The prevention of social groups from monopolizing political power has gained new constitutional significance and meaning after the collapse of the authoritarian systems and in the wake of the abuse of state power in the twentieth century. This is why the German Basic Law institutionalized the principle of *militant democracy*. With the same idea in mind, immediately following the fall of the communist systems, the constitutions were amended everywhere, prohibiting any one party or organization from gaining exclusive governmental power. The same provision was generally echoed in the new constitutions.

[35] A common example of the nongovernability due to unstable parliamentary factions is the multiparty Third Republic of France. Here the absence of a majority completely paralyzed the work of the government. But in this system there was nothing that could have induced the members of Parliament to cooperate. The executive did not have the right to dissolve Parliament and thus was completely at the mercy of the anarchic assemblies devoid of party discipline. The Council of Ministers was a true reflection of parliamentary discord. The ministers were under no obligation to act upon the decisions of the Council of Ministers, not even when issues were put up for vote in Parliament (understandably, because they had personal responsibility).

According to classical constitutionalism, constitutional regulation means the submission of state institutions to the law to ensure that they do not interfere with liberty. Constitutionalism requires that freedom as self-government be institutionalized through the formation of branches of power that is accountable to the citizenry. In the twentieth century, when state benefits became important, it was expedient to include the fundamentals of governmental-services regulation in the constitution. There was a simple and logical reason for this. It was necessary to clarify the compatibility between the institutionalization of state-welfare services and the limits on government authority, which was the original constitutional objective. Since until the mid-nineteenth century no one imagined that the state would undertake such a wide range of social tasks, constitutions gave it a free hand, thinking that a minimum of protection of basic rights was sufficient for liberty. On the other hand, new constitutional requirements were formulated with an eye to the state's new activities. Social groups that had an interest in the new activities sought to elevate these functions into constitutional rights and duties. The constitution and constitutionalism came to a crossroads. If one takes the restriction of state activity and limits to government too seriously, the prohibitions on intervention and regulation, which ensure the state's neutrality and protect individual rights, will conflict with the new requirements, making the institutions protecting legal rights the insurmountable obstacles to welfare services. Consequently, twentieth century constitutions had to find forms that would facilitate constitutional monitoring of the welfare state's activities, but at the same time, they had to reconcile the right to benefits with the classical civil rights and liberties that are endangered by the demand for benefits. Indeed, the dependence on benefits, recognized as a social right, presents new threats to individual autonomy and may undermine the conditions for participation in the establishment of democratic state organizations and the definition of their democratic functions. After all, what kind of governmental decision can be expected from those who depend on the state's services?

When reading modern constitutions, one has the sense that they are not about the basic principles of governing and the institutional limits of power. There is perhaps more concern about organizing and guaranteeing the basic institutions of the social structure. Contemporary constitutions are full of special arrangements pertaining to the state's operations and services and the privileges of certain groups. In the socialist constitutions the predominance of a visionary social order was quite obvious. Such constitutions were blueprints for the future and sketchy descriptions of the Potemkin-like functioning of state bodies. Their programmatic nature was one of the characteristic dogmas of socialist constitutions. This distortion, as shown by the state-socialist structure, threatens freedom at its roots.

The classical constitutional order is satisfied with the legal sanctioning of the fundamental arrangements necessary for the functioning of the state. These arrangements are instrumental to the minimum peace, the guarantee of the protection of minorities, without which even the majority would feel itself threatened. This is not to be confused with including special social values or objectives in the constitution. Classic liberal constitutions did not consider such particularism to be their task. Apart from universal liberties, which were taken as a given, the liberal draftsmen did not want unity on a moral basis, nor did they prescribe special tasks for the state. They left the state's tasks to be determined by daily politics, because politics went beyond the constitution, which simply provided the structure of government. According to this liberal conception, the state is by and large neutral, at least at the constitutional level. The state should not interfere with everyday socioeconomic relationships and the shaping of the economy, and it should not set goals for the nation. The public sphere is a hermetically closed world. It is another issue that state neutrality supports the status quo of the existing power and its domination; the rich will become richer, and in the best of times, it is all the poor can do not to lag behind.

Liberalism presupposed that politics would play a moderate social role. Political philosophies that advocate social engineering perceive the state and the government as the means to furthering and achieving certain social objectives.[36]

> Within that structure the primary bond of the state is not the rule of law, but common commitment to a shared purpose; and for implementing that purpose, control and decrees are more appropriate than laws, while administrative bodies, inspectors and tribunals, planning agreements and various types of interest group "intermediation" are preferable to an independent judiciary and police force.[37]

[36] Beyond rational economic objectives, states may strive for spiritual aims, like glory through conquest or salvation.

[37] Noël O'Sullivan, "The Political Theory of Neo-corporatism," *The Corporate State: Corporatism and the State Tradition in Western Europe*, eds. Andrew Cox and Noël O'Sullivan

Separation of the private and public spheres disappears, or at least it becomes blurred, as do the parliamentary institutions and the political responsibility that goes with parliamentarism. Such separation is considered an indication of the inefficient management of affairs and an obstacle to integration.

These attempts at social management, if they are constitutionalized or if the constitution does not provide adequate protection against them, can ruin constitutionalism, which does not usually promise discernible short-run advantages. The state as a task-solving machine follows its own pseudonaive logic. This logic dictates that short, consequently, efficient ways of problem solving should be chosen. This logic wants to and can make itself believe (and unfortunately, the unsuspecting uninitiated, too) that, with its partially corporatist solutions, it can give direct and efficient answers to social problems. Compared with the "simple" and spontaneous solutions of direct-interests representation, the negotiations of classical constitutional and parliamentary deliberation flounder. Classical representative government and legislation are seen as mere formalities that result in a loss of time and money.

After all, why should a privatization process be slowed by court appeals? Why should privatization decisions be run through a parliament that does not understand the first thing about cash-flow? In addition, lurking in the shadows, and not without interests, are the organizations, chambers, trade unions, professional associations, churches, and stamp collectors' clubs that are able to determine among themselves, "in a professional manner," what the "best" solutions are for "interested" parties. Governmental bias often plays a role in determining which interested parties are to be involved in the decision-making process, in selecting the organizations genuinely representing interests, or in choosing from *among* competing representations. The advocates of "social participation" are ready to forget these decisions concerning interest representation, just as they are ready to forget that the organiza-

---

(Aldershot, Hants, England: Edward Elgar, 1988), 23. According to O'Sullivan, the constitution and instrumental (objective-oriented) politics are compatible if the administrative aspect of politics does not become dominant, though the administrative approach will always remain neutral toward the rule-of-law statehood. Modern constitutionalism may be able to confine administrative policy within given borders, provided that clearly corporatist solutions are excluded, and that in the system of values, there is a social group committed to classical constitutional values and their legal protection.

tions representing interests are not necessarily democratically authorized even within the given interest group. In neocorporatism, employee representation is often granted to a government's favorite trade union, and the law determines how the trade unions are to select a representative from among themselves. The advocates of "socialization" enthusiastically rediscover the concept of order (*Ordnungsdenken*)–so widespread under fascism–and promise that all those who are not apparently represented in the representative democracy will receive direct and successful representation through the organizations representing interests. Unlimited representation for everyone! In places where the constitutional structure has not yet had time to grow strong, endeavors to assert interests easily prevail. The proponents of interest representation deny, of course, that the deals made by interest groups and sanctioned by the state are struck at the expense of society as a whole. Some of these interest groups consider themselves to be the only ones who know their area well, and in the assumed possession of this knowledge, they are the only ones who have the right to regulate their area of life. It stands to reason that the knowledge and interests of these groups are circumscribed by their viewpoints, and because of their considerable investment, stemming from their direct interest, these interest representations, in complex societies, can occasionally gain an important role in decision making and regulation, terminating political responsibility and shutting the general public out of politics.[38] That a solution seems predominate or that it fits well into the everyday logic of the interested parties, that is, it is dead simple, is not an argument for its acceptability. A slap in the face is dead simple, but simple slaps are no guarantee of successful social engineering. Organizing the state along corporatist

[38] From a strict political science perspective these are not neocorporatist structures, because the neocorporatist structure typically characterizes decision-making triangles (e.g., employers–trade unions–the state). Although in an attempt to distinguish itself from fascism, neocorporatism emphasizes that, in this instance, there is no state-selected corporation with mandatory membership. According to Schmitter's original definition, corporativism can be defined as a system of interest representation in which the constituent units are organized into a limited number of singular, compulsory, uncompetitive, hierarchically ordered, and functionally differentiated categories, recognised or licensed (if not created) by the state and granted a deliberate representational monopoly within their respective categories in exchange for observing certain controls over the selection of leaders and the articulation of demands and supports. Philippe C. Schmitter, "Still the Century of Corporatism?," *Review of Politics* 36 (1974): 93–94.

lines is incompatible with democracy and the popular representation ingrained in modern constitutionalism.

The state undertakes to perform a number of socioeconomic tasks, and in the end, it finds it is unable to carry them out. For this reason it "transfers" part of the regulatory work to organizations representing interests that in part it controls. If these representations become constitutionally recognized organs of power, the separation of power collapses.

This does not necessarily mean, in theory or in practice, that the constitution cannot include certain social values that are supposedly linked to the homogeneity of society, and that, when the constitution was formulated, were felt to be endangered. For example, such was the section in the Irish Republic's Constitution on the prohibition of divorce. With the state's role increasingly more significant, state goals are included in the constitution, fundamentally threatening neutrality because, in this way, the state's role is to carry out certain tasks to the advantage of some people. This can divide society. By undertaking such objectives and making respect of certain values obligatory, social peace may be threatened, especially if society is divided over the values appearing in the constitution. There is a high probability for disagreements over the tasks, seeing that the prescribed values represent the demands of the current political victors. On the other hand, constitutionalizing welfare is often justified with the argument that society is dangerously divided, and without governmental provision of services, even greater division is inevitable.

By including state objectives in a constitution, they become political in the way that everyday politics is.[39] True, in exchange for this, political issues may be decided not entirely on the basis of power relationships but instead are given a constitutional dimension that makes possible more balanced solutions and may confine political conflicts within the legal framework. But this is an extremely dangerous game because legal forms do not easily adapt.

[39] In 1917, in an effort to perpetuate the armed victory over the conservatives who were supported by the Catholic Church, the Mexican Constitution radically restricted the independence of the Church (not touching upon the free exercise of religion). In the name of justice, the Constitution made land reform permanent, and the Institutional Revolutionary Party gained power. As a result, social division was institutionalized and, to a certain extent, economic backwardness was, too.

Why is it wrong if a constitution includes the demands of social justice? After all, even the American Constitution was written to promote the public good.

The answer is that there is a basic difference between *what is hoped* the constitution will advance and *what is prescribed* in the constitution as an objective to be realized through legislation and other state activities. If a constitution is to be taken seriously, the prescription of an objective has far-reaching consequences, though there is little danger in taking it seriously when it declares objectives and values. Asserting values and objectives may tie up those for whom a constitution promised freedom in a straitjacket. It can happen, naturally, that some will look upon the straitjacket as a piece of warm clothing (consider again the example of homogeneous values in Ireland, where a restrictive value declaration may count on social support until the value's unconditional affirmation exists).

But the state's objectives in its constitution disrupt the functioning of society, because the freedom of social initiative is subjected to centrally determined objectives and means, and such projects may endanger the freedom that the constitution originally sought to protect. The objectives may fundamentally determine the definition of public liabilities. In the name of objectives and values, liabilities and competencies are increasingly assumed.

One could respond to these concerns with the argument that they merely show a disdain of a liberal outlook. The state may have a different, noble mission that goes beyond leaving the citizens' individual autonomy undisturbed. Liberals sanction the given, biased, and unjust social outcomes and divisions. According to their view of neutrality, it is a bad thing if the state follows justice or other abstract collective values and objectives on a constitutional mandate. But who are the liberals to demand the right to determine what the *proper* social order is? State neutrality is not only an unjustified requirement but a fatal mistake, too. After all, it denies and excludes redemption by objecting to the institutionalization of those values that will bring salvation.

To be sure, what is a real value and salvation for one group threatens another group's redemption, and to a third, it is a damnation. In reality, any truth elevated to a generally binding official truth affects the basis of the constitutional order, which is founded on tolerance, on leaving one another in peace. To this extent the state's neutrality is desirable. This is independent of the fact that there is some sort of deeper attraction between classical liberalism and constitutionalism as a limit to state interventionism. Not all liberals claim that the constitutionalization of all sorts of state objectives ruins constitutionalism. The guarantee of certain welfare services and the "social rule-of-law state" can be accommodated in constitutionalism. Within certain limits, constitutionalizing welfare *may* be compatible with the protection of freedom. Early on, many liberals recognized the right to a minimum (subsistence) standard of living, and not because of some Christian duty or because this was how they hoped to ensure social peace. Among other things, they held that this is what transpired from man's right to exist. Legally guaranteeing a subsistence existence is obviously not the same as what is offered by the Russian Constitution of 1993: the right to free university education, free housing, and receiving credit to buy a house on advantageous terms. But a state's objectives, such as "another Great Chinese Wall has to be built in ten years"–and legislation will determine how much work people have to put into this–do not constitute part of the liberal constitutional concept.

It is a rather risky endeavor if a constitution tries to find and encapsulate social consensus beyond basic rights (which can be universalized) and the pragmatic conditions of social peace. Such ambitious projects are but an opportunity to impose biased points of view. Constitutional history indicates that social systems often continue to exist by *concealing* conflicts among values and not by endorsing a special orientation. In some instances the conflicts were resolved; in others civil war was held at bay for decades. Such was the case in the United States, in 1787. The compromise on the slavery issue was that it would not be dealt with on a constitutional level until a new generation was ready to address it. The Constitution itself contained a moratorium until 1808. When the gag rule was no longer followed, a deadly civil war erupted.[40]

[40] Stephen Holmes, *Passions and Constraint* (Chicago: University of Chicago Press, 1995), 202–234. For a century, Belgium treated the denominational-schools issue with the same reticence (because it would have divided the country completely). When the issue finally surfaced, it proved unmanageable.

1.8. THE LEGAL NATURE OF A CONSTITUTION

1.8.1. THE SUPREMACY OF THE CONSTITUTION: PROTECTING THE CONSTITUTION BY MAKING AMENDMENT DIFFICULT

The constitution is primarily effective when and if it is binding. Mere declaration, if not strengthened by some form of religious belief, cannot influence actions. As the creations of modern states, constitutions assume prevalence in the legal sphere.

In itself, a constitution's normative nature, and the fact that it is made legally binding, says very little. To have the ability to determine the legal system, a constitution must be above all other legal regulations. It is the starting point and the closing argument of a legal system.[41]

In England, the laws guaranteeing constitutionalism, if these principles have been written down in laws at all, can be amended at any time by other laws. In other political cultures this would render constitutionalism impossible. The supremacy of the constitution as legal regulation has to be ensured with the help of legal, technical means.

1.8.2. AMENDING THE CONSTITUTION

No matter how technical it may seem, amending a constitution is an essential element of the document itself and of constitutionalism. The current and latent crisis of Hungarian constitutionalism is proof of this. If the constitution can be changed like any other law, as is the case in Hungary (with a supermajority), then there is nothing to guarantee its supremacy in the legal system. In the absence of rigorous amendment procedures, a constitution can become the victim of incidental considerations at any time, if any one of its prescriptions were to obstruct a current legislative improvisation or a prevalent legislative interest. The blessed self-restriction dictated by the constitution would cease to exist,

[41] The U.S. Constitution (Art. VI, sec. 2) declares that it and the laws of the United States (together with the international treaties adopted by Congress) are the supreme laws of the country. This principle refers to the supremacy of federal law as opposed to the laws of the member states and not to the relationship between the Constitution and other legal regulations. The Founding Fathers, however, agreed on the Constitution being above all laws. This is the principle upon which the Supreme Court acted.

whereas it is the task of the constitution to ensure it. With an easily amendable constitution all its guarantees would cease, too. The intimate relationship with the people's sovereignty, which was so important when it was created, would discontinue. The legitimacy of the whole political system would be threatened if the content of the constitution were to appear as, or become part of, the ordinary political bargaining process.[42]

Of course, constitutions are not immutable. In the name of democratic justification, Thomas Jefferson held that all generations should have the opportunity to amend their constitution; because what they inherited was not formulated with their participation, and earlier generations had no right to determine how future generations should live. Obviously, Jefferson's ideas did not win the day. The U.S. Constitution has proved one of the most stable texts in legal history. New generations simply grow into its neutral order, which can adapt to changes by judicial and administrative practice (with support from Congress) without having to modify the text.

Since 1787, the U.S. Constitution has been amended only seventeen times. It is even more remarkable that the original text, with the exception of the provisions on the Senate and presidential elections, has not changed. The text has only been amended, that is, supplemented. (Of course, a supplement may add something that results in major change, like women's suffrage). On the other hand, during the past forty odd years, the German Basic Law has undergone several major amendments and has changed in at least one hundred and twenty points. The Austrian Constitution, during the past seventy years, has been amended or supplemented with a stunning six hundred constitutional laws.

[42] From a technical point of view this is exactly the principal problem with the uniquely ambiguous Hungarian Constitution. Besides the "leniency" of these provisions, the theoretical problem with this solution is that there is no strict rule protecting the regulation on amendment itself, consequently, it is void of self-binding force. (The regulation on amending the constitution should be more severe than the procedure of amendment itself.) It is easy to see that an incidental political coalition could quickly amend the Constitution at its discretion. Examples from the first eight years of the new democracy are telling. Between 1989 and 1994, at least 10 percent of the Constitution has been changed or has been supplemented; there was no year without amendments (except 1993). After a moratorium, a new set of amendments was adopted in 1997. Without exception the amendments were linked to the introduction of laws that went against the current Constitution or simply served personal views and convenience.

If there is a general social and political consensus, the technical difficulty of constitutional amendment is not a real obstacle. But no doubt a large number of amendments indicates that amendment procedures can be rather lax. On the whole, the German Constitution is easy to amend, with the exception of a few seemingly unamendable basic-rights provisions and the provisions on the rights of the member states. All that is needed for amendment is a two-thirds majority in both houses. This, at first glance, is hardly more than is prescribed by the Hungarian Constitution. But in Germany, approval of the majority of the member states (member-state governments) is necessary.

Even if the amendment power is reserved for the parliament, amendments can be made difficult. In the Norwegian and Dutch systems, whenever a modification proposal is accepted, the legislature is dissolved, and it is the new parliament that has the right to adopt the proposed amendment, turning the elections into something like a quasi referendum. Politicians and MPs will obviously not risk their mandates in the middle of a term for the sake of an anticonstitutional law, be it so dear to them.

A referendum seems to be a more "democratic" procedure than the Norwegian and Dutch practice because, in reality, in most cases it makes the amendment of the constitution easier. The referendum method is applied by a number of the American states, Switzerland, Australia, France, and wherever the Fifth Republic is a model (for example, the current Russian Constitution). But even the French are careful with referenda. According to French law, the unanimous approval of both houses is necessary to initiate an amendment to the Constitution, and a referendum can be avoided if the two houses act as a "congress" on the recommendation of the president. In such instances, three-fifths of the votes of a "congress" are enough to adopt an amendment. This makes the French Constitution, whenever the candidate of the parliamentary majority becomes the president (as in 1995), one of the easiest to amend in the world.

Amendment of the Swiss Constitution may be initiated by the public, too (at least one-hundred thousand signatures have to be collected within eighteen months). The Swiss federal legislature has initiated the amendment of the Constitution in more than one hundred cases, in the last one hundred and thirty years, with about a 70 percent success rate. By contrast, the public initiative was successful only eight times during the last one hundred years, an indication that this form of constitutional amendment is not really promising.

In many federal states, the results of a referendum in the given majority of the member states have to be favorable to the amendment. The U.S. Congress can recommend (with a two-thirds majority in both houses) amending the Constitution, or two-thirds of the member states may convene an assembly to make a recommendation. A proposal has to be approved by three-fourths of the member states' state legislatures or at conventions held specifically for this purpose. (In this respect the legal regulations of the member states are applied.) No wonder that in 1787–88, with the exception of the previously planned first ten amendments (the Bill of Rights), there were practically no other modifications, and with the exception of the amendments after the Civil War (when those who opposed equality lacked political representation), amendments have been concerned with the technique of government. A second exception is the Prohibition Amendment, which was passed on "moral" grounds.

Easy amendments result in loss of prestige. It is more than a matter of expediency to structure basic rights as unamendable, at least in the sense that they cannot be narrowed. This is the approach of the German Basic Law as interpreted by the federal Constitutional Court. Compared with the amendment through referendum, more security is offered by the Dutch method of amendment, which is based on the mandatory dissolution of its Parliament. Amendment by referendum might still be appropriate in matters regarding national sovereignty and government structure. Simplified and easier methods of amendment might be expedient regarding specific issues. The Russian Constitution of 1993, for example, recognizes different procedures of amendment, offering more protection against changes of fundamental rights. The application of simplified and easier procedures may not only be permitted but also desirable, when amendments concern the transfer of sovereignty to an international organization in matters of economic legislation and when they concern further amendments stemming from membership in the organization. This condition is an express prior constitutional authorization, referring to the joining of the given organization and a preliminary constitutional review of any specific proposal. Such a mechanism is required for joining the European Union. It is the specific state's constitution that should lay down the ratification process for joining the Union.

1.8.3. Binding Nature and Direct Applicability

The fundamental law's features and its supremacy are in themselves not enough to determine for whom the constitution should be considered binding. Does it refer only to legislation or to all state organs? And, as a consequence of this binding force, is it possible to quote the constitution in all courts? To what extent is it possible to apply the constitution's prescriptions directly?

Socialist theory considered the constitution a programmatic document. It was a program and a guide for legislation. This suggests that it could not be directly applied in a court of justice.

In contemporary rule-of-law states the constitution is binding as the state's fundamental law (its supreme law) because of the manner of its making or ratification. The popular mandate of the draftsmen or the subsequent ratification procedures make the constitution the most general expression of popular will, a nation's highest ranking legal norm. But this popular-social compact, or at least the acceptance of submission, is not without its problems, because a respectable constitution is made respectable not only by its superlegitimate adoption but also by its aging. Contrary to Jefferson's opinion, use will consolidate a constitution. But even if there is no popular revision of the old constitution, it needs current application and practice (judgments) to give it strength and contemporary meaning.

A rule-of-law state accepts that its constitution has normative binding force, but because of the differing views on the structure of the legal system and the function of the courts, widely differing meanings are attributed to its normative character. In countries where judicial review is accepted practice, the application of the constitution means by and large that in a court hearing a given case may examine whether the law to be applied corresponds to the prescriptions of the constitution. Further on, in the absence of other concrete and applicable legal prescriptions, in case of direct applicability of the constitution, the relevant provisions of the constitution will apply as the basis for decision making in given cases.[43] According to a more conservative opinion, only specially formulated constitutional provisions can be applied directly:

[43] If a rule can be applied directly, Anglo-Saxon terminology defines this as a self-executing rule. In the European Union this is referred to as direct effect.

> A Constitution is primarily a declaration of principles of fundamental law. Its provisions are usually only commands to the legislature to enact laws to carry out the purposes of the framers of the Constitution, or mere restrictions upon the power of the legislature to pass laws, yet it is entirely within the power of those who establish and adopt the Constitution to make any of its provisions self-executing.[44]

This assumption may be true, but the majority of classical constitutional rules either expressly declare a right or are rules of competence, and as such they contain clear-cut obligations. It is relatively easy to interpret constitutional prohibitions, too. The effect of prohibitions is direct, which means that a regulation violating a prescription does not need to be heeded, provided judicial review exists in the given constitutional order. The situation is different when a state's constitution lists the general tasks of government. These sections may be read as gospel, because, according to prevailing views, no court, even in fully fledged judicial-review countries–save special cases–can make the state carry out state objectives and tasks in a prescribed manner. This seemingly technical problem of wording may undermine the prestige of a constitution and that of its courts.

Let us take Section 27 of Article I of Pennsylvania's state constitution as an example:

> The people have a right to clean air, pure water, and to the preservation of the natural, scenic, historic and aesthetic values of the environment. Pennsylvania's public natural resources are the common property of all the people, including generations to come. As trustee of these resources, the Commonwealth shall conserve and maintain them for the benefit of all the people.[45]

What is the effect of this rule? Can a Pennsylvania court apply it directly in order to settle a dispute? If there is no law on the protection of historical landmarks, can a court say that the legislation is guilty of negligent omission on the basis of the state's constitution? Can it induce the legislature to legislate? Constitutional courts are the ones that have such authorization, but not ordinary courts. Even if a court has such

[44] *O'Neill v. White*, 22 A. 2d 25 (Pa.1941).

[45] Section 27 of the Constitution of the State of Pennsylvania was adopted by a referendum.

powers, what can a constitutional court do, or any court that has a right to conduct judicial review? It can register the omission, but it cannot make a law.[46] What is more, a court will lose its prestige if the opportunity to blame legislation for omission is taken advantage of too frequently.

A Pennsylvania court of first instance declared a building permit to be valid because, according to the jury, the building did not violate the right to a historical memorial site. On appeal, the court held that since there was no specific law on the protection of historical monuments, there was nothing that could be applied in the given case. The Supreme Court of Pennsylvania could have held that it would apply the Constitution's relevant provisions and that it would judge for itself whether the building in question violated the memorial site. But the court declined to do so, arguing that if they admitted the possibility of direct application of the Constitution, then the executive could make decisions on the issue without any further legislative guidance.[47]

Determining the tasks of the state creates a specially tense situation because it prescribes constitutional obligations, the realization of which cannot be forced by courts. If a court takes it upon itself to decide which actions the government should take to satisfy the government's constitutional mandate, it will usurp the powers of the legislative or the executive branch, like the American judge who prescribed state financing of a school in order to provide competitive education for the children of the poor attending it and to enable them to have access to the same kinds of educational facilities as students living in more affluent districts. If a court fails to reach decisions on merit but declares and mandates that the constitution shall be specifically implemented by the legislature, that court condemns the legislature, perhaps without any result. Although judges lend credit to the constitution's principles, they

[46] According to the Swiss Civil Code, the judge, in the absence of a legal regulation, may act as a legislator. French law expressly prohibits judges, citing the absence of a pertinent legal regulation, from refusing to decide on merit.

[47] *Commonwealth v. National Gettysburg Battlefield Tower*, Inc. 302 A. 2d 886 (Pa. Commw.) Aff'd 311 A. 2d 588 (Pa. 1973).

In the U.S. it is not common at the federal level to find that the legislature has an obligation to legislate on a specific issue, because in conformity with the text of the Constitution, the states do not have *positive* obligations to further the course of justice or to carry out governmental tasks.

do not enforce the provisions of the constitution in actual cases and do not provide remedy to those concerned by the promises of the constitution. This is a loss of prestige for the entire legal system, including the courts.[48]

Enforcing the constitution becomes a seemingly more straightforward matter if the constitution indicates that a given issue *needs* further regulation (for example, "this matter shall be regulated by law," or "the law shall determine the details"). Such a norm obviously says more than some general formula, like "the Hungarian Republic respects the institution of the family." But, as is the case with the Hungarian Constitution, the delegation technique may prove counter–productive. Ostensibly, in order to protect various basic rights–or in other areas in order to exclude legislative delegation and to strengthen parliamentarism–the Constitution in many cases uses the phrase "the law shall provide for [the given issue]." For example, Art. 57 (5) of the Hungarian Constitution reads: "according to the pre–scriptions of the law [statute] everyone may request legal remedy…" If there were no reference to the law, the rule in the Constitution would be directly applicable and only the selection of the competent forum would require specification. But here, in the absence of an appropriate "enabling" law, there is no recourse. At most, the Constitutional Court can declare–to be taken into consideration or not–that Parliament committed a legislative omission.

Paradoxically, the above wording does not usually serve the purpose of making a right unenforceable, permitting the constitution to be depreciated by the legislature. (Such ill-willed intention would be difficult to deny in connection with the declaration of the right of asylum in so many–"as-determined-by-law"–constitutions.) By allowing the fundamental right or the basic institution to be regulated by legislation, the executive is prevented from exercising direct regulation. Hence the executive's inevitable rights-restrictive tendencies are curtailed. But there is a price: What if the legislature fails to pass the required laws? Sometimes legislation is politically incapacitated. In many

[48] Certain alleviation is brought to this nonenforcement if the court can order the state to pay compensation for damages caused by the negligence of the legislature, as is the case in the United States. Since the 1991 *Francovich* case, if a member state of the European Union fails to transfer the community norm to its legal system, it is liable for any resulting individual losses (Francovich v. Italy [1991] ECR).

instances, for safeguard reasons, a two-thirds majority is required to pass certain laws. If one did not insist on the idea that without the state there would be no liberty, we would not have to interpret the words of the constitution in a way that makes us think that a law needs to be written for every freedom, because without this crutch, freedom would only be able to limp along.

For instance, the Hungarian Constitution reads: "a two-thirds majority vote of the MPs present is required for the adoption of the law on the prevention of media monopolies." As the victim of this obsessive idea–that constitutionally stated freedoms need legislative enactment–the Constitutional Court held that such a *law had to be passed*, otherwise the monopoly would never cease. This would logically follow from the fact that the government actually never did anything on its own initiative to end this state of affairs, namely, it failed to allocate frequencies for commercial broadcasting, and in conformity with the logic of no-direct-applicability, the inaction could not be challenged in an ordinary court. On the other hand, broadcasting without a license was considered illegal.[49] In theory the media monopoly would have ceased to exist by a simple government declaration and through governmental auctioning of frequencies. Of course, if all freedom is expected to come from the state and from its encouraging-enabling and protective actions, the result–in the absence of an appropriate legislative act–will be the consolidation of an anticonstitutional situation. A preferable situation would have had the government at its own discretion (and while still abstaining from making concrete decisions) let the private media in. A more straightforward solution would have been for the Constitution to prohibit media monopolies. Either there are no legislative tasks here and everyone consequently may broadcast (like in Romania after the 1989 revolution) until the participants manage to come to an agreement, or, because of the pressure to put an end to the chaos, the legislature resigns itself to action, regardless of a constitutional obligation to do so. The dictates of legislation are political; only their limits are constitutional.

[49] A similar fact pattern resulted in the condemnation of Austria by the European Court of Human Rights in the *Informationsverein Lentia* and others. *v. Austria* case (Ser. A 276 (1993)).

Chapter 2

THE TAMING OF DEMOCRACY

At present the biggest danger is
the tyranny of the legislature.
Thomas Jefferson

2.1. DILUTED PEOPLE'S SOVEREIGNTY AND WEAK DEMOCRACY

Constitutions are about the restriction of government power. At the beginning of the evolution of the modern state, government power was said to be a force that could be neither restricted nor resisted. According to Bodin, the ruler is not bound by anyone or anything. In the first attempts to separate the state from the ruler, the state "inherited" the ruler's unresistable and supreme power. State sovereignty means that the authority of the territorial state prevails exclusively over the people living within its borders. Another state or external forces cannot have say in the lives of the subjects of a given state nor can they interfere with the decisions pertaining to the given territory.

According to the democratic principle, government can function only if it has the approval of those governed. The most perfect form of approval is where the citizens themselves apply self-government, obeying laws they created for themselves. "Self-government" may take the form of representative or direct democracy. Democratic government for the people is realized by the people, with the laws embodying the wishes of the people.

Rousseau inverted the notion of the sovereignty of the monarch and the state for the sovereignty of the people. This is a wonderful idea if it means that no one has the right to rule the people and that the citizens only may govern themselves.

But people's sovereignty was too big a bite; so great a power can be managed only if it is sliced up. Rousseau, however, seduced by the totality of power, did not want to hear of the division of powers.

Before the shift to the sovereignty of the people, the power of the state or that of the monarch was derived from the original power that the nation, or the people, had over themselves in a manner that the ruler was assigned in a contract the right to dispose over the people by the people themselves. According to Locke, this contract does not mean a complete resignation of rights. The people will retain at least as much power as will enable them to take back the rights they assigned, if the government does not live up to the trust placed in it and violates the original contract. Rousseau went one step further. In his opinion the people cannot lose their freedom through the social contract. Citizens continue to exercise their rights even when organized into states.

At this point, partly because the direct expression of a people's will would present insurmountable technical difficulties in an area larger than a city state, Rousseau's reasoning takes a strange turn. In a society organized by the state, the original freedom that prevails in the state of nature would become unimportant; because after the political society has been established, the individual's moral character will become fully developed. Consequently, in the civil society, the general will pertains to society. It would be wrong to say that the will of the majority will express the general will. The standard formulation that occurs in many constitutions, namely, that the people are the source of all power, does not satisfy Rousseau's ideal.

Rousseau turned his mysterious notion of the "general will" into the source of law and linked popular representation with the legislative function, providing the basis for the misbelief in the supremacy of legislation where supremacy originates from legislation being the manifestation of the will of the people. Rousseau's ideas allow for many interpretations. One of the interpretations suggests that the general will has to be manifest in the law. The minority simply failed to recognize the general will, and the citizen belonging to the minority has to be grateful when the will of the majority is imposed on him, because this frees him from having to suffer his own mistake–failing to recognize the general will.[1]

[1] Undoubtedly, in many cases people tend to follow after a time what they voted against as a will coinciding with their own. Thus once a contested bill becomes a law, it becomes a respectable reality, getting nearer to the expressed majority will because of the well-known normative force of facts. In the normative sense, the "partial" will in-

That the citizen might be divested of his fundamental rights on account of the above "correction" of his mistake, did not concern Rousseau. Benjamin Constant, on the other hand, said that the realization of the French Revolution's objectives–the program of the Enlightenment–was derailed by Rousseau's idea of the people's will. He held that Rousseau was almost indifferent to how the general will was expressed. It is not necessary for the people to exercise power as it is not the people who continuously determine and form sovereignty.

According to Rousseau's ideas, as the people and the state converge, it is not important to build a wall between the individuals comprising the people and their state. Indeed, in certain cases he expressly opposes this in the name of the establishment of a unified will. People's sovereignty cannot be transferred, so there is no call for representation. But since there is no solution to the expression of absolute and monolithic power, in the end it is irrelevant how the people's will is determined as all will expressed by representation is distorted. Rousseau is pathologically afraid of revolt, and of his favorites–the people–he says all that they need to do is indicate what they think, especially if they find that the government has become estranged from the constitution.

Here Rousseau created a deadlock: because for people to be able to create laws that comply with the general will, they must become what they would become as a result of the law created by themselves. A cheap solution is used to show the way out–a man sent by Providence becomes Rousseau's legislator. What begins as universal participation ends as one man's rule. Surprise, surprise: the passage on the providential messenger who brings the law onto us–a prophecy, perhaps?–became Napoleon's favorite quotation from Rousseau. It is also not surprising that the sovereignty of people remained an attractive ideal for politicians. If the politician wins, if he acquires the representation of the sovereignty of the people, he gains total power.[2]

When Abbé Siéyes replaced the "empirical" people with the *nation*, he simply changed the form of the basic mistake hidden in Rousseau's concept of people's sovereignty. This substitution divested the people of

---

deed becomes the only accepted, enforced and, in this sense, "general" will, which is binding to all people.

[2] Benjamin Constant, *Political Writings*, trans. and ed. Biancamaria Fontana (Cambridge: Cambridge University Press, 1988), 175.

its direct influence, but the abstraction of the nation, replacing or ousting the people, as applied between 1789 and 1815–and since then–has turned into a nationalist slogan. The rule of those declaring themselves the representatives of the nation is just as despotic as the rule of those who represent no one but themselves.

The state and society become one in the idea of the sovereignty of people and the sovereignty of the nation, which replaces the people. Or do they just get mixed up? Their homogeneity or *concordia* is upset by the antidemocratic separation of powers advocated by nasty liberals and by the restriction of power demanded by constitutionalism. This objection appears in the works of Carl Schmitt, too, disguised as description. But it was the state-socialist order that came the closest to the indivisible unity of state power. It served the unity of the workers and peasants, with the intellectuals graciously included in the holy trinity, conjuring up the image of a harmonious society.

It was the result of a long evolutionary process that constitutionalism managed to incorporate democratic elements, including popular representative democracy, into its system restricting despotism. Liberal thinking considered Rousseau's ideas dangerous. According to the advocates of liberal constitutionalism, indivisible sovereignty puts the individual at the mercy of the state because it eliminates the separation of power that protects the individual in favor of an imaginary social unity. The concept of liberal constitutionalism was formulated by those who suffered totalitarian persecution during the French Revolution. Later supporters of the constitutional state shared these victims' contempt of the popular will. Max Weber considered popular will a fiction and democratic self-government impossible. "It is like the customer's knowing when wanting to buy a pair of shoes what kind of abilities the shoemaker should have. The customer knows where the shoes *pinch*, but never knows how to make them a perfect fit."[3]

[3] Letter to Michels, 4 August, 1908, quoted in Wolfgang J. Mommsen, *Max Weber and German Politics: 1890-1920* (Chicago: University of Chicago Press, 1984), 395.

Weber's reservations concerning democracy represent a view that was not only widespread in Germany. In Leo Strauss's view, Hegel's *Legal Philosophy* had already discussed constitutional monarchy as a system where legitimacy is not related to democracy. The system is legitimate because power is in the hands of highly qualified officials appointed by the monarch, and human rights are respected. Leo Strauss, Preface (1962) *Spinoza's Critique of Religion* (New York: Schoecken Books, 1965).

A certain democratic interpretation of popular sovereignty, namely, that all power comes from the people and with their collaboration, was nevertheless linked to the idea of constitutionalism. This relationship precedes the times of mass revolutions. The U.S. Constitution supports the separation of powers and the will of the people simultaneously.[4] Whether this is a realistic possibility or a mythical marriage, and to what extent people believe in it, is a different matter. But at least from the U.S. perspective, both separation and popular will serve freedom and suppose that popular will takes the form of self-government:

> We Americans think of ourselves as politically free. We believe in self-government. If men are governed, we say, then the governing must be done, not by others, but by themselves. So far, therefore, as our own affairs are concerned, we refuse to submit to alien control...Governments, we insist, derive their just powers from the consent of the governed.[5]

Constitutionalism is suspicious of democracy, but this does not necessarily mean that there is animosity. Putting aside what its individual representatives thought of popular power, constitutionalism is basically neutral on this issue so long as democracy does not threaten to become despotism. In general, modern constitutions expressly recognize equal and universal voting rights as the basis of the political system and of the legitimate exercise of political power. The American Founding Fathers believed in the nation (after they had shrunk the circle of those who belonged to it). Constitutionalism and constitutions cannot simply disregard the most popular legitimatizing theory of our age—namely, democracy. Nevertheless, exercising democratic power could also pose a threat to liberty and basic rights. Constitutionalism, though it has adopted under modern conditions some of the elements of the democratic political process, attempts to tame the people's democratic rule. Constitutionalism offers such institutions for the exercise of power, which prevent, to a certain extent, democracy's despotic inclinations. By doing this, constitutionalism is not an enemy of democracy, though it

[4] In the Social Contract (II.2.) Rousseau furiously attacked Montesquieu because he considered sovereignty divisible. Jean-Jacques Rousseau, *The Social Contact and Discourses* (New York: A. A. Knopf, 1993).

[5] Alexander Meiklejohn, *Political Freedom: The Constitutional Powers of the People* (New York: Harper, 1960), 9.

does not adulate it. According to Leo Strauss, "...the reason why we cannot allow ourselves to be the bootlickers of democracy is because we are its friends and allies."

Constitutionalism considers certain basic rights and values inviolable, as opposed to the majority principle of the sovereignty of people, which claims the supremacy of laws passed by the majority. The constitution, instead of declaring the sovereignty of people, settles on the appropriate restrictive institutions.

No matter how many internal contradictions there are in Rousseau's writings, he found an awesome follower in democracy's articles of faith. Democracy and constitutionalism cannot be considered in any way the same. At best, their relationship can be characterized as a tension bordering on animosity. But the ideal of democracy has proved so effective that a modern constitutional system cannot exist without democratic legitimation. Hence the modern constitutional ideal does not refute the sovereignty of people, and, instead, it incorporates into its system certain expectations and principles of democracy.

> It is necessary to radically change the perspectives which can be found both in liberal and democratic thinking. The source of legitimacy is not the predetermined will of the individuals, but more a process of change: deliberation and discussion. The legitimate decision does not represent everyone's will, but it is the result of everyone's discussions, where all citizens are entitled to participate. The process shaping everyone's will is where the legitimacy of the result originates from, and that is not a collection of previously formulated wills. The principle of deliberation is individualist and democratic at the same time...We expressly allege, even if this means our opposing an old tradition, that legitimate law is the result of general deliberation, and not the expression of the general will. With this, the burden of proof is shifted from the morality of the citizens to the procedures of the formulation of wills and opinions, which have to provide grounds for the assumption that the outcome is reasonable.[6]

Democracy in this reading becomes constitutional, i.e., limiting of power; it is exactly because the people are the sovereign that no one and no institution can claim sovereign power for itself. What power the constitutional institutions have was vested in them by the people. On the other hand, the sovereignty of the people does not mean that those who

[6] Bernard Manin, "On Legitimacy and Political Deliberation," 1987, *Political Theory* 15 (1987): 351 ff.

exercise this sovereignty may take sovereign decisions on the individuals' existence.

> Rousseau overlooked this truth, and his error made of his Social Contract, so often invoked in favor of liberty, the most formidable support for all kinds of despotism.[7]
>
> At the point where independence and individual existence begin, the jurisdiction of sovereignty ends... The assent of the majority is not enough, in any case, to legitimize its acts...[8]

2.2. MAJORITY RULE

If the will of the majority prevails, there is still a danger that it will oppress the minority. Moreover, the rules of democracy do not guarantee the prevalence of a government of the majority, even in a representative system. Based on the principle of majority, in parliamentary representative systems, for a representative to be elected to the parliament, winning 50 percent of the vote is necessary at most. Fifty percent of the representatives (as in the Belgian Constitution) or half of 50 percent (as in Hungary) is enough to pass a law. Thus it can well happen that a law, even under the stricter (Belgian) conditions, represents only the will of one quarter of the franchised. In other places, the votes of MPs representing 5 percent of the population are practically enough to pass a law that allegedly is an expression of the sovereignty of people and the general will. It is sufficient that the conditions of democratic legitimization are met.[9]

[7] Constant, 177.

[8] Constant, 177.

[9] The validity of elections is either not dependent on a required minimum of participation at all, or the threshold is 50 percent at most, whereas this would be the condition of the expression of the majority will. In only a few countries is voting compulsory. Belgium is one of the few exceptions.

A relative majority is enough to win a seat in a parliament; thresholds and other election techniques lead to further distortions. There is nothing unique in Margaret Thatcher's winning, in 1987, 58 percent of the parliamentary seats with 42 percent of the popular vote. It is somewhat more odd, however, that in 1979 she got fewer seats, despite winning a larger popular vote, and that in 1974 Harold Wilson got more seats with fewer votes than the Conservatives with a larger number of votes.

The majority of the representatives representing the majority of the voters is acceptable for most constitutions as the source of legislation. It is better to say that constitutions generally are silent on this issue, because from the point of view of constitutionalism, democracy defines itself as it wishes. There is only one condition, namely, everyone should have an equal chance to participate in the democratic decision making. This is a very modest condition, especially as it has to prevail only in the long run. In other words, the current majority can determine how the next majority should constitute itself, with the condition that the so-created majority can again determine how the following majority is created.[10] Modern constitutions generally require only that an equal right of political participation be observed, and they also provide the rules on how the majority is formed.

In 1994, the Hungarian Socialist Party got 53 percent of the seats with barely one-third of the votes. The actual turnout was about 60 percent. This means that the will of 20 percent of the voters "equals" the will of the majority and that of the sovereign people. This does not necessarily make the procedure antidemocratic because it gives an *opportunity* for majority representation. Under such circumstances, however, it is ridiculous to continue referring to the *general* will and the sovereignty of people.

Presidential systems, despite the direct expression of the popular will, are no different. It common to elect a president with 32–35 percent of the total votes cast.

In the case of individual constituencies, two-round election systems make actual majority representation more realistic. But they do so at the expense of having to limit the choices available.

[10] In a rule-of-law system, and this is all that constitutional review requires here, the majority, *after* the elections, cannot change the number of parliamentary seats to be allotted to the given proportion of votes. The threshold number of votes cannot be subsequently raised, nor can some of the elected members of parliament be excluded and the seats reallocated. Such shenanigans were extensively used in 1947, during the Communist takeover in Hungary. As late as 1994, following the elections in Slovakia, the parliamentary majority attempted to declare illegal one of the parties that participated in the elections and reallocate the remaining seats to itself. Had it succeeded, a majority coalition would have been the result. The example illustrates how crucial the separation of the branches of power is. It is unacceptable that a parliament be authorized to carry out such "little" operations. Nevertheless, this is extremely dangerous ground, since the parliament's independence could be endangered if it cannot determine its own coming into being and cannot be responsible for confirming its mandates. It might be the task of the courts to decide whether electoral nominations are legal but only if a complaint is made before elections, and complaints have to be dealt with before elections begin.

2.3. CONSTITUTIONAL LIMITS TO DEMOCRACY

When speaking of representative government–the expression of the general will in elections and people's sovereignty–in effect we accept that it is equal to what the majority voted for. What is more, in all political systems this majority is the rule of a multiplied minority. The majority principle prevails insofar as everyone may participate equally in the elections under the rules that bring about this distorted result. In principle everyone has the chance to put their mark on the (democratic) system, where even the rule of the numerical majority could prevail. When we say everyone through personal participation has the opportunity to accept the system, we acknowledge that citizens, as individuals, do not in general have the opportunity to reject the system "in which they were born." Except for general and equal participation, the rules of democratic politics are in practice beyond the citizens' determination, even if the constitution determining the fundamental order is confirmed by referendum. Owing to their political significance, the rules of democracy are not an issue typically regulated in the constitution, though they would have a place there if the constitution's task were to settle the politically important issues (which is only partly true at best). The electoral system is the politicians' closely guarded domain, and they do not let outsiders interfere with the rules.

On what grounds can we say that the expression of the will of the majority, in a referendum or by a parliamentary majority elected by a part of the nation, represents the will of the people, of the whole, and, consequently, that it is binding to everyone?[11] Locke and Rousseau gave an extremely practical explanation: the majority will is acceptable because it is impossible to reach a unanimous agreement.[12] Another argu-

[11] It would not be possible to satisfy Rousseau's conditions even if everyone's vote were behind the law (and not just a simple majority), because in Rousseau's view the general will, which makes the law binding to everyone, is not simply the will of everyone. In Rousseau's metaphysics the reverse of the argument is important, namely, it is *not necessary* that all the wills agree to make up the general will.

[12] John Locke, "Second Treatise of Government." In *Two Treatises of Government*, ed. Peter Caslett (Cambridge: Cambridge University Press, 1991), § 140. Rousseau, 278–279. It is truly surprising that such a basic rule of social order like majoritarianism has such poor theoretical foundations.

ment for the majority principle is that it puts society's members less at the mercy of power than other principles of decision making. After all, Lenin demanded and got the dictatorship of a *minority* vanguard. Hitler's *Mein Kampf* substituted the majority principle with the decision of the "competent people." This idea of "the experts' decision," as it is termed today, has been around since Plato. But whereas Plato wanted the rule of the wise (through the influence exercised on the ruler), Hitler advocated the rule of a chosen leader of the "superior race."

It appears as if the majority principle was supported by linking the principle of equality with an argument originating in social contract theory. The representatives (and all voting citizens) are equal in constitutional democracies. They have equal voting rights and have agreed to act in accordance with the operational rules derived from equality and to accept the outcome. The reason why the majority rule prevails in elections is that the majority rule always allows an unequivocal outcome for the decision-making process. Majority rule may be applied on the condition that all decisions be formulated as an answer to a binary alternative. In other words, a decision is either adopted or rejected.[13] Since it is impossible to know on the basis of equal opportunities who will constitute the minority, this is a fair rule. What is more, all other rules on decision-making would violate equality.

It is rather intriguing that electoral systems that aim at creating a parliamentary majority capable of operating the legislative system under a majority rule are either satisfied with a relative majority in the case of a mandate or strive only to apply the majority principle within an area that has rather artificial geographical boundaries. On a national aggregate the allocation of parliamentary seats could be completely different with the same total number of votes cast. It could happen that between two

---

Hans Kelsen also came up with a practical explanation in *Vom Wesen und Wert der Democratie* (Tübingen: J. C. B. Mohr, 1929). The rule of the minority is unacceptable because, while it is possible on the basis of the numbers to determine who the majority is, there might be several (indeed many) minorities, the uncertainty of which would undermine social integration.

A cognitive argument may also be raised: the more people agree on something, the less the danger is of making a mistake. (This may be applied only to facts, however, and not to values.)

[13] The situation is more complex if there are several options from which to choose, as is the case in parliamentary and municipal elections.

parties, party *A* wins by a close margin in half plus one of the constituencies. In the remaining constituencies, party B's candidates overwhelmingly win the majority of the votes. Party A takes the majority of seats in the legislature, whereas party B won the majority of votes.

In reality, the acceptance of the majority principle stems from certain assumptions about the minority, as Jefferson points out:

> All, too, will bear in mind that this sacred principle, that though the will of the majority is in all cases to prevail, principle, to be rightful, must be reasonable; that the minority possess their equal rights, which equal laws must protect, and to violate which would be oppression.[14]

The rule of the majority, be it a faction in the parliament of a majority social group, can only be acceptable if the minority has a chance under the prevalence of the majority rule to become part of the majority at least when it so wants, and if being in majority does not lead to the oppression of the minority. If the minority has no chance in the long run to succeed, the system will be unacceptable to them. If the minority's status is unbearable, then comes revolt, because for them there is nothing to lose. The constitution is to provide guarantees of the social peace, which is its own prerequisite. If for no other reason than the maintenance of peace, constitutions have to protect minorities. A constitution should guarantee, therefore, partly by electoral provisions, that the minority's status be endurable and, in theory, that it be only temporary.

If the majority principle is merely a matter of agreement and acquiescence (a convention), however, then following this principle of decision making, the participants may accept that further rounds of decision making will take place under different rules.[15] Consequently, a constitution may institutionalize any deviation from the majority principle until it is accepted under the given rules of the constitution, provided that at least the first decision was made along the lines of democratic (majoritarian) principles. As a limiting condition, it may be concluded from the

[14] First Inaugural Address. In Thomas Jefferson, *Writings*, ed. Merrill D. Peterson (New York: Viking Press, 1984), 492–93.

[15] This line of argument is problematic because it does not answer what "acceptance" is. Does it mean agreement by all or acceptance according to the majority principle? Or does the acceptance of the constitution mean that everything may be considered constitutionally accepted if it is ratified in the constitution-making process by the majority, regardless of actual acceptance?

rules on equality that the participants cannot be excluded unilaterally and arbitrarily from any of the decision-making rounds.

Once equality became the dominant mood of the twentieth century, all citizens were given an equal opportunity to take part in the democratic decision making process in their constitutions.[16] The constitution, however, makes no mention of the concrete conditions and rules under which a citizen's democratic participation should take place. Nor does it say anything about the assessment of the result of the participation. In order to enforce constitutionalism, the content and the sphere of decisions reached through the democratic participation of citizens are restricted. Here, in particular, constitutionalism must protect the minority against the majority. Such devices are even more important when what is termed as majority is in reality the rule of a minority. Paradoxically, therefore, the restrictions of the majority rule to a certain extent protect the majority and democracy against legitimate minority rule, which could easily emerge in representative democracy. As it was stated in a leading U.S. free-speech case, the extrication of certain issues from majority decision making goes to the heart of constitutionalism:

> The very purpose of the Bill of Rights was to withdraw certain subjects from the vicissitudes of political controversy, to place them beyond the reach of majorities and officials and to establish them as legal principles to be applied by courts... [F]undamental rights may not be submitted to vote; they depend on the outcome of no elections.[17]

The numerical majority voting in favor of a rule does not reveal much about the importance of this decision to a group, whereas, in theory, the intensity of the needs behind the vote is also important. It could well happen that each member of a 20 percent minority would be willing to pay ten dollars for a given outcome, while each member of the not-too-interested 80 percent majority would sacrifice only one dollar for

[16] The democracy principle will apply to nearly all collective governmental decisions. Democracy permeates constitutionalism inasmuch as the constitutions and the organs enforcing and protecting them will stand up against antidemocratic organizations (those that do not operate in accordance with the one-person-one-vote and the majority principles and accept some kind of "*Führerprinzip*" in the leadership). See the Socialist Reich Party Case in Germany 2 BverfGE 1 (1952).

[17] *West Virginia State Board of Education v. Barnette*, Jackson, J., 319 US 624, 638 (1943).

the opposite outcome. Smoking is allowed not only because such a ban would perhaps violate fundamental freedoms but because the smoking minority's will to keep on smoking is stronger in intensity than the nonsmoking minority's will for a smoke-free environment. In a similar manner, in a democratically neutral, secular school system the members of a minority religious denomination may be entitled to run a school where the traditions of their belief prevail because they are willing to die for their belief, while the whole issue is unimportant to the majority.

Taking into consideration the intensity of the will of the minority may present difficulties leading to tragedy when the minority and the majority are playing a zero-sum game and when the wills of each group may only be enforced at the expense of the other. The majority may believe, for example, that they would be damned if they allow certain rituals of the minority's beliefs be practiced. In the Balkans, the national language issue is played as a zero-sum game when the national language is made the official language of the country. In this instance, the basic rules of the "game" predetermine a fatal outcome. Only mutual concessions can lead to a way out.

The constitution must provide for the protection of minorities. To a certain degree, protecting fundamental rights does this, and certain group rights and minority-protection privileges can be added to this. But, completely excluding all disadvantages–all (ab)use of majority power–is impossible. Consequently, the constitution offers institutional and procedural solutions in an effort to protect minorities. Such institutional protection may be provided by constitutional adjudication, if the court enforcing the constitution supplements the legislation's enactment with the minority's concerns left out of consideration by the legislative majority. No wonder then that the majority-representation principle is not considered, or violated, when constitutional adjudication is established. In the United States, the justices of the Supreme Court are appointed by the president. In other countries, the various branches of power, in various proportions, delegate their candidates to the courts. But procedural guarantees are perhaps even more important.

> The first, intended by the Framers [of the American Constitution], was to impede the operation of majority rule. In few other democratic countries are there so many obstacles in the way of the government by electoral and legislative majorities.[18]

[18] Robert Dahl, *Dilemmas of Pluralist Democracy: Autonomy vs. Control* (New Haven: Yale University Press, 1982), 190. According to Dahl, these obstacles go against democ-

Separation of powers also serves as the majority-restricting constitutional solution insofar as it is not the same majority that prevails in all three branches. Although the legislature is commonly considered to be the expression of majority rule, even parliamentarism may restrict majoritarian excesses if the representatives with their unbounded mandate significantly move away from the will of the majority of the voters in a manner that moderates this will. This is one of the most contradictory areas of restricting constitutional sovereignty because the parliamentary majority that moves away from the majority of the voters may also facilitate the enforcement of minority despotism. Further, minority protection is derived from the representatives' time-limited mandates (Madison's argument). The danger of minority tyranny is limited, too, as the parliamentary majority has to negotiate with other branches and departments of power (e.g., a second house), or a popular initiative may result in overruling the majority of the parliament, if in one of the laws the majority in the parliament forced a minority opinion onto society.

The rule of the majority threatening the minority, and likewise the antimajoritarian government of the minority which has a parliamentary majority, may be prevented by various joint decision-making mechanisms (including veto) and through nonproportional representation. For instance, all U.S. states send two representatives each to the Senate, regardless of the unequal size and population of the states, which provides for additional rights and protection for the sparsely populated states. This was a difficult initiative to push through during the making of the American Constitution in Philadelphia. Similarly, in the German Basic Law the governments of the smaller member states are given a proportionately larger representation in the *Bundesrat*. Likewise, small states in the European Union's Council of Ministers have disproportionate voting power. Qualified majority decision-making rules and presidential veto, wherever applied, also provide for minority protection.[19]

---

racy; they primarily serve the minority's interest in preserving their privileges. Dahl recommends abolition of the presidential veto and supports unicameralism in order to make democracy widespread. See "On Removing Certain Impediments to Democracy in the United States," in *Democracy, Liberty and Equality*, ed. Robert Dahl (Oslo: Norwegian University Press, 1982), 133.

[19] U.S. presidents from Washington to the present have applied the presidential veto 2,500 times, and only in 6 percent of the cases were they overruled.

Constitutionalism is about limiting power. This implies that constitutionalism excludes winner-take-all forms of political competition. (In this respect, constitutionalism may be threatened by any political arrangement that drives the winners to pillage, like in a spoils system, be it the political allocation of jobs or party financing where the winner may legally fill up the political party's coffers with state subsidies.)

The constitutional division of power restricts the kind of democracy that favors the winners, and through checks and balances it facilitates the operation of democracy. The U.S. Congress must have a qualified majority to override a presidential veto and pass a bill. This supermajority requirement brings us closer to the "general will." If a simple majority in the Congress brings about the president's or the Supreme Court's resistance, it may well be an indication to the voters that the majority's exercise of power is of dubious value.

If parliamentarism is a zero-sum game, the winner that manages to line up the numerical majority takes all, regardless of the proportion by which he wins. Constitutionalism, however, represents values that may divert the winner from this logic of victory. If constitutionalism serves the stability of government, it could be in the winner's interest to prevent situations of complete defeat. The possibility of total destruction could turn the participants of the political and social game into enemies, whereas they should be cooperating and learning to live with one another.

In certain decision-making situations, it is possible to include–as a result of political thinking or because this is the custom–the minority, or a large part of the minority, in the decision-making process, giving it a larger role than would be warranted by its numbers. A national-unity government in wartime is a good example. If the general will cannot be logically similar to the will of the numerical majority, then solutions acceptable to the minority have to be found, too. The need for inclusion and the seeking of consensus leads to the consociational, or consensual, form of democracy. Consociationalism, at most, has been institutionalized on the level of constitutional practice and often because of lasting divisions in parliament, as in Holland and Belgium. In Switzerland, all parties with a convincing representation in the National Council are drawn into the government. Besides the consensus-seeking national character, at least two conditions are necessary for these systems to work well: no one group can be much stronger than the others, and the strongest group can be only slightly stronger than the second strongest.

2.4. REFERENDUM AND DESTABILIZATION

Constitutions tamed popular sovereignty (as well as democracy) and incorporated it into the concept of constitutionalism. By making the people the source of power, constitutions exclude the possibility of anyone making himself the origin of sovereignty. Some constitutions make a specific point of including this idea. According to the German Basic Law, the people are the *source* of all governmental power, whereas the framers of the Hungarian Constitution thought it sufficient, in 1989, to drop the restrictive adjective "working" from the original 1949 version. In that version it read: "In the Hungarian People's Republic all power belongs to the working people." Hence there is no place for mediation. The German text states that the people exercise state power through elections and through the given legislative, executive, and judicial organs. In contrast, in Hungary and in many other countries, the people exercise sovereignty through their elected representatives as well as *directly* (through referendum).

Although the actual institutional practice lessens the danger of popular rule, the Hungarian Constitution creates the impression that the representative Parliament embodies popular sovereignty. The arrogant Article 19 adds to it that "[t]he Parliament is the supreme organ of state power and popular representation in the Hungarian Republic." This makes establishing a balance among the branches of power difficult. In the Hungarian Constitution, the referendum, as an alternative way of expressing popular sovereignty, counterbalances representative popular sovereignty. However, the technical conditions of referenda are not determined in the constitution, which allows legislators to limit them nearly at their pleasure.[20] Certainly limits may be needed.

A referendum may be a destabilizing factor if the constitution does not include prescriptions for its use, that is, if it does not draw out the poison, divesting it of the illusion that in it the people are sovereign and

[20] If the constitution fails to provide basic rules of operation on referenda, it may fall easy prey to legislation. The laws on referenda contain procedures for initiative/validation that are a great opportunity for someone who wants to destabilize and who does not in an earnest way want a referendum to exercise any kind of serious control over legislation. The legislator is in the position to institutionalize a popular initiative with requirements that are easy to satisfy or may prescribe a 50 percent participation for a referendum to be valid, letting the failure discredit democracy.

unimpeachable because it embodies their direct will. No wonder, then, that the American and German constitutions do not recognize referenda on the federal level (except in one very specific matter–territorial change–in Germany) and that the Italian one permits only an abrogative referendum, that is, it is possible to appeal to the nation *against* a law.

Sometimes constitutions limit the people's referenda rights by granting exclusive referendum-initiative or admissibility powers to one or another branch of power. In France, for example, the president has the power to initiate referenda. De Gaulle, who had considerable popular support, often turned to the electorate to overrule and discipline Parliament.

It is extremely risky to make someone the exclusive depository of popular sovereignty. In the former Soviet republics, the directly elected presidents, claiming to follow the French model, defy their parliaments on the grounds that they directly represent popular sovereignty.

No matter how attractive the referendum is in light of democratic slogans, it cannot really be used to restrict power, nor can it be used for the nonmanipulated popular control of power. Switzerland is frequently cited as an example where the opposite can be true.[21] It was the French who imported the referendum (1798) to Switzerland, when the Swiss had to vote on their constitution written under French military occupation. They voted for its acceptance, as is usual under such circumstances (as the people voted, for example, for the Brezhnev Constitution). True, the French had to resort to trickery, inasmuch as all abstentions were counted as "yes" votes. Had they been harder pressed, no doubt they would have taken all nonappearances as "yes" votes, too.

Over the years, eight forms of referenda were institutionalized in Switzerland. In addition, in the case of certain issues, the population–in a referendum–voted that they did not want to take certain decisions by referenda (for example, an optional referendum on military expenditures).[22]

[21] In discussing Swiss referenda, I draw on Olivier Duhamel, *Les Démocraties, Régimes, Histoire, Exigences* (Paris: Éditions du Seuil, 1993), 68–74.

[22] An *optional referendum* may be requested only within 90 days after the adoption of a law, and (in the case of a federal law) 50,000 signatures have to be collected. Issues concerning emergency, constitutional, or expenditure matters are excluded. (The Weimar Constitution recognized the optional referendum but without the above restrictions.)

The commentators find that the Swiss participate with sufficient frequency (around 40 percent), especially if one takes into consideration how often they are called to the ballot box, though participation is steadily declining (before the war, participation was around 60 percent). The Swiss reject slightly more than half of the laws. The *possibility* of calling a referendum is perhaps more important from the point of view of legislation than for referendum itself. Since legislators have to consider the possibility of a referendum, they strive to involve as many people as possible in the preparation of bills. Among the achievements of popular initiative, one may recall the sober ban of *absinthe* and the enlightened vote to refuse the kosher slaughtering of animals. Today, popular initiative is mostly resorted to by certain interest groups to have their corporate interests accepted. This recourse is usually made when parlamentarians forget special interests for the sake of public interests. Popular initiative is the last resort of isolated political groups and movements; their sacred causes are put on the agenda, and people talk about them, generally without short-term practical impact. Some parts of a rejected proposal, however, may be lifted by politicians into the "regular" legislative process, as it happened with the restriction of the rights of guest workers after the referendum rejected some xenophobic proposals. What comes of all this?

> In Switzerland the referenda from 1874 to 1939 showed the Swiss people to be anxious for liberal political rights, severe to murderers, unfriendly to the process of centralization, in favor of tariff duties, occasionally anti-Semitic, a drag on state activity in the control or management of industries, supporters of domestic virtue (in the marriage and liquor laws), steadily austere (especially in the cantons) in relation to the payment of public officials, and unenlightened regarding public health measures. On the whole one may say the effect has been gradualist; or, in other words, the assemblies were ahead of the people. Moreover, the people have certainly not acted spontaneously, but have, in fact, been strongly incited and whipped up and informed by the same processes of electoral campaigning by political parties...as we find in democracies without direct legislation.[23]

If we add to this the tendency experienced in various American states, namely, that certain groups attempt to use referenda to codify their anti-constitutional biases (that is, against illegal immigrants, homosexuals,

[23] Herman Finer, *Theory and Practice of Modern Government* (1949; Westport: Greenwood Press, 1970), 562.

and the like), we can understand constitutionalism's reluctance to accept the referendum, even if we do not consider its destabilizing effect. The referendum, because of the susceptibility of people, is the enemy of the political elite (and the constitutional values they represent).

A poet may be allowed to disregard the vices of the people, and at most he will simply lose in an election and write a disillusioned narrative poem. But the politician that denies the short-sightedness and emotional susceptibility of the "people," who are understandably incompetent in most issues concerning legislation, and that fails to appreciate this–as opposed to the process of legislation, which at least in principle is based on a rational discourse of the controversial points and conviction–is most likely thinking of taking advantage of these shortcomings. At this stage, one cannot deny that there is a certain *elite-consciousness* in constitutionalism, which can be justified on moral or utilitarian grounds but hardly on the basis of popular feelings or democratic egalitarianism. If a nation's spirit is one with the conservativism or radicalism instigated by demagogues expressed in a referendum, then there is a pinch of the elite's dictatorship of taste in constitutionalism, no matter how incompetent the result of a referendum is and no matter to what extent constitutionalism, in which there is a hint of elitism, is directed against oppression.

If one has elite values that are universal and would be of benefit to all, we are not denying the dignity of the individual as a member of the crowd. What we might simply say is that, in a crowd, a person is not always worthy of his own dignity. In this particular case, even Rousseau may be enlisted as one of the supporters of constitutionalism: "Our will is always for our own good, but we do not always see what that is; the people is never corrupted, but it is often deceived, and on such occasions only does it seem to will what is bad."[24]

Admittedly, because elections are few and far between, the possibility of turning to the people to counter a legislature that is detached from the people and is often corrupt and one-sided can be a means of restricting power. One could say that the referendum and popular initiative are conservative and/or radical indicates certain political or ethical value choices but this criticism is irrelevant from the constitutional perspective. Whether the referendum can be incorporated in an actual political system without damaging constitutionalism depends, above all, on the

[24] Rousseau, 203.

citizenry's democratic culture. Hitler used referenda on three occasions, and in each instance it was initiated by the government, including the adoption of the *Anschluss* (the incorporation of occupied Austria into Germany). All three initiatives were adopted by an overwhelming majority. Democracy, on the other hand, remains operational even if the referendum is excluded.

From the point of view of constitutionalism, it is of primary importance for what the referendum is used. It cannot be one of the accepted, ordinary tools of legislation, but it can be part of constitutional control, and it can be the means of countering an *impasse* in legislation (for example, it would be a possible solution to let the "people" decide when the two houses of a parliament cannot agree).

Chapter 3

DANGEROUS LIAISONS: CHECKS AND BALANCES AND THE SEPARATION OF POWERS

How could one part know the whole?
Pascal

3.1. THE BALANCING ACT

The constitution's purpose is to restrict the state and the people who constitute the state. Taken on its own, a constitution is nothing more than a dead letter or a negligible tradition. What kind of protection will the constitution provide? Can it serve as a limit to power if people do not believe in it or if the interest of the stronger is to bypass it? No matter how important and indispensable belief in the constitution is, constitutionalism, as the antithesis of despotism, requires institutional guarantees. To provide such guarantees the various branches of power need be arranged in a manner that they restrict each other.

Article 16 of the French Declaration of the Rights of Man and Citizen of 1789–copied in several constitutions–reads as follows: "Any society in which the separation of powers is not determined, has no constitution at all."[1] As for the division itself, governments and their constitutions show significant differences. There is neither one correct recipe nor one ultimate solution.

For those who advocate that "power is in unity," separation does not come naturally, and they attack separation as a structural complication that needlessly delays necessary decisions and impairs the efficiency of government. This idea dates back to Rousseau, and it was supported by the revolutionary framers of the Pennsylvania Constitution of 1776 and the French revolutionaries of 1792. Following Robespierre, Marquis de Condorcet attacked the system of balanced but separate powers in the

[1] References to the English translation of the French & German originals can be found in *Constitutions That Made History*, eds. Albert P. Blaustein and Jay A. Sigler (New York: Paragon House, 1988), 359–387.

name of unity, which was badly needed in France at that time.[2] Condorcet claimed that only a functional division was acceptable.

In all cases, wherever a dictatorship is being institutionalized, the issue of the unity of power immediately arises. But as demonstrated by the inefficient operation of Hitler's government, the separate parts are in no rush to merge into the primordial "original" unity of power. Theorists laying the foundations of Nazism held that the dictatorship of the *Reichspresident* was the means to preserve the nation and to achieve the sovereignty of the German people (not the individual). "Dictatorship is pure government, IMPERIUM in the original meaning of the word, that is disposition over the totality of state power."[3]

The Communists advocated monolithic state power. The dictatorship of the proletariat is simple, and it is simplicity that makes it so attractive: it implies strength and does not require too much work from the gray matter. That the state was subjected to the communist party dictatorship–in Stalin's case, the dictatorship of a single person–made matters much easier. Easier, to be sure, is not always nicer.

Undoubtedly there are emergencies and crises that call for immediate, firm, and directly executed state actions. The first form of the modern state was absolutism, and it was this despotic form of government against which Montesquieu suggested the introduction of checks and balances.

To avoid dictatorship, power should be counterbalanced with power. Hence some form of division of state powers is desirable. In this regard, a constitution dictated by constitutionalism is essentially more than the allocation of authority among state organs. Drawing only the demarcation lines of power is insufficient.

"Ambition must be made to counteract ambition."[4] Wandering cattle are not restrained by a clear boundary, only by a barking dog on the

[2] *Plan de constitution, presenté a la Convention nationale*, vol. 18, *Oeuvres* (Paris, 1804), 185; 201.

[3] Johannes Heckel, "Archiv des öffentlichen Rechts" in Clinton Rossiter, *Constitutional Dictatorship: Crisis Government in the Modern Democracies* (Princeton: Princeton University Press, 1948), 62.

[4] *The Federalist Papers*, No. 51: Madison (New York: Mentor Book, 1961), 322.

Montesquieu was of the same opinion: "...it has eternally been observed that any man who has power is led to abuse it; he continues until he finds limits... So that one cannot abuse power, power must check power by the arrangement of things." In Charles Secondat, Baron de Montesquieu, *The Spirit of the Laws*, trans. and ed. Anne M. Cohler,

neighboring property. The leaders of each branch of government have to be given the appropriate means to restrain interference into their sphere of authority. Is there anything more tempting than possessing these means? And isn't the temptation too great for those who dare to will, and those who dare to act, to become the judges of their own desires and actions? Who would be a good judge in his own case? Can a person entitled to determine the law and, therefore, to make people rich and powerful resist the temptation? Can he resist the temptation to give preference to his own desires?

The risk of self-interest is mitigated only in part by the constitutional principle that the law applies to the legislator. The legislator, contrary to the king, is not above the law, but he can still be given preferential treatment *under* the law.

The desire for power is thwarted only if the person with the desire is not identical to the one who controls the means to fulfil that desire. The ambition of the one who wants power is checked because he is not in a position to act without any further consideration or transfer, and because it is not he who can dispose over the act's result. In addition, as he who acts is not the one who desires, the "executor" of the desire has the possibility–within certain limits–to control the person who is responsible for "devising" the desire. After all, the "executor" has to execute only what complies with the previously stipulated conditions. No matter who has the means with which the actor is physically able to transform living conditions, perhaps even through force, these means cannot be used without due authorization.

The modern division of power among the classical branches of government–legislative, executive, and judicial–first appeared in England. However, in the eighteenth century the relation among the branches was not perceived as the relationship of the governmental branches divided according to areas of operation or function but rather as a problem of balancing the *social forces* constituting the country.

The upper house represented the aristocracy, while the lower house stood for the taxpayers; the decisionmaker was officially the "King in Parliament." In other words, the three social forces of the country could make decisions only together and could pass laws only together. With

---

Basia Carolyn Miller, and Harold Samuel Stone (Cambridge: Cambridge University Press, 1992), XI. 4.

time, a division of labor in operations came about.[5] The executive branch, partly based on the king's personal privileges, was separated from Parliament and was exercised by the king's "servants."

Montesquieu described the English system as one where the freedom of the people is guaranteed: where the branches of government–and the people involved–are distinctively separate from each other, and as a result, the branches are able to counterbalance each other.[6] In reality, by its separation, the executive branch became independent, which made possible its despotic use of power, for example, in colonial matters. When opposing British rule, the American revolutionaries followed Montesquieu's principles.[7]

Madison hoped that fundamental governmental bodies would operate in a way that would enable them to become stronger only at each other's expense, so that they would control each other's activities. The antagonistic interests of state officials would permeate institutions with jealousy. As officials of the various departments are at the mercy of their institutions and as their power depends on the power of their organizations, they are not indifferent to how powerful their branch of government is. The design of the system is such that officials should truly de-

[5] At this time the administration of justice was not considered a separate branch of power, although English common law, as precedent law made by judges, existed independently of the legislature. According to earlier legal theory, even the king was bound by the rules of common law.

[6] Although Montesquieu, together with Locke, was the most prominent expert on constitutionalism in the eighteenth century, his teachings do not, as we see it today, fully satisfy the requirements of constitutionalism. Montesquieu does link freedom and the separation of power, but his views on freedom are rather contradictory. Sometimes this concept simply means that life is in conformity with the prescriptions of the law (there is no despotism and the rule of law in a formal sense prevails); sometimes it means that people do not have to be afraid of one another and sometimes that all people govern themselves. It is because of the latter that the need for representation arises. Montesquieu, however, also advocates a representative mandate in general issues and the multiple representation of the aristocracy to counterbalance the people. The executive is primarily engaged in the management of foreign affairs and in conducting wars. The legislature may only investigate these matters subsequently, while the executive may intervene in the legislative process whenever it wishes. Finally, the judicial branch is despotic without being separated, but as a branch of government, it is a lightweight.

[7] The French constituents, in 1789, just like the Americans two years earlier, fought with a moving resoluteness for the separation of powers. They deemed separation the guarantor of freedom.

pend on their particular branch of government. For constitutionalism, the importance of the right to appointment and personal incompatibility stems from here. The various branches of government press each other to correct possible violations of the law and to refrain from such violations, showing due regard for each other.

There are various ways to divide and arrange the branches of power, and any solution is viable so long as the possibilities for the restriction of freedom are precluded or headed off. From a constitutionalist point of view, the democratic nature of government operations is of secondary importance. Democracy, here, means the prevalence of the public's own views instead of those of the institutions. Under certain circumstances the efficiency of government is of secondary importance, too, though the state's impotence in settling frictions among its various organs will in the end endanger security and, in this way, freedom. The American Constitution, however, never sought to avoid conflict between and among the branches of government:

> The doctrine of separation of powers was adopted by the Convention of 1787, not to promote efficiency, but to preclude the exercise of arbitrary power. The purpose was, not to avoid friction, but by means of the inevitable friction incident to the distribution of the governmental powers among three departments, to save the people from autocracy.[8]

Undoubtedly, accepting friction and conflict has a shrieking resonance in the ears of those who advocate order and consocial joint decisionmaking.[9] But even where shared societal processes are of vital im-

[8] *Myers v. United States*, 272 U.S. 293 (1926) (J. Brandeis, dissenting).

[9] Accepting conflicts does not mean the acceptance of an impasse in decisionmaking. A constitution that leaves room for such an impasse is inappropriate in a technical sense because it destabilizes. Requiring a qualified majority in certain areas of legislation may cause such a destabilizing impasse. This is a well-known phenomenon of the Hungarian Constitution. The disadvantage of having a qualified-majority requirement is that it does not provide a solution in a number of cases (the result is a nondecision that does not necessarily amount to a flat rejection). When a two-thirds majority is required to restrict fundamental rights, there is no problem because a decision to the negative is a simple rejection. The basic right cannot be restricted, so everything remains as it was, hooray for freedom. (Complications arise if the law was meant to promote a basic right. Even such promoting motions contain a little bit of a restrictive element, so there is less to worry about.) But where the aim is to establish an organ or appoint a person, a destabilizing impasse may easily arise.

portance, the preconstitutional decisions that determine the need and sphere of consocial decision making follow from the shared understanding that the country in question cannot bear and survive certain conflicts.[10] Consocial structures usually evolve in the shadow of potentially fatal conflicts. (Allowing the religious and ethnic divisions to spiral into unlimited conflict, in Belgium, for example, would be disastrous, as all parties recognize.)

There are two models to illustrate the above-mentioned division of powers. One is based on the separation of powers and the other on the distribution of powers among the various state organs. In the first model the separation of the branches of power is, in theory, complete. The branches of power are separate, that is, *independent of each other*, but not autonomous, because they cannot operate on their own.

Powerful presidentialism is what the U.S. separation-of-powers system is usually associated with. This political-science approach is mostly concerned with what kind of allocation of power serves best (most efficiently and without fail) the operation of the political system without crises, the realization of the political trends "supported" by voters, and the implementation of some kind of collective program.[11]

[10] The need for consensus may arise from social traditions. Thus in Japan, in matters particularly important to the majority, decisions made by the parliament have to be acceptable for the minority (the opposition), too, assuming that the opposition concedes something from its own views. When Prime Minister Sato wanted to extend the Japanese–American defense treaty, the Socialist opposition stood up and left the chamber in protest. Sato put the issue up for a vote only after the Socialists left, and his party affirmed the treaty. As a consequence, Sato had to resign (Courtesy of Professor Michael Young, Columbia University, New York).

[11] The term presidentialism is misleading when applied in connection with the United States. The American president is considered "strong" only by those who are not familiar with the Latin-American constitutions. Looking at the issue on a theoretical level, it is evident that the president of the U.S. lacks important powers. For instance, the president cannot initiate laws (hence the lack of the privilege of special legislative procedures for executive initiative and executive emergency legislation), his appointment powers are subject to consent by the Senate, and he does not have interim legislative rights. Nor does the U.S. Constitution allow the president to declare a state of emergency. *Cf.* all these powers in the Peruvian Constitution even before Fujimori's self-initiated coup d'état. See Cynthia McClintock, "Presidents, Messiahs and Constitutional Breakdowns in Peru," *The Failure of Presidential Democracy: The Case of Latin America*, eds. Juan Linz and Arturo Valenzuela (Baltimore: Johns Hopkins University Press, 1994).

Complete separation is a misleading term in itself, too, and no political system could likely exist on this basis. Moreover, if an organ is allowed to operate in a restricted area without any further control, this would trigger autocracy. It is difficult to tolerate even judicial power, though the "least dangerous branch," because it is counterbalanced by the other branches only to a lesser degree, and there is little democratic control over it. The weight of a judge's power can be eased only with the possibility of appeal.

In the case of complete separation, the other branches of power would not play a role in the selection, management, control, and accountability of those working within another branch. In existing systems, even when in all the above-mentioned matters the executive is left on its own, it may be directed through the threat of bills and budget modifications. But there is no doubt that in checks-and-balances systems there is less emphasis on the division of power at the personal level: the conflict of interests between the executive and the legislative is not a matter of principle. Here is a certain degree of functional differentiation among the branches of power: the basic activities of the branches differ from one another. In its operations each branch gives priority to its own basic functions; however, limits on the power of the branches originate from the fact that one branch cannot act without the cooperation of the others.

Checks and balances exist in separationist systems owing to the prevailing close interrelationships.[12] The U.S. Constitution, in reality, is a

[12] Madison was forced into an apologetic mood about the close relationship of the two principles (separation and checks and balances). Since then, as a result of the duality, the U.S. Constitution is interpreted in two ways (formalist and functionalist) in Supreme Court decisions. This is the practice followed in several other countries, too. According to the formalist approach, based on the literal interpretation of the text, the constitution clearly states who should do what. This view was adopted by the Hungarian Constitutional Court. There is, however, one minor failing: in reality the Hungarian Constitution, like other constitutions, does not always state clearly who should do what. Even where the language seems to be unequivocal, interpretation may turn it upside down. The Hungarian Constitution, for example, states that the president of the Republic of Hungary is the commander in chief. A commander has appointment powers in his division. This is not so according to the Hungarian Constitutional Court, as far as the president is concerned. The Constitutional Court held that appointment should be interpreted "functionally." According to the functionalists, functions should not necessarily be interpreted according to the constitution's "incidental" solutions (outdated in a modern state). Functions should be divided functionally, and this should be the yardstick.

mixture of these two principles. The result is a "government where the divided institutions share the branches of power."[13]

At this stage a comment about balance is in order. Balance is by its nature dynamic, and, consequently, it is imperfect at any point in time. Dynamic balance means that interbranch disequilibria exist within constitutionally acceptable limits. Dynamism originates in the workings of the political system. The imagined or accepted order in the constitution may be modified by election outcomes or may be reinterpreted by the courts.

Here the focus is primarily on the balance between the legislative and executive branches. In this relationship the "more-directly" elected branch of power considers itself to have the mandate over general policies because of its "more-democratic" legitimization. Accordingly, the parliament would like to dictate politics, too, while the directly elected president would like the parliament to adopt the policies approved by the people through his election. In this see-saw game, balance occurs when the see-saw is level. When one of the players is heavier, the see-saw falls out of balance, tilting toward the heavier player. Problems crop up when the player on top falls off and the seat at the lower end hits the ground, crushing the freedom that was hanging around. Meanwhile, the elf of judicial review tries to strike a balance between the two extremes by running around the center of the see-saw.

Without intending to blur the difference between the parliamentary (division of powers) system and separation of powers (presidential systems and constitutional monarchies), it must be stressed that, paradoxically, it is not only in the American system of separation of powers that there is a need for joint decisionmaking. British parliamentarism and German chancellor democracy have resulted in more centralized executive decisionmaking, while, on paper, the executive is subject to the parliament.

The actual relationships may be interpreted only by observing the two dimensions simultaneously. The powers of any given branch should be interpreted both at the level of decisions concerning the composition of organizational structures and in terms of carrying out actual functions. The two dimensions are (1) *organizational* (including personal)

[13] Richard E. Neustadt, *Presidential Power: The Politics of Leadership* (New York: Wiley, 1960), 33.

dependence and (2) independence in *decisionmaking*. One branch of power, in its formation, may be independent of the other but will nevertheless be dependent on the other if it cannot realize its function alone. Although one branch can make the "final decision" on its policies, the decision depends on conditions pertaining to another branch, therefore, in reality the power-limiting balance is not based on the apparent separation.

In the relationship of the branches of power, it is the dependence or independence appearing in the above two dimensions that makes a real difference. The two major models used in introductory political science and government classes–the presidential and the parliamentary systems–refer to specific combinations of the above dimensions. It is difficult to get a clear overview because the separation of the branches of power would imply that each function has its own organizational system. In reality, both the functions and the organizations may be divided. For instance, an organizational unit or a function of the legislature may be taken over by the executive, or vice versa, the legislature may be granted the authority to adjudicate over certain units of the executive (like impeachment).[14] Indeed, the legislative branch may itself establish its own executive organizations that do not belong to the executive.

3.2. SEPARATION AND DEPENDENCE IN CREATION AND TERMINATION

3.2.1. Creation

At various stages of its existence an organization (a branch of power) may relate to the other branches in different ways.

In England and in most other early constitutional monarchies, the creation of the executive branch was independent from the legislative, but this was not so the other way around. The executive branch (the king) was not only separate from the legislative body but remained so in each and every stage of its existence, because the king's person was sa-

[14] According to the French Constitution of 1958, the executive branch exercises certain legislative functions.

cred and because the usual (but not necessarily) hereditary character of the monarchy prevented Parliament's intervention in the event of a vacancy in the executive.[15] The king could appoint and keep ministers even after the 1848 revolutions; it took decades for rulers to accept Parliament's initiatives and wishes as to appointment or dismissal of ministers.

In Britain, the king (as the head of the executive) could not be deposed. Nevertheless, according to an eighteenth-century doctrine, he could dissolve Parliament whenever he desired, provided that he convened a new session within three years at the latest. As the members were cautious enough to vote on taxes only for the subsequent year, Parliament had to be convened more frequently.

Contrary to the British system, in the United States, in theory all branches of power are independent in their establishment from the others, including also most judges, who (with the exception of federal judges) are popularly elected.[16] In the American system, both the legislative and, in essence, the executive (the president) are directly elected by the people. Contrary to the eighteenth-century English doctrine, the Americans advocated separate institutions in each branch of government. The president cannot dissolve Congress, and by the same token, Congress cannot oust the president, except by impeachment. Congress cannot dissolve itself; presidents can only be shot. The president's sole institutional right pertaining to Congress is that he may convene it in cases of emergency. The executive branch is not directly involved in the legislative process. In cases of emergency–if the electoral vote is unsuccessful–Congress may, however, elect the president and, by exercising the right of impeachment, oust him.[17] There is evidence that, on the

[15] The political conditions of modern parliamentarism were established by the Glorious Revolution, inasmuch as the ruler did not accede to the throne as a result of family inheritance but was invited by Parliament to take the throne with certain conditions attached.

[16] The confederalists advocating a looser state structure, among other things, held that the 1787 resolution was not consistent enough because, for instance, federal judges were appointed by the head of the executive. (On the perfect separation of judges, see Chapter 7.)

[17] Impeachment refers to the calling to account of elected officials and federal judges for gross violation of the law or the constitution. The proceedings are launched as a result of a resolution passed by the House of Representatives. At the end of the proceedings, held in the Senate, the official is removed from his position.

other hand, in the parliamentary system, exceptionally, the executive may be established independently of the legislative, and yet the government (cabinet) will depend on the parliament, according to the principle of confidence. In Israel, since 1996, the head of the executive branch, that is, the prime minister, is directly elected by popular vote.[18] The cabinet, as a responsible institution, continues to rely on Parliament's confidence. Thus we are faced with the constitutionally patented, checkmate situation. What happens when the council of ministers resigns but the prime minister cannot because his mandate is from the people?

In the cases examined thus far, the executive and legislative branches were established independently of each other, that is, the relationship is symmetric as far as it relates to the process of creation. The rights pertaining to dissolution make the eighteenth-century English model asymmetric. The king had the right to dissolve Parliament but not vice versa. This particular semiseparation (more due to social-political reasons than merely because of the imbalance of government) resulted in structural tension. Parliament's defenselessness became untenable. The "solution" was brought about by another structural disequilibrium, resulting partly from a revolutionary change and partly from a slow, organic one. The point of departure was the supremacy of the legislative branch. In eighteenth-century England, the argument was that the country's political forces and forces of power came together in Parliament, and this is where decisions on taxes were made. It was on this basis that Parliament was declared an omnipotent and supreme body. Following Rousseau's doctrines, in the French Revolution the legislature, as the expression of the will of the people, was accorded the leading role.

By declaring the supremacy of the legislative branch, a part of the executive branch (which on the rights of the crown wanted to gain supremacy for itself) fell under legislative supervision and became depend-

[18] The Knesset passed this strange law as a result of public outrage over the resignation of the government; because two members of the Knesset followed the advice of their extremist rabbi who in turn unexpectedly dissociated himself from the government. The majority found it unacceptable that the will of a rabbi, who was considered an extremist by the majority, could force a government to resign.

This idea is not new. It was none other than Condorcet who put forward the idea of a government elected directly by the people and accountable to Parliament when the Constitution of 1792 was under draft.

ent on it. Paradoxically this process was the result of a royal initiative. William of Orange, who was invited by Parliament to occupy the throne because of an international conflict, deemed it especially important to gain the support of Parliament, which was responsible for the stipulation of taxes, among other things. Consequently, William appointed four gentlemen to become members of his team of personal advisers, in other words, his cabinet, which he thought had the influence to inspire understanding in the House of Commons for the king's ideas. Later the situation changed, and as a right of tradition, only those members who were supported by Parliament could be appointed to the cabinet (which by that time had real executive authority).

In republics where the king's power was not transferred to the head of state, the parliament is wholly responsible for deciding who becomes the prime minister, and in some cases it votes on the members of the cabinet. In the Third and Fourth French Republics, the convention was that the government presented its program to the parliament, which voted on it.[19] As a result of this practice, most French governments were obliged to resign for lack of support almost immediately after they had presented their program.[20]

The above decision-making power also includes the termination of the government's mandate. In parliamentary systems, this dominance of power–at least on paper–is decisive as far as it relates to the existence of the branch.

As to termination, the executive branch may, however, have considerable counterweights. According to some models, if the parliament has expressed its no-confidence, the executive "dies," but it may still dissolve the parliament. In certain countries and circumstances the executive has no authority to do this, but if a new government is not formed within a

[19] The standard communist solution was that the parliament *elected* the government but, in order to avoid any problems, only on the recommendation of the presidium of the parliament. Between parliamentary sessions (about 360 days a year) the presidium, composed of the most trusted Communists, exercised all legislative power.

[20] The first three governments of the Fifth Republic continued this practice, inasmuch as the prime minister read the program; but there was no vote because the government, as a matter of form, was primarily subordinate to the president of the republic. In the early 1980s, the socialist government, in an attempt to revive the government's responsibility, returned to the earlier practice of inaugural voting. Between 1958 and 1993, 9 of 25 governments requested this vote.

longer period of time, some automatic mechanism dissolves the parliament, and new elections are held.

In continental parliamentary systems these logical models represent, at the same time, various stages of development. The picture became more complicated when parliaments began to elect cabinets that stood by the king, resulting, to a certain extent, in the duplication of the executive branch.[21]

At the beginning of the nineteenth century, the constitutional problem was how to monitor the king, who could not be challenged in his person, in his capacity as the head of the executive. The ministries accountable to the parliament were set up with exactly this objective in mind. It was the creation of these ministries that the liberal opposition demanded with so much perseverance in the early nineteenth century.[22] The king remained the head of the executive in most European monarchies, almost until the end of the Second World War; but he could not, even according to the French Constitution of 1791, act without the *approval* of a minister in whom the parliament vested its confidence.

The Dutch and Belgian models, stemming from the former solution, are especially interesting from the point of view of the constitutional requirements of the original separation of the branches of power. In the Netherlands, the monarchy was established after the French occupation of 1813, before which the country had republican traditions. According to the Constitution of 1814, the king made laws together with Parliament, but besides this, he had legislative privileges. The ministers were the king's advisers.

Disputes over religion and language use led the Belgians to establish an independent state, in 1830. The Belgian Constitution of 1831 became a model for the liberals, whereas it merely prescribed ministerial approval for all royal acts. The principle of ministerial responsibility was included in the text of the Constitution, but this meant only that if the minister carrying out the king's orders violates the law by signing a legal

[21] In British constitutional law the privileges of the Crown still exist. Parliament has no right of control over these privileges, meaning they cannot be challenged by a vote of no-confidence.

[22] "If you want complete confidence to exist between nation and government, let Hungarians establish constitutional, in other words, accountable, executive power..." József Eötvös, *Reform* [1846], *Reform és hazafiság*, vol. 1 (Budapest, 1978), 524.

document, he could be called to account under criminal law, and the king could not grant him pardon.[23]

There is still no trace of modern political and governmental responsibility. Indeed, there is no government either, only ministers who are independently and individually responsible under criminal law. It remains the king's right to appoint and to relieve ministers, and the idea that the government should be appointed and "recalled" by a parliamentary majority does not even arise. There was no prescription whatsoever saying that, if the government's proposal is rejected, the government should resign. The king could dissolve Parliament whenever he wished.[24]

Until 1848, the Dutch persisted in the original 1814 system: there was no ministerial responsibility in the Constitution at all. As a spillover of the revolutions of 1848, a second, directly elected chamber was institutionalized, but the government could dissolve the parliament. (It is worth keeping in mind that these arrangements stemmed from the separation of the executive from the parliament and their militant opposition toward each other.) In 1866, the king, at the cabinet's request, relieved one of his ministers, provoking the second chamber (the lower house) to protest in a resolution. The executive considered this move anticonstitutional and revolutionary, consequently it dissolved the lower house. The new parliament, still in the shadow of its dissolved predecessor, remained silent. A year later, however, the government's position on the status of the Grand Duchy of Luxembourg prompted the parliament to pass a resolution in which it criticized the cabinet, so the latter resigned.[25]

[23] In the past 164 years there has yet been no time to pass a law on the responsibility of ministers in accordance with Article 90 of the Belgian Constitution. For more detail, see the section "Myth of Ministerial Responsibility."

[24] The currently prevailing situation is based fundamentally on convention. The king can appoint anyone as a matter of form, provided he has ministerial approval. (There is one minister in office at all times.) In practice, however, the king appoints the candidate of the party coalition. Should Parliament make a no-confidence motion, the government either resigns or new elections are held. See Belgium in *International Encyclopaedia of Laws, Constitutional Law*, ed. André Allen (Deventer: Kluwer, 1991).

[25] A Supreme Court decision in the Meerenberg case (1879) and another amendment of the Constitution (1887) were necessary to repress the executive's original legislative power, which was not based on delegated power.

It was only in republics–at least at the beginning and under revolutionary circumstances–that the parliament ruled over the executive branch.[26] In many cases it is the legislative power that provides the president of the republic with his mandate.[27]

The parliamentary system, therefore, is asymmetric with regard to the establishment of the branches; the executive is created by the parliament. This dependence, however, as a result of the various methods of termination, is tempered in a variety of ways. Although by expressing its lack of confidence the parliament may make the cabinet resign, it is often the cabinet's choice whether it retaliates by dissolving the parliament.

In parliamentary systems that follow the Westminster model, the cabinet or its prime minister is chosen by the parliament and cannot function without its support, even if the appointments were made by the president. If the parliament expresses a loss of confidence in the cabinet, it must resign.

The vote of confidence keeps the executive branch dependent on the parliament. But what is considered to be a vote of confidence? In bicameral systems, for example, the Third French Republic, both houses passed separate motions of no-confidence, nevertheless, the cabinet remained in place. It is not a sign of a loss of confidence if a proposal of the cabinet is rejected, though until the end of the nineteenth century this was considered so.[28] Today the rejection of a cabinet proposal does

[26] According to the influential German Imperial Constitution of Frankfurt, which was drafted during the 1848 revolutionary period but never put into effect, the cabinet would have been elected by the lower house of parliament. The lower house was to be elected by popular vote. Under the Weimar Constitution of 1918, the chancellor (prime minister) is appointed by the president of the republic; however, the prime minister has to resign if the parliament passes a motion of no-confidence.

[27] According to the Swiss Constitution of 1848, the Federal Council, which exercises federal executive power, is elected by the National Council (a directly elected chamber) for three years (Art. 84).

The president of the Third French Republic was elected for seven years by a joint session of the two houses (with a simple majority).

According to the current German Basic Law, the president is elected for a period of five years by a joint session of the two houses, while the Hungarian Constitution says the president is elected by one house, with a majority, for a period of five years.

[28] Even in the early 1960s it was a widely held view that the cabinet should resign if its proposal is rejected. As a result of this assumption, the members of Parliament consti-

not necessarily mean that it will resign and that new elections are called. Today, members of Parliament know that they do not risk provoking a call for new elections by voting no.[29]

According to an express provision in the Italian Constitution, rejecting a cabinet's proposal does not mean a lack of confidence. A motion of no-confidence has to be launched separately. The Constitution of the Fifth French Republic, similarly to the German Constitution, prescribes specific restrictions on the no-confidence vote.[30]

The constitutional arrangement of parliamentarism, which tries to bind power by setting a special relationship between the executive and legislative branches, looks good on paper but is rather outdated in practice. In the typical Continental parliamentary system, the executive and legislative branches do not, as a rule, stand in opposition to each other. Instead, it is the political parties that divide and structure the government. It would be extremely difficult, relying solely on constitutional checks and balances, to successfully counterbalance the closely interwoven relationships established on a party (political) basis, something that is almost induced by parliamentarism. Thus the "soul" of parliamentarism seems to be "dead," and there is no more balance of powers.[31]

In theory the solution to the above problem would be a kind of separation where the branches of power would be established independently of each other, consequently, the possibility of party collusion would be minimized, while their existence and operations would be mutually dependent. This model advocates a balance of the branches of power of

---

tuting the government majority were extremely careful in following party lines. When, however, on one occasion a proposal of the Labor Party, which had a marginal majority in Parliament, was rejected and the cabinet did not resign, party ranks loosened.

[29] In 1994, the "eurosceptic" conservative members of Parliament were against Britain's contribution to the EU budget in accordance with an EU automatism. Prime Minister John Major, in an attempt to win the support of the dissenters, announced that the government would resign if it did not win the vote. The majority dissenters emphasized that their vote regarded a matter of principle and forced the government to set certain conditions in exchange for their support.

[30] For a discussion on the restriction of votes of no-confidence and the resulting increase in the independence of the executive branch, see comments in Chapter 4 on constructive no-confidence in connection with the prerogatives of the executive.

[31] Robert Redslob, *Die parlamentarische Regierung in ihrer Wahren und in ihre unechten Form* (Tübingen: J.C.B. Mohr, 1918) 179, quoted in Mommsen, 350.

equal weight. In order to achieve this, the branches of power are said to originate independently and directly from democratic sources. The way this is realized is that some vestiges of the royal power are divested to the elected president.[32]

The president of the republic, who is elected by the people and who appoints the organizations and the members of the executive, helps the balance of powers move out of stalemate. De Gaulle's constitution, adopted by referendum in 1971, was drafted along the lines of this model. According to his constitution, the president of the republic is directly elected, and he appoints the cabinet, which can be toppled by Parliament. The president of the republic may, on the other hand, dissolve Parliament (National Assembly) at any time.[33]

The instability caused by the democratic nature of this solution (popular election of all branches) is alleviated by the fact that the cabinet might provide a "ferry service" between the directly elected head of the executive and the directly elected parliament. As for the formation or dissolution of such a cabinet, it may depend on the president or the parliament. For example, the cabinet is appointed by the president but can be toppled by the Parliament. According to Max Weber, the cabinet should be elected by the parliament, which would also be responsible for monitoring its activities, while the republic's popularly elected president, who relies on referenda, would exercise executive powers partially independent from the parliament. This setup would be directly legitimized by the people. Weber's ideas, which recur from time to time, originate from the political need to have a charismatic leader who implements a program for which he received "authorization" from the people and a parliament that helps to realize the rule of the parties.[34]

[32] One of the fathers of this idea, Max Weber, claimed that the president of the republic, who was elected for seven years, should succeed the German emperor *and* Chancellor Bismarck. The best example of the legal succession of a king and a president is the case of a president elected for life. Napoleon was a consul for life before he became the emperor. Simon Bolivar drafted several constitutions in a number of Latin American republics, which made him president for life. He had to move from one country to another every year or two.

[33] Such was the prevailing system in Germany under the Weimar Constitution (from 1919 to 1933). This model was also adopted by Russia in Yeltsin's constitution.

[34] The role of the parliament in this model is to control the power of the administration. Weber rejected the American presidential system because he thought there was no one to keep a watchful eye on administration. Weber died in 1920, and since then the

A mutually restricting balance of the branches of power does not occur only where there is a separation of powers. Such balance may be established by "equalizing" and dividing, as a result of which the branches of power may have, in opposition to each other, symmetric rights of establishment and dissolution. In theory this would mean that the executive power and the legislative power have to be in equal positions. If the cabinet is elected by the parliament, we are facing "parliamentary absolutism." According to Redslob, who influenced the thinking of the drafters of the Weimar Constitution, "pure" parliamentary systems exist only in places where the balance of powers is mechanical.[35] The American separation does not permit the balancing act because the relationship among the branches is not close. "Real" (as defined in textbooks) balance occurs if the parliament can recall the cabinet and the cabinet can dissolve the parliament. The minister's responsibility (the fact that a minister may be called back) may be counterbalanced by the fact that the parliament may be dissolved at any time by the cabinet. Balance requires that both branches of power possess their own source of power of existence. The head of the executive, similar to the parliament, is elected by the people or, as in constitutional monarchies, is legitimized by the will of God. If the people elect both branches, they have the opportunity to impose their will on one of the branches by turning to the other. Should this not be ensured, the people's counteropinion can in no way be enforced against the parliament after an election, as the parliament will be the only power with supremacy.

---

idea and practice of having a permanent administration has been adopted in the U.S., too. Hence the danger of the operation of a spoils system (that is, the allocation of administrative positions to the winners of the elections) has lessened. The direct democratic control (hearings) of administrative procedures has a moderating effect, too. The role of courts in controlling the administration has significantly increased. All this points to the diminishing importance of legislation in its function as a controller. On the other hand, since Weber's death, the experiences with charismatic leaders led to the need to exclude the charismatic male. It is exactly this leaning toward Caesarism and the possibility of spoils that makes post-Soviet systems so appealing. On the other hand, anticesarism may have its weaknesses. In parliamentary party systems it may happen that leaders without any charisma may prove even more powerful than the president.

[35] Redslob.

3.2.2. Personal Dependencies

The appointment, supervision, and calling to account of the members of each branch of government is a matter of organizational relations. But given the personal nature of power, this dependence was one of the major problems in the early stages of Continental constitutionalism. Perhaps the excessive importance attributed to the system's separating and dividing the branches of power stems from this period. Constitutions that separate the branches of power emphatically reject the possibility of one person serving in two branches of government, while most parliamentary systems do not consider this important.

In the case of the separation-of-powers model, it is usually a constitutional requirement that the members of one branch cannot serve in another branch. In addition, the American Constitution (Art. I, sec. 6, clause 2) forbids senators and representatives from holding paid positions in the administration. The French Constitution of 1791 (Tit. III, ch. 2, sec. 4, par. 2), similarly to the American, attributes considerable importance to the separation of powers, even on a personal level. (The current Dutch Constitution adopted the 1791 French model in 1815.)

Such a prohibition would be welcome in parliamentary systems, too, because the lack of conflict-of-interest rules enables the administration to "buy" representatives, and the interests of the administration prevail directly. In the Austro–Hungarian monarchy, in theory a member of parliament could not be appointed to an office where appointments were made by the Crown or by the offices of the Crown or by the government and which came with a salary (Law XXIV of 1901). Ministers were exceptions to this rule.

Personal incompatibility can extend as far as stipulating that the representative of the executive cannot appear or make a verbal contribution in the operations and on the physical premises of the other branch. The American president and kings, in their heyday, appeared in the parliament only on ceremonial occasions. They were "barred" from entering the corridors of the legislature lest they took it upon themselves to interfere. But in parliamentary systems, cooperation always demanded that ministers be admitted to sessions and be allowed to make oral contributions.[36] In some instances the basis for letting them in was that they

[36] In modern parliamentary democracies where the parliament's role as a controller should prevail, the problem is more that ministers do not attend sessions. Sometimes

were the parliament's principals with special powers, but more often it was because they were the king's special envoys. In some parliamentary systems (primarily influenced by the British tradition) it is found important that the members of the executive come from among the parliament's members, because the ministers are thus available in person and there is greater potential to control and influence them. Undoubtedly this principle clashes with the dogmatic theories of separation. Parliamentary practice offers examples of both models. There are parliamentary countries (Norway and Holland) where a member of the cabinet cannot be a member of the parliament, whereas in other countries, for example, England, it is practically a requirement that a member of the government be a member of the Commons.[37]

The Belgian Constitution of 1831 permitted ministers to be MPs. According to the Bulgarian Constitution, a minister's parliamentary mandate has to be suspended upon entering the government. Most Continental constitutions refrain from taking a stand on this issue.

An obvious outcome of separation would be that the branch itself has the right to determine its own structure and organization, as well as to make its own appointments. However, according to a rather cryptic paragraph in the American Constitution, the president does not have an exclusive right to appoint the officials of the executive. Higher officials may be appointed by the president upon "the advice and consent" of the Senate. The right to appoint junior officials ("inferior officers") may be delegated by Congress by law to the president and the courts or "heads of departments" (chief officers of the administration). There is nothing in the American Constitution on how the person thus appointed may be dismissed. According to the Supreme Court, if someone is employed only in the executive branch, he can be relieved only by the president, regardless of the law and in accordance with the Constitution.[38] The president does not have this right in the case of an administrative office created by the legislature and where the appointment was also made by

---

special regulations need to be introduced to make them attend. This requirement applies at "question time."

[37] As a minister should be a member of parliament, but as members of parliament cannot sit in both houses of the legislature, Lord Home had to resign his title in order to become prime minister.

[38] *Myers v. United States*, 272 U.S. 52 (1926).

the legislature and where the person is engaged in quasi-legislative or quasi-judicial activities.[39]

The principle, therefore, is that an official in a given position belongs to the branch of government that may, on a discretionary basis (that is, beyond removal for crime), relieve him. Indeed, the right of appointment is irrelevant when it comes to concrete decisions that are taken by officials already appointed. By comparison, the function realized is secondary in the characterization of the pertinence to one or the other branch. Still, as a consequence of the disparity of the function and the dependence of the office holder, the areas of competence of the branches of government overlap. This is typically the situation when the legislature orders an official whom it may relieve to implement a law.

The results are paradoxical. In a parliamentary system, the appointment of the cabinet is the parliament's competence. The cabinet, however, may appoint to the administration anyone it so desires, provided the appointee meets the requirements stipulated by the legislature. By comparison, in the American system, which emphasizes separation, the president cannot make appointments to his own branch without the approval or authorization of the other branch. The appointments requiring joint approval of the branches serve constitutionalism so long as there is no risk that any of the tasks allocated by the Constitution to a given branch are jeopardized.

3.3. SEPARATE OPERATIONS AND JOINT DECISIONS

Although making and unmaking the determination of the organization and the persons in a given branch are important, this does not determine in itself the relationship of the branches of government. The actual limits to, or excesses of, power stem from the interference of the autonomy of existence and the autonomy of decision making. Even if the legislative branch is separate and independent, this will amount to little if it cannot enforce its will with laws; if the executive uses constitutional means to force the legislative to accept its will, or, simply, if the executive has the constitutional privilege to legislate in certain matters.

[39] *Humphrey's Executor v. United States*, 295 U.S. 602 (1935).

According to the principle of separation, each branch of government may operate within a given framework. The organization comprising the given branch carries out its allocated task and only this task. The executive may be directed only via laws and (with the exception of the "case of political accountability" enforced through elections) is accountable for breaching the law only to the court and not to any of the divisions within the executive power.

In terms of separation of powers, the U.S. presidential system, in reality, is not watertight either. The president may intervene into the legislative process in a negative way: with his veto he may, for any reason, refuse to sign a law (as was recommended by Montesquieu). To override his veto, a two-thirds majority vote of the Congress is required. But the limits of Congress's power are also uncertain. Congress regularly passes laws in which it delegates its power to legislate in merit, whereas according to a strict interpretation of the Constitution, no other body may assume this power. Many consider that congressional committees of enquiry, special counsels, and administrative bodies (for example, the Federal Reserve Board) set up by the legislature do exercise judicial and executive functions. But the major problem in the separation of the branches of power is not caused by the uncertainty of the relationship of the various branches but rather by their separation as such. From time to time there is a gaping void between the legislative and executive branches, threatening to paralyze the decision-making process.

Only in cases of emergency (civil war, world war, economic crisis), and even then only for a temporary period, does the executive gain unquestioned control. The nature of this control, even in such critical times, is one where the legislature accepts the initiatives of the executive, practically without question. For instance, the legislature enacts statutes that set forth broad objectives; on the basis of these enactments the executive may, in effect, issue orders that will provide for substantive rules. Even in these instances a special kind of balance may set in. The dominance of the executive (and the party behind it) may be restricted because the autonomy of the judiciary is upheld, and within certain limits, it may intervene if power is centralized in any of the branches of power in a manner that threatens civil liberties and minorities.[40]

[40] The conservative Supreme Court declared two laws constituting the basis of President Roosevelt's New Deal economic policy null and void. True, this happened

Various combinations of checks and balances exist in different countries and at different times. Based on the rules governing the formation of the branches, it may seem that the legislative branch plays a dominant role in the checks and balances system existing in parliamentary regimes. This dominance is enhanced by the legislative and other (for example, financial) instruments with which the government may be influenced. The cabinet is not only established by the parliament; but, what is more, the parliament is instrumental in its continuous existence. By resorting to the motion of confidence, the legislature is able to impose its political will on the executive. But the vote of confidence is too drastic a measure; it is a bomb that (in the event new elections are called) may blow up its engineers. Other institutions of supervision–some of them constitutionally entrenched–are preferred instead; these remain essentially political in nature. The control over government takes advantage of public opinion's influence. The members of the cabinet may be questioned; it is possible to interpellate where, in the end, a vote is taken on the acceptance or rejection of the answer given by the (member of) government. At this stage, the technical consequences of the confidence issue do not come into play. Parliamentary committees may investigate the actual activities of the executive, which may result in a scandal, or perhaps a legal procedure, or a political calling to account.

The above picture is misleading, however. In systems of checks and balances (parliamentary systems), the executive has made its operations considerably independent and has become dominant without parliamentary direction. In addition, it is able to influence the legislation and the parliament's other activities that are in theory aimed at directing the executive. In other words, the executive operates by using the parliament as the formal director of its actions. The tail takes its revenge on the dog.

The cabinet counteracts not only the legislature's formal powers but, in certain cases, manages to reverse them.[41] The executive has a privileged position in submitting bills and preparing the budget. According

---

two years after the laws were passed, and by that time most of the economic policy objectives had been realized. The Supreme Court gave up the fight at the point when it came under too much political pressure.

[41] Even a question asked in the parliament may be applied in this manner. In the British Parliament it is customary for the minister to make use of a question planted by a member of the majority when attempting to explain his views to the public.

to the French Constitution, under certain circumstances it is possible to pass a new law initiated by the government without the National Assembly ever voting on it. The executive acts as an original legislator without any special authorization. The French Constitution goes as far as to list the cases in which laws can be passed by Parliament. All other cases can be regulated *only* by the executive, and the organization "representing the people" is expressly forbidden to interfere.[42]

Monitoring of the executive is seemingly more restricted in the separation of powers system, that is, in the United States. Establishing the executive is not a competence of the legislative branch. Moreover, in strong presidential systems, the legislature routinely accepts most of the bills initiated by the executive.[43] The United States is a genuine exception to this rule. It has no direct executive initiative, and the members of the president's party may turn against him without any repercussions (for example, expulsion from the party). In a "real" presidential system, however, despite the separation of the branches of power, the legislature does not enjoy more independence, and it can rarely counterbalance the president's power. On the other hand, creating balances to the executive's legislative interference, by interfering into the administration, is difficult in practical terms. Unlike the executive's constitutional privileges in influencing legislation and its political opportunities to do so, the U.S. Congress cannot determine the concrete decisions of the person or organization in whom the power of the executive is vested, because this would be tantamount to it making decisions on execution.[44]

[42] Paradoxically, the French Parliament pays more attention to its remaining, limited legislative power than it did when it had unrestricted and "officially" nondelegable legislative powers under the Fourth Republic. On the other hand, the government does not insist on the delegation of legislative power to the government, a move often made in the early years of the Fifth Republic.

[43] David M. Olson, *The Legislative Process: A Comparative Approach* (New York: Harper and Row, 1980).

In Peru one can study a "real" presidential system in action. In the two presidential terms between 1980 and 1990, from 50 to 70 percent of all bills were put forward by the executive, and from 65 to 75 percent of these were passed by the legislature. (McClintock, 383). In the United States, 30 percent of all bills passed are initiated by the president (formally originating from a trusted congressman), while 20 percent are put forward jointly by the executive and some members of Congress.

[44] According to the U.S. Constitution, the bill of attainder is prohibited. From time to time, however, Congress may make concrete decisions. In Britain, private acts, once

> The Constitution does not contemplate an active role for Congress in the supervision of officers charged with the execution of the laws it enacts ... To permit the execution of the laws to be vested in an officer answerable only to Congress would, in practical terms, reserve in Congress control over the execution of the laws.[45]

The legislature's supervisory role is terminated by the appointment of executive officials (with consent from the Senate), so the legislative cannot become a permanent director. The table on p. 94 shows some possible models designed on the basis of the issues reviewed thus far. Compiling the five examined issues allows for twenty-five possible combinations. In the real world it is unlikely that a clearly separated or a clearly subordinated system can be found in the actual relationships.

---

the most common form of enactment, are still important as special rights of local authorities. In the Austro–Hungarian monarchy such enactments were made for the construction of railway lines.

[45] *Bowsher v. Synar*, 478 U.S. 714, 726-727, 732 (1986). The Gramm–Rudman–Hollings Act sought to balance the budget and would have authorized the comptroller general to put forward to the president certain recommendations to reduce the budget deficit. The president would then have been obliged to adopt these recommendations. The problem with the comptroller general was that, according to the act, after being appointed by the president with the consent of the Senate, Congress retained the power to remove him by impeachment or by a joint resolution in case of inefficiency and the like. If Congress is responsible for the removal of the officer, then he pertains to the legislative branch and cannot be entrusted to carry out executive tasks. The Supreme Court did not question in this case that Congress may have organizations that are dependent on it.

The principle behind the act was that all final budget decisions are made by Congress. The president's sequestration order to reduce the budget deficit would have become final only after a period of grace, unless Congress enacted other measures to cut the deficit. Consequently, the executive took only initial steps and the comptroller general did not have the right to make a final decision on his own.

Actual models for the possible connection between the executive (presidential) and legislative branches

Solution \ Models	1.	2.	3.	4.	5.	6.	7.	8.
directly elected head of the executive	+	+	+	+	+	-	-	-
government appointments are made independently of the parliament	+	-	+	-	-	-	-	-
government is not answerable to the parliament (absence of no-confidence)	+	+	-	-	-	-	-	-
the executive may dissolve the parliament at any time	+	-	+	+	-	+	-	-
the executive may propose laws	+	-	+	+	+	+	+	-

1. Absolute presidential; 2. USA; 3. Fifth French Republic; 4. Weimar; 5. Bulgaria (1991); 6. Westminster; 7. Third French Republic; 8. Absolute parliamentary system

3.4. ADDITIONAL COUNTERBALANCING FACTORS

3.4.1. The Role of the Judiciary in the Balancing of Powers

When we speak of checks and balances with regard to the judiciary, we find interdependencies again. Often it is another branch of power that makes decisions concerning the appointment of judges and the establishment of judicial organizations. But the other branches rarely have the authority to make judgments. Similarly, they lack the authority to intervene in concrete matters or to exercise any form of supervision.

Members of supreme judicial organizations are frequently elected by the parliament, while other judges are normally appointed by the executive, which may influence their careers in certain cases.[46]

All this is not of an imperative logic. There are systems (like the Italian Supreme Council of the judiciary) where self-governing bodies of judges decide on these issues. Elsewhere, the cooperation of the other branches is required. The U.S. president must seek the Senate's approval when appointing Supreme Court justices.

[46] This is the reason why judges may be transferred (and promoted) only if the person concerned agrees. It also illustrates the constitutional significance of the permanence of their positions and income.

In terms of its operations, the judiciary does not depend fundamentally on the other branches (at most it depends on them for its budget). The judiciary acts in accordance with regulations stipulated by the other branches, but its decisions may affect the operations of the other branches.[47]

In traditional parliamentary systems, court decisions do not affect the legislature but could have an effect on the executive branch's operations. In the post-World War II era, a new trend emerged demonstrating that politics was no longer satisfied with the judiciary's traditional role of merely applying laws. Breaking from Montesquieu's teaching, according to which judges are the law's mouthpiece and which relegated them to a level lower than that of the legislature, various forms of constitutional adjudication began to question the supremacy of legislation. Judges not only make law through precedent, though they still maintain that they do refrain from this. In addition, they now have a significant influence on legislative trends and on the meaning of the constitution.

3.4.2. The Federal (Vertical or Lateral) Separation of Power

In certain cases the restriction of government power also prevails on a vertical level, irrespective of the fact that on the horizontal level, that is, among the branches of government that are on the same level, separation or checks and balances exist. The state may be divided and restricted both at the "center" and the "periphery." This is offered by the separation that stems from federalism. In the face of central state organizations, some local representative bodies may be granted original powers, and these limit the central government's power. The central (or federal) legislature may make decisions only regarding matters stipulated in the constitution. In all other cases the prerogative is left to the provinces, regions, or member states. In a different arrangement the center has legislative powers in all matters not expressly attributed to the constituent states, or the states may dispose of residual powers only. There is a great variety of actual solutions.

[47] As an exception to the rule, the courts are left by and large to determine their own rules of procedure.

The U.S. Constitution (Art. I, sec. 8, clause 18) recognizes only legislative powers of the Congress on enumerated issues and in cases where legislation is "necessary and proper for carrying into execution" the enumerated powers. In the past two hundred years, the brief list given in the Constitution of 1787 has been considerably expanded, even arguing that commerce among the member states is a federal matter. (It is on this basis that, for instance, employment relationships can be federally regulated.)

In specific matters listed in the German Basic Law, the federal legislature has exclusive rights; in other areas there are matters of concurrent legislation. (Concurrent power means that if the federation does not pass a law, the member states have the right to do so.) The federation has the right to enact laws in concurrent matters if the matter can be better handled at the federal level. (Until recently, nearly all issues were thought to be better handled at the central level.) Finally, the federal legislature has no power to make decisions in matters not mentioned in the federal constitution or expressly reserved to the *Länder*.

Russia is seeking to introduce a system in which the approval of the federation's "subjects" (that is, the republics and the other territorial entities) will have to be sought in certain legislative matters before federal laws can be passed. According to the Russian Constitution, the supremacy of the federation subjects should prevail in legislative matters not classified as federal.

In federations, the member states, as far as they have real power and their own resources (sources of income, administrative bodies, and the like) are, within certain limits, capable of protecting their rights against central legislation and execution. Sometimes the center's weakness helps. In some instances the executive branch is constitutionally divided and in others the member states are responsible for execution, or the central executive cannot give orders to the local executive. According to the German Basic Law, for instance, to prevent the otherwise strong central government from becoming too dominant, the central executive bodies, as a rule, have no executive apparatus, that is, there is no subordinate apparatus under most of the federal ministries. If the center wishes to apply sectoral policies, provided a few important exceptions, it has to ask the provinces (*Länder*) for support. The officials executing central policies are employees of the *Länder*.

The extent to which provinces and member states act as actual counterweights has varied over time and across systems. The first decades of

American federal statehood were overshadowed by the member states' continuous efforts to prove that the federal Congress could not pass laws that applied to them without their approval. In the end, President Andrew Jackson, in connection with the Nullification Crisis made a straightforward declaration to avoid any misunderstanding, namely, that the federal government, in order to preserve the Union, was ready to fight even its own citizens.[48] Jackson's message to those who refused to recognize federal authority in South Carolina was the following:

> Tell them from me that they can talk and write resolutions and print threats to their hearts' content. But if one drop of blood be shed there in defiance of the laws of the United States, I will hang the first of them I can get my hands on to the first tree I can find.[49]

Clearly this indicates that limitations to the federal separation of powers might themselves be limited.

As welfare services and international relations became increasingly important, the weight of the central government increased. Those who shaped Germany as a federation in 1948 would hardly recognize their design today. The same could be said of the United States. But the trend is not necessarily universal. In the past two decades, Belgium successfully transformed its unified central government into a federation, or confederation. This move by and large created a peaceful area of activity for the national separatist movements.

3.5. WHEN DOES THE COUNTERWEIGHT BECOME EXCESSIVE WEIGHT?

On the European continent, as the antagonism between parliament and the executive passed away and while the existence of the organization of the executive depended unquestionably on the legislature, the executive gradually became more important, even if it was not manifest in the

[48] Some member states refused to implement federal resolutions. In 1832, several southern states fell into controversy with the Union over demand for customs rights and became the advocates of separation.

[49] George Fort Milton, *The Use of Presidential Power* (Boston: Little Brown, 1944), 91.

constitution like that in the French Constitution of 1958. The strengthening of the executive is partly the result of changes in election systems, which came to favor party rule, and partly of the changes in the functioning and influence of parties (considerably affected by the role of the media in influencing the outcome of elections). The less parties support the executive, the more unstable the government's majority and the more difficult for the executive to exert its influence. But this goes beyond the issue of constitutionalism.

Several other factors, for example, party systems, electoral systems, and the role of public administration, influence the power relationships among the branches of government.[50] Here it is sufficient to note that the interconnectedness of the branches of government limits the power of each.

Modern parties and electoral systems can play a decisive role in the relationship of the branches of government. The number of parties in the parliament depends to a considerable extent on the electoral system. As the number of parties in parliament increases, the independence of the legislature increases accordingly, though in certain cases this happens at the expense of governability. According to Duverger's classical premise, in single-round elections, the first-past-the-post electoral system is advantageous in forming two-party systems, while proportional representation is advantageous for multiparty systems. Constitutions, however, are mostly silent on electoral systems, meaning that the making of actual political power, which heavily influences checks and balances, falls outside the fundamental law.

If we assume that the political parties are well disciplined, any separation of powers may seem an impossible venture in the process of es-

[50] Olson and Mezey put forward other hypotheses on how the relationship of the branches of government will develop. If the executive is centralized, the representatives' chances of pushing through independent legislative initiatives become slimmer. If the executive's initiative is put forward by a relatively lower-level organization, the legislature has a greater chance of rejecting it. Some ministers may be defeated by government members, too, partly because there is no direct consequence in terms of existence, that is, there will be no elections. Where the government is formally entitled to legislative initiatives, there is a greater chance for the initiative to be accepted, as all rejection will be looked on as going against the government. See David M. Olson and Michael L. Mezey, eds., *Legislatures in the Policy Process: The Dilemmas of Economic Policy* (Cambridge: Cambridge University Press, 1991).

tablishing constitutionalism. It is advantageous in terms of the separation of powers if representatives do not depend on their party for campaign financing and the nomination of candidates but are continuously dependent on the voters and if they–in case all else fails–can be recalled. But this is difficult to reconcile with the principle of indivisible representation of the unified nation, stability, and other constitutional values.

If as a result of election, a modern party manages to draw both the legislative and executive branches within its sphere of influence, the party leadership can "unify" the two branches and there will be only one center where decisions are made. This can be moderated only by the separation of the constitutional branches of government. It has a limiting effect, for example, if the executive needs time to acquire, in accordance with constitutional procedures, the legal authorization required for the realization of the party's policy. In such circumstances, the elements of a constitutional system that grant political rights for minorities become especially important, because they prevent the legislature from becoming completely subordinated to a single party or to a dominant party coalition. A second legislative chamber elected at a different time and according to different principles, the weight of the member states in the federation, and a constitutional court (with members appointed earlier by different political groups) may have such a counteracting role. In an attempt to restore the constitutional balance, parliamentary minorities with their constitutional complaints involve the constitutional court in the process, which may render the dominant party's rule through the executive more difficult.

3.6. SEPARATION AND FREEDOM

The most appropriate basis for assessing the relationship of the branches of government is to determine whether freedom is preserved. To the extent that it is possible to draw normative conclusions by looking at past experiences, constitutionalism, as a limit to despotism, may also be efficient if one of the branches is given a certain role in determining who should be employed by another branch and it is given leave to participate in carrying out the duties of the other branch. It does not follow from the practice of cooperation that there is a need for joint decision making. Under certain circumstances, co-determination may lead to a breakdown in the decision-making process. Division of government powers will result in moderating exercises of power, if the influence of the various branches is directed toward the various stages in the decision-making and execution processes.

What is critical is maintaining separation regarding the core of a specific government function. This is demonstrated in the way the executive's quasi-legislative power may lead to the restriction of civil liberties. At the beginning of the American Civil War, in 1861, as the commander in chief of the army, President Lincoln issued a confidential order authorizing the commander of the army to take into custody anyone acting suspiciously, without having to observe the rule of habeas corpus. The commander, in turn, delegated this power to lower ranking commanders, a move that resulted in the detention of thousands of private citizens. As the order was adopted in practice without first obtaining congressional approval, no objection could be raised as to its breaching of the Constitution. The order, which was originally intended for application in the theater of war, was soon extended to apply in areas that were broadly termed "war-operation zones," and, indeed, it was applied in a much wider circle. Mass deportations in Missouri followed.[51] The source of anticonstitutionalism, in this case, is the absence of separation.

A number of similar examples can be offered besides the United States. It is a fact, however, that in England, a country of quintessential

[51] Mark E. Neely, Jr., *The Fate of Liberty: Abraham Lincoln and Civil Liberties* (New York: Oxford University Press, 1991), 9.

This story was repeated, albeit under different legal, technical conditions, during World War II when American citizens of Japanese descent were deported. Nevertheless, it would be unjust to consider the American model of the separation of powers as one that is less concerned with civil liberties than parliamentarism. As shown below, the situation is fully the reverse. An American example is given because it shows that at times not even separation is enough, especially if it can be skirted by citing the powers of the commander in chief of the army. The incident points to a characteristic imperfection in the U.S. Constitution. It fails to admit the need to apply special rules in cases of emergency. It does mention rebellion and invasion, in which cases the "privilege of the Writ of Habeas Corpus" may be suspended.

The more recent Continental constitutions tend to stipulate who may declare states of emergency and under what conditions. In such cases, the executive assumes most of the authorities of the legislature and stipulates the extent to which civil liberties may be restricted.

parliamentarism, fundamental rights and liberties are not violated either. Nor did the lack of strict separation (under normal circumstances) lead to the restriction of civil liberties in other parliamentary states on the Continent. In most cases, it is the parliament's exclusive right to restrict or regulate civil liberties. Liberties are observed no matter what the executive–legislative relationship is. On the other hand, it is the parliamentary party majority that matters; partisan influence may be detrimental to liberties. Civil liberties are threatened by party dictatorship and, indirectly, by the will and tastes of the alleged majority. The threat of modern dictatorship is not actually presented by the autocratic rule of one of the branches of government. The real danger consists in the overwhelming dominance of one party, or party group, over all the branches of government.

Under certain circumstances the separation of powers still makes some difference, especially when the separation is more characteristic, making control over the executive more likely. In cases where civil liberties can be restricted only by law and a qualified majority is required for the passing of such, it is quite often necessary to win the support of the parliamentary minority, that is, the support of the opposition, because the government's support and the party behind it are not enough.

The separation of the branches of power is more appropriate for moderating party dominance than are checks and balances.[52] In this respect the American experience is more favorable, though, according to a broadly held view, it is not the separation that is the primary reason for the singularly weak influence of the American parties on political decision making. In the United States, the separation and the democratic electoral system act together in exerting their influence. This is due to the fact that the Congress elected under the presidential term and the continuously renewed Senate show a party preference that deviates from what was current at the time of the presidential election. This offers a further possibility for the institutional balance to facilitate the parties' restricting influence on each other. The United States, however, is an exception. According to the experiences with the increasingly presidential and more "separated" South American systems, the separation, paradoxically, has no real significance because the political parties are *not* sufficiently strong.

[52] This does not contradict the objections mentioned concerning presidentialism.

No matter how outdated and unimportant the principle of the separation of powers and the juggling with checks to power may seem, many observers continue to consider them of fundamental importance as far as the prevalence of constitutionalism is concerned. Without separation of powers, that is, in the case of a homogeneous power, it is much easier for the power to become biased and then, later on, despotic. In addition, in the past forty years, judicial review and independent constitutional adjudication have become effective barriers to the concentration of power in Europe. It can happen that the constitutional courts strongly support the separation, or at least the division, of the branches of government against the tacit conspiracy of the other branches to blur the difference. Court decisions may force the legislature and the executive to take steps against each other to protect civil liberties.

Modern constitutions are aware of a number of additional methods which enhance the effect of the measures that result from the separation of powers in an attempt to curb despotism. These include the institutions for the division and depoliticization (party independence) of the executive as well as the partial control by the constitutional court of the decisions of the executive and the case-related democratic control (participation in the decision-making process) of given executive institutions.

Chapter 4

PARLIAMENTARISM AND THE LEGISLATIVE BRANCH

Your Representative owes you not his industry only but his judgment, and he betrays, instead of serving you, if he sacrifices it to your opinion.
Edmund Burke

4.1. THE TRANSFORMATIONS OF PARLIAMENT

4.1.1. THE EVOLUTION OF PARLIAMENTARISM AND ITS TRANSFORMATION INTO A REPRESENTATIVE SYSTEM

Among the late medieval predecessors of the modern parliamentary system is the English Parliament, which had the most lasting impact on later developments. In early days, Parliament was an informal gathering of the nobility and feudal lords. It functioned primarily as a consultative body with the right to administer justice and vote for the introduction of special taxes. The members represented themselves (their families, in the House of Lords) and the towns and counties, often at the request of leading officials of a town and not necessarily as directly elected representatives. The elected representatives became members of parliament with only a fraction of the population having the right to vote.

The English Parliament's real power sprang from its members' military and economic power as well as their social status. Occasional royal recognition increased the self-confidence of the institution well before the representative system, with its democratic legitimacy, became popular.[1]

[1] "The power and jurisdiction of parliament is so transcendent and absolute, that it cannot be confined, either for causes or persons, within any bounds." Sir Edward Coke, 4 Inst. 36. in Sir William Blackstone, *Commentaries on the Laws of England*, vol. 1 (Chicago: University of Chicago Press, 1979), 156.

During the English Civil War Parliament became a real, indeed exclusive, power, assuming at least in theory the responsibilities of the executive. This Long Parliament became a monolithic power to the extent that nearly two generations later, during the Glorious Revolution (1689), it seemed unthinkable that this chamber could again exercise supreme power, although this would have been the simplest solution for the dethronement of the Stuart king. A monarch was sought because experience indicated that

> ...where the legislative and executive authority are in distinct hands, the former will take care not to entrust the latter with so large a power, as may tend to the subversion of it's own independence, and therewith of the liberty of the subjects.[2]

The centrality and supremacy of the legislative power became the dominant theory in the mid-eighteenth century. Locke's contention that there remains with the people an inherent supreme power to remove or alter the legislative was refuted: "we may venture to affirm, that the power of parliament is absolute and without control."[3] Blackstone described parliament as "the place where that absolute despotic power, which must in all governments reside somewhere, is entrusted by the constitution of the kingdoms...It can, in short, do anything that is not naturally impossible."[4] Parliament, however, was only able to pass laws together with the monarch. Not long after Blackstone's commentaries were published, the English Parliament itself began to believe that it was omnipotent, an opinion, however, that soon proved to be untenable, at least as far as the American settlers were concerned. Among other things, its stubborn refusal to restrain itself explains why antagonism between the American colonists and the mother country flared. The sovereign despotism of the English Parliament (coupled with that of the monarch) deeply wounded the Americans. One of the main objectives when drawing up a new constitution for the frustrated colonists–Englishmen by birth–was to find ways in which this omnipotence could be restrained.

[2] Blackstone, 142.

[3] Blackstone, partly on the basis of Montesquieu's theories, considered the balance of power the foundation of the English Constitution. This balance, however, is a mixture of various forms of government (democracy, aristocracy, and monarchy). Blackstone, 157.

[4] Blackstone, 156.

Despite its alleged omnipotent supremacy, Parliament was subject internally to constraints. According to Blackstone, Parliament is comprised of His Majesty, the House of Lords, and the elected House of Commons. The branches of power, that is, the people at large, the peers, and the executive power (the monarch), balance and restrain each other through the need for mutual agreement. The powers of the two parliamentary houses to investigate and impeach the monarch's counselors further serve to uphold the system of checks and balances. It is also part of parliament's operations as an institution that members cannot be called to account for statements made *within* the chamber, that is, they have personal immunity. It is the privilege of the House of Commons to initiate bills related to taxes and finance, which may be rejected only by the House of Lords. The reason for this privilege is that, in such a manner, the people impose burdens on themselves. The Commons are elected "that herein consists the exercise of the democratical part of our constitution," because it is through elections "which is the declaration of the people's will."[5] People exercise their sovereignty by choosing their representatives. To ensure that the right to vote was not abused, only those who were not influenced by others could vote; consequently, the right to vote depended on wealth.[6]

In most respects today's parliaments are the opposite of the eighteenth-century model. In constitutional systems, the executive branch is not part of the legislative branch, although continuing with the monarchical tradition, in many parliamentary systems the president of the republic often monitors legislation.

The second house of the parliament–where it exists–does not represent a defined social group or estate. In the federal system this is the forum of the autonomous regions, provinces, cantons, member states, or it is simply elected by a procedure differing from that of the election of the House of Commons (or the lower house). It represents the people in a different manner, consequently, it plays primarily a controlling and restraining role in the parliamentary process, although in some systems it is an equal part of the legislative branch.[7]

[5] Blackstone, 164.

[6] Blackstone, 165.

[7] In the United Kingdom, the House of Lords' role in the legislative process and in shaping politics is restricted, especially since the reform of 1911. At the very most it can

Members still enjoy immunity and the executive can still be influenced by parliamentary inquiries and impeachment. But in Blackstone's time parliamentary democracy as the major force of influence on the executive was unknown. Eighteenth-century parliaments were not concerned with the principle that the executive could not operate without the *trust* (confidence) of parliament and that, all in all, the executive power acts as the representative of the legislative power. Nor did the reverse of parliamentarism exist, that is, the executive could not initiate bills and did not enjoy the privileges pertaining to finance bills. Today's parliaments are no more a forum of complaints about, and the means for remedy of, irregularities reported by their members. Based on its own representative-democratic legitimacy, parliament intends to determine politics.

Finally, and in theory most importantly, membership in parliament today is subject to popular *election* (life terms in the House of Lords and senatorships for Italian presidents are negligible exceptions). The majority of parliaments are formed as a result of direct elections, in a system where all adults have the right to vote. (In federal systems it is often the case that federal councils are comprised of the representatives of the governments of the member states, as in Germany, or they are elected by the state legislatures, as in the U.S. before the Seventeenth Amendment of the Constitution was adopted in 1913.)

Supposing that the separated legislative and executive powers are able to control and restrain each other efficiently, it is almost irrelevant from the point of view of constitutionalism how they relate to each other or what their internal organizations are like. Our standard minimum conditions are fulfilled, so we can rest assured that neither will capture absolute power. Nevertheless, the kind of political system we live in is not without importance because, in order to feel that the state is to some extent our own, we need to be able to identify with it, and for this we need to have the ability to influence and monitor the government. In this regard the roots of the need for a representational-parliamentary government and liberal constitutionalism are identical, and the two are related. Moreover, popular control of government does not make limits to power through separation unnecessary.

---

obstruct the passage of money bills sent by the House of Commons for no more than a month.

Parliament is the body of (general popular) representation from where, in parliamentary systems, the special legitimacy of the legislative power and its supremacy over the executive power derives. Of course, if the head of the executive is elected by the people, the parliament's supreme legitimacy resulting from its representative character is lost, and the relationship of the two branches of power will be determined only by the logic of the division of labor and the contingencies in the text of the constitution.

On event of a constitutional division of power, it is almost without doubt that laws will be passed by the parliament, that is, an elected body that represents the electors (in a modern democracy, the whole public). More precisely, parliament mostly represents the public, however, the people or nation with political rights cannot automatically be associated with the whole public.[8]

People need some sort of legislative and governing body elected by them if they do not want to relinquish the right and let somebody else keep an exclusive watch over the constitutional order. While it seems a natural consequence of democratic ideals that the legislative branch is chosen by "popular" vote, it seems less unequivocal but compelling that the executive power or the person in charge of it should be elected by the people. It is consistent with the democratic exercise of power that the executives, at least in part, operate as parliament's "executive committee."

4.1.2. The Cooling off of Popular Sovereignty in Parliamentary Systems: The Free Mandate

It can be said that parliament exercises its legislative function as a consequence of its popular, representative character. Its crucial role in determining executive policies also follows from its popular democratic legitimacy. Unfortunately popular representation, which is the basic article of faith of modern parliamentary democracy in a nutshell, probably has not one single element that is not in need of correction.

[8] Poland and Hungary, for instance, had strong parliamentary systems with deputies representing the self-governments and the nation; but before 1848 the *natio* of the nobility was small in number compared with the whole population.

However odd the institution of constitutionalism is, parliament is in itself a means of restraining the will of the people and popular participation, while at the same time it is an institution that also needs to be restrained.

In accordance with the democratic foundations of power, all people are equal and autonomous, thus only they themselves are able to decide their fate.

The sovereignty of the people and democracy require that the citizens' will have a decisive impact on their own affairs and that their will should directly govern the state. This point of departure surprisingly and stubbornly prevails, though it is not at all certain that people truly want to continuously maintain this constant participation. The conditions of a complex society impede the emergence of the general will, and the reduction of the common will to that of a majority renders the popular demand uncertain. Constitutionalism is not in favor of the direct unmediated operation or, quite often, volcanic eruption of popular sovereignty.

It is at this stage that the parliamentary system comes into the fore–arm in arm with constitutionalism–and acts as an intermediary between the people and the assertion of their will. Parliament becomes the body of the expression of the general will and of legislation.[9] As the state works according to its laws, it is enough to issue commands to the state through laws. Democratic principles may support the election of other bodies by popular vote, but this is unnecessary for the operation of popular sovereignty. For the general will of the people to prevail it is enough if that will dominates the legislature.

The English Parliament–the ideal of the eighteenth-century prophets of constitutionalism–created the impression that parliament was

[9] It is partly a "historic" coincidence that the representation of the people's sovereignty was invested in parliament. In theory the majority of people may invest this right in one person (if the majority's will represents the common will of the people), but it is easier for the one-man regime to turn into absolutism. A dictator or president could be elected who would then present to his people the laws dictated by the general will, an idea expressly advocated by Rousseau. But when the democratic need for popular sovereignty arose, the monarch was already there as the sole expression of the people's will. Given that the whole of the popular-will theory was used by the enemies of the monarch, he could not in any way have been accepted as the representative of the general will of the people.

omnipotent or, at the least, that it was endowed with privileged, supreme powers. Locke, who summed up the experiences of the Glorious Revolution earlier, said that the government's power originated from the people. He held that, under a compact, the people transfer the power to government and the bodies stipulated in that compact. But according to Locke, "there remains still *in the People a Supreme Power* to remove or *alter the Legislative*, when they find the *Legislative* act contrary to the trust reposed in them."[10]

The eighteenth-century legislative body, notwithstanding its medieval "delegation" principles, was capable of adaption to the requirements of democracy and the democratic electoral system. Such accommodation enabled the political system to avert the danger of *direct* popular will and popular rule. A second major change of parliament was necessary to remedy the dangers of democracy. Until the emergence of constitutionalism, power was transferred by the people to a body or person exercising it under a compact. With parliamentary representation–even if indirectly–the people themselves exercise this power. If the constituent does not want the people–be they the source of all power–to exercise and institutionalize the most horrific, mass *absolutist* despotism of the masses growing above everyone, the legislative body cannot remain the "supreme" body. This principle, for that matter, ensues from the separation of the branches of power, but in the shadow of popular rule, only the separation of the branches into equal powers seemed reassuring.

Parliament with its–elected–actors can reflect society's diversity. The representatives of this diversity may debate issues and exchange opinions, and in this manner the general will can be formulated. It is not something that is given but something that can be formulated and is acceptable to everyone. In accordance with these ideas, at the beginning parliamentary representation was considered the virtual manifestation of society.

Parliament, as the body of the legislature, can restrain the otherwise constitutionally desirable democratic-majority rule exactly because it is a *representative* government. It is based on the principle of representation

[10] John Locke, "The Second Treatise of Government" in *Two Treatises of Government*, ed. Peter Laslett, (Cambridge: Cambridge University Press, 1991), § 149. For Blackstone's legalistic mind this was not supported in existing law.

not direct democratic rule. As Madison said, the legislative branch, as an independent actor, stands between the majority of electors and the law. For parliament to be able to distance itself from the majority, it must cease being the virtual representation of the electors. This is ensured by the representatives' free mandate.

The *binding mandate* was a typical feudal phenomenon, and when the ambitious delegates of the French feudal lords, who had binding mandates, transformed the feudal parliament (Estates General), in 1789, into a constituent National Assembly, their first act was to rid themselves of the binding mandate that came from their provincial representation. Thus they became representatives of the whole nation. This is why the idea of national sovereignty could be so successful: the individual who is elected to represent the whole *nation* is independent of every individual elector or constituency.

This was Abbot de Sieyés's fine trick. The representative serves the nation and not popular sovereignty. This is advantageous as, otherwise, the people and the electors comprising the people, or a majority of the people, may come with their empirical and mundane will and take the representative to task, asking: "What are you doing with my will, in my name, and with the power I invested in you? On what grounds have you replaced my will with yours?" After all, contrary to representation and delegation in private law, the representative is not bound by the electors' will any more than the electors are bound by the representatives' statements and votes.

> Parliament is not a *Congress* of Ambassadors from different and hostile interests; which interests each must maintain, as an Agent and Advocate, against other Agents and Advocates; but Parliament is a *deliberative* Assembly of *one* Nation, with *one* Interest, that of the whole; where, not local Purposes, not local Prejudices ought to guide, but the general Good, resulting from the general Reason of the whole.[11]

[11] Speech at the Conclusion of the Poll, 3 November 1774, in Edmund Burke, *The Writings and Speeches of Edmund Burke*, vol. 3, eds. Paul Langford and William B. Todd (Oxford: Clarendon Press, 1996), 63. In eighteenth-century England, it was easier to reject the idea of the binding mandate than at a later period in the French Assembly, which prepared and passed the constitution in the name of popular, or national, sovereignty.

There were no party lists in the eighteenth and nineteenth centuries. The voter and their representatives could only be identified within the constituencies, thus in theory it was possible to attribute a specific meaning to the mandate received from the electorate in the constituency. However, once the member represents *the whole population*, *or nation*, his mandate is not bound. Whose moneybags actually influence the representatives' votes is not discussed in constitutions. Incompatibility–as long as it does not affect checks and balances–is the "private business" of the representatives and not a constitutional problem of representation.[12]

This logical twist has been of little concern since 1789, as it was already evident at that time that the binding mandate would render the working of the political system too particularistic if not impossible. The uncertainties in the Declaration of the Rights of Man and Citizen of 1789 show that the shift was a difficult one. But Sieyés's brilliant idea, the consequences of which were horrific, made the *nation* the subject of sovereignty: "the source of all sovereignty is essentially in the nation" (Art. 3 of the Declaration). The service of the nation will allow the reconciliation of popular election and nonbinding mandate. The Declaration treats direct and representational legislation as completely equal (Art. 6), but the French Constitution of 1791 does not really permit direct democracy. The nation, which is the sole source of all power, may exercise these powers through representation *only* (Tit. III, par. 2), and the representatives, because they represent the whole nation, cannot be given instructions (Tit. III, ch. 1, sec. 3, par. 7).[13]

[12] It is plain to see that here the inclusion of the handling of modern political dependencies in the constitution has been omitted. Modern constitutions are prepared by representatives or party mouthpieces who must pay attention to the representatives' joint private interests, so the possibility of including strict and "virtuous" regulations on incompatibility is slight.

[13] Beginning with the French Constitution of 1791, liberal constitutions generally prohibit binding mandates and electoral instructions. Such rules can be found, for instance, in the Spanish Constitution of 1812, where the indirectly elected regional representatives have to work in the interest of the whole Spanish nation (Art. 100), and in the Frankfurt Constitution of 1848 (Art. 96).

The free-mandate concept was included in many constitutions for reasons other than liberal principles. In 1814, the Dutch Constitution accepted this principle because the delegates to the earlier General Estates (Assembly) were actually the delegates of the provincial parliaments, and the work of the Estates was virtually paralyzed because the

4.1.3. Parliament: A Club for the Finest Gentlemen

"In the beginning," that is, at the end of the eighteenth century (and in the early liberal constitutions), popular representation had not yet been tamed and only very few politicians and thinkers considered the lower social classes acceptable participants in the political decision-making process, the parliaments of representative governments had no desire to represent the people not even in principle. How could this order be justified against democratic republicanism, according to which the constitutional systems that did not recognize the binding mandate or at least the principle of recalling representatives were simply wrong? From where did the legitimacy of parliamentary decisions originate in the eyes of liberal constitutionalists in Europe?

The theory of parliamentary representative government is built on the assumption of the early-nineteenth-century restrictive electoral system. In this system it was assumed that voters, who were small in number, could come to know their candidates well. The elected representative could not be ordered to act in one way or another. He was free to commit himself to his principles and plans. On this basis, it is possible to choose from among the candidates. It was at this time that institutions of public opinion, like the free press, became more robust. It was assumed that public opinion would be informed on who did what in parliament, thus voters could make enlightened choices based on their candidates' past performance and credible campaign promises.

The electoral decision is based on one's intellectual performance, in other words, how convincing the candidate is in the eyes of other members of the legislature, the voters, and public opinion.

---

delegates, as if they were attending a badly organized diplomatic conference, had to go home for instructions (after the amendment of 1983 the rule can be found in Art. 67. (3)).

At times constitutions emphasize that the members represent the whole nation, and *all* they need do is act in accordance with their conscience: Art. 38, Germany (1949); similarly, Art. 21, Weimar; Art. 27, France (1958); and similarly in the Third and Fourth French Republics. The hypocrisy of national representation is shown by the rather widespread practice that the member elected from the party list gives his party a signed declaration of resignation, which comes into effect on event of insubordination. Courts are reluctant to accept these documents (the first such case went to court in Weimar Germany, when a communist representative rebelled).

As opposed to the legitimization of popular representation and radical republicanism which later became rather disreputable because of the dangers of unlimited popular sovereignty, liberal thinkers in the nineteenth century saw the advantages of the parliamentary system in the *decision-making* process itself and not in the fact that those affected by the decision had the possibility of participating in the decision-making process, albeit through their representatives.[14] Beginning with Edmund Burke and ever since the end of the French Revolution, it has been denied that parliamentary representation is a binding private-law mandate given by the voters.

In an effort to justify parliamentarism or the legislature in general, without the will-of-the-people reason, democracy's critics (Guizot and Tocqueville) and its liberal interpreters (J. S. Mill) found a new, anti-democratic or, from the point of view of democracy, at least a neutral role for parliamentarism. Parliament is not the organization of the *will* of the people but that of the *thought* of the people. Parliament is a forum for *political debate* where the social processes of cognition, necessary for rational decisions, occur.[15] Parliamentary debate is the means to political

[14] The republican passion was paradoxical because nowhere did the majority of the population have the right to vote, thus, in the absence of general suffrage, it seems rather strange that the contemporaries spoke of *popular* representation. In the United States, some groups (slaves and Indians) were excluded on a "formal" basis. They were not considered fully mature beings (with an adequately developed mental capacity). But such denial was considered an extremely dubious move even in those days, in comparison with property or tax qualifications that were accepted in the constitutional states of the nineteenth century. The fears of the propertied classes continued to prevail. It was argued that the person who did not have property and who depended on others for his existence did not have the freedom to make decisions, thus he could not vote. Women were excluded from the electorate on various and, for a long time, only exceptionally contested grounds.

[15] The advocates of a moderate will of the people reached this conclusion, too. The majority of the French Constituent Assembly, following Sieyés's teaching, were in favor of social and parliamentary debate. The debate helped to formulate the general will. It was held that the will of the majority, which was generated through proper debate, was the general will, which could not be restricted or questioned.

The British parliament of the eighteenth century, as well as today, might appear as a party-driven voting machine. Nonetheless, during the years leading to and following the Reform Act of 1832, deliberations in the parliament among "men of wisdom and ability" became intense. "The ideal member of Parliament, like the ideal constituent, was the

understanding, at the end of which the representatives will have got nearer to the truth. A free press is the external condition of the success of truth finding.

In the parliamentary representative system, (1) the powers that be were forced to search for the truth together; (2) the powers to be were forced to carry out this search in view of the public because of the publicity given; and (3) due to the freedom of the press, citizens themselves took part in the search for the truth and the result of this search was presented to the powers that be.

Before becoming himself a member of government, Francois Guizot, in the constitutional monarchy of Louis-Philippe of France, held that the representative system had to be the parliamentary representation of rational people only. The legislative process had nothing to do with the blind will; it had to do with intellect, consequently, liberal parliamentarism had to be antidemocratic.[16] General suffrage was absurd and impossible. For people like Guizot 220,000 (well-to-do) electors were the French nation.

John Stuart Mill also considered parliament an appropriate venue for the exchange of political views. But contrary to the antidemocratic Guizot, he considered representative government part of a wider social program. This form of government fitted into the general intellectual development and was justified inasmuch as it was the best means of this development. "The position which gives the strongest stimulus to the growth of intelligence is that of rising into power, not that of having achieved it."[17] Mill advocated a system of universal but graduated suffrage. Representative government facilitated self-determination and national determination.

But representative government, in itself, and without the appropriate constitutional restrictions, is dangerous. If parliamentarism in accordance with democratic principles means the dominance of the majority

---

independent rational man." Samuel H. Beer, *Modern British Politics: Parties and Pressure Groups in the Collectivist Age* (New York: W. W. Norton, 1982), 39.

[16] Francois Guizot, *Histoire du gouvernement representatif en France*, vol. 1 (Paris: Didier, 1851), 14. Guizot originally held the lectures beginning in 1820.

[17] John Stuart Mill, *Considerations on Representative Government* (Buffalo, NY: Prometheus Books, 1991), 190. Hegel, another opponent of the system of popular representation, attributed considerable importance to the *educational* role of parliamentary debates.

opinion and the rule of the majority, one should guard against it, because the rule of the majority leads to the utter defenselessness of the minority and the individual.

Mill saw further faults in representative government. A representative parliament could not operate without the continuous services provided by a permanent administration composed of experts. The impossibility of restricting the power of a bureaucratic state also presented a threat. Bureaucracy destroyed individuality and prevented the development of individual potential when, in the name of uniformity, it persecuted deviation. Under such conditions, representative government could only be successful if it consisted of those with sufficient education.

Parliament is the place where in-depth discussion of issues takes place, with occasional bargaining, which also requires rational reflection.[18] In parliament the factions counteract each other, thus the minority's views influence the majority's, lifting some of the barriers resulting from one-sidedness to facilitate the in-depth examination of issues and helping to avoid mistakes in decision making. The variety of views has a beneficial effect on parliamentary decisions, though it sometimes happens that because of the diversity of views, the decisions made are not, or are just marginally, appropriate. Parliament's special role, then, is due to its role as a forum for free debate.

Parliamentarism has been continuously losing its prestige since its victory in the second half of the nineteenth century. With the rise of multiparty systems a permanent instability became characteristic of parliamentary governments. Parliament, as a club, was seen increasingly incapable of making decisions. Originally, traditional party-based parliaments–like the Hungarian one in the last third of the nineteenth century with its whip-abiding, obedient MPs and its fundamentally politically homogeneous electorate, or the bi- or tri-partisan English parliament of the Disraelis and Gladstones–stood in sharp contrast with the nineteenth-century French parliamentary assemblies, in which there was much less party stability and the obedience of the parliamentarians to the faction was far less stringent.

[18] Hamilton held similar views. But his concerns were more practical. *The Federalist Papers* No. 70 (New York: Mentor Books, 1961).

4.1.4. A Critique of Classical Parliamentarism. Party Rule and Corporatist Assemblies

By the beginning of the twentieth century, parliamentarism seemed to have lost its steam. The earlier insufficiency, namely, that only a small number of civilians were represented, could be remedied by general suffrage, but the cure, though it may not have been worse than the "illness," lead definitely to a new de-legitimization.

It became nearly impossible to reconcile the idea of reason-dominated deliberation, the model of the parliament as a debating club, with the way parliament actually worked. The difference between the principle of a parliament as a forum for debate and the way parliament actually worked became evident, ironically, once general suffrage and, consequently, popular representation were institutionalized. The *general right to vote* brought with it the development of modern mass parties.[19] This, hand in hand with the proportional electoral system (Belgium, 1899; Sweden, 1907), transformed parliament along strict party lines.

The parties were on their way to becoming efficient machines. Where the modern party system led to a firm parliamentary majority, democratically controlled party rule was established. Democracy in this context meant that the government, which was granted almost dictatorial rights, could be called to account and dismissed every four to five years by the population. The chances of a democratic party dictatorship increase especially when there are no strong constitutional checks

[19] In France, after the Commune of 1870, the bourgeois republican groups granted workers the right to vote because in this way it was possible to counteract the royalist votes of the property-holding franchised peasants in the provinces. Bismarck granted workers the right to vote in order to counteract the representation of the *Junkers* in parliament. The difference between the active and passive voting right was abolished already during the French Revolution (August 10, 1791) because of the war and "in the interest of national defense." All men over 21 (with the exclusion of servants) who swore allegiance were granted the right to vote. The same principle was applied in many countries during and after World War I. It is difficult to deny the person, whose responsibility it is to defend the state and die for it, the right to have a say in what is to happen in his country in peacetime. By the end of World War I, in nearly all states that were to a certain degree constitutional, the right to vote was granted to at least the male population. The armed cannon fodder had to be given something in exchange for its sacrifice.

and balances and power is not restricted. This is what happens in all Westminster-type systems.

"John Stuart Mill wrote a book on *Representative Government* without mentioning parties. A realistic survey of the British Constitution to-day must begin and end with parties and discuss them at length in the middle."[20] To a certain extent, England still has a party parliament; however, like in most countries the number of party-membership fee payers and party-meeting goers has declined, and the inherited party loyalty has weakened. As the weight of the media increased, a new kind of intellectual manipulation was introduced. Parties now try to win supporters through advertisements and not by operating clubs and holding meetings to exchange ideas with members. They do not work with organizations for the masses but try to manipulate opinion directly outside their own organizational structures.[21]

The parliamentary system lost its obvious, "natural" constitutionalism, something that was thought to be an integral part of it.

The bargaining among groups or factions of parliamentarians, which follow party lines, did not correspond to the principle of the debating forum, neither did it satisfy the requirements of efficiency in terms of the traditional rules of parliamentary procedure. On the other hand, the popular nature of the new party-dominated representative democracy does not yield the expected legitimating power. What point is there in talking about popular representation where the representative follows the party line, where he cannot act according to his conscience, and where the "nation" can have a chance of being taken into consideration? The

[20] Ivor Jennings, *The British Constitution* (Cambridge: Cambridge University Press, 1962), 29.

[21] Party democracies embody the worst fears of the advocates of liberal parliamentarism: the Caesaristic rule of the democratic leader has been brought to the fore. Max Weber, though an advocate of liberal constitutionalism, considered classical parliamentarism unacceptable and, as the advocate of Caesarism, declared in 1917 that democracy, as opposed to parliament, meant the direct election of supreme powers ending in Caesaristic acclamation. He wanted to replace the parliamentary system with a democracy elected by popular vote, even if it led to a one-man despotic rule. If parliament reaches a deadlock, one has to turn to the people. Without a president, a crisis in parliament, which is most certain to occur if there are four or five parties, cannot be solved. Max Weber, *Parliament und Regierung im neugeordneten Deutschland, zur politischen Kritik des Beamtentmus und Parteiwesen* (München–Leipzig: Duncker und Humblot, 1918), 114.

fundamental myth of parliamentary popular sovereignty today, namely, that the members represent the people or the nation, cannot be sustained, in view of the party system and the system of proportional representation.

The dissociation from those represented, in the traditional meaning of representation, has become complete. The myth of the representation of the nation ceased to operate because the representative, who was above the mandate given by his electors, was now obliged to obediently follow his party's wishes if he wanted to be reelected. Naturally, there are mitigating circumstances to party rule: the election system, too, determines how important it is to gain nomination to the party list; where the individual constituencies are not replaced by party lists and/or if nomination is a local party matter, the influence of the party center might be less; and the factions in parliament do not always depend on the party center.

If someone at the beginning of the twentieth century–not long after general suffrage was granted–were to have examined what was happening in the parliament of a continental constitutional state, he would have found the values of nineteenth-century deliberative parliamentarism irrelevant. Parliamentary debate had lost its importance; the persuasion of the public was and is carried out outside parliament. Debate based on argument was replaced by sheer propaganda. The member who stands up to speak in parliament does not want to convince other representatives. The seats in parliament are empty, bar the hours when members are required to vote. In brief, political persuasion is replaced with attempts to win the voting public. "As, in keeping with the law, everyone is allowed to speak, no one else is allowed to speak but the person who manages the (PARTY) machinery. This has ruined parliament's original objective, it has broken up its technique and has reduced its operation to a farce."[22] The discussions in merit, if any, are no longer public but done in committees, and any real work has been shifted to these committees; at least this is the case according to critics.

The members are impossible to persuade because they are now merely obedient servants of their parties, as it is only with their backing that the members can hope to be elected or reelected. Dependence on the voters has disappeared. In a proportional electoral system this is even

[22] Joseph Schumpeter, "Sozialistische Möglichkeiten von Heute," *Archiv für Sozialwissenschaft und Sozialpolitik* 48 (1922): 329–330.

formally true, because in this system there are no individual constituencies, no one has her own voters; instead, the voters vote wholesale for the candidates on the party lists.

In mass democracies it seemed inconceivable to think of parliament as a forum for debate. To janitors emancipated into voters debate in parliament, or "government by discussion" did not amount to much.[23] A partisan, party-based democracy did not seem attractive either. "I want the monarchy," wrote Thomas Mann in 1917. "I want a tolerably independent government, because it alone guarantees political freedom in the intellectual and in the economic spheres... I do not want the parliamentary and party economic system that causes the pollution of all national life with politics... I do not want politics. I want objectivity, order and decency."[24]

The man in the street was not satisfied either, even though he was considered a voting citizen who had the power to determine the course of politics. From the beginning of the twentieth century, people though franchised, could conclude that none of their real concerns were solved in parliament. The whole debate in parliament was a farce. There was a general impotence, there was no strong government, and necessary laws were not passed. There was no strength and vigor. This antiparliamentary sentiment was further stirred up by Marxist and other radical socialist and anarchist movements among their followers in the working classes, the *petty bourgeoisie*, and among intellectuals. Parliamentarism was considered the pastime and force of the ruling classes. At times the idea of realizing the rule of the working classes by capturing parliament crops up. But Lenin, who in this regard is the most authentic authority, at the first given opportunity dissolved the revolutionary Duma because the Bolsheviks lacked an (absolute) majority. Instead he institutionalized a system of "representation" that completely excluded parliamentarism:

> The way out of parliamentarism is not, of course, the elimination of representative institutions and electivity but the conversion of the representative institutions from talking shops into "working" institutions. "The Commune had

[23] Harold Laski, *The Foundations of Sovereignty* (New York: Harcourt, Brace and Co., 1921).

[24] Thomas Mann, *Reflections of a Nonpolitical Man*, trans. Walter D. Morris (New York: F. Ungar, 1983), 188–189.

to be not a parliamentary but a working institution, passing and executing laws at the same time."[25]

Besides Leninism, other totalitarian forces appeared attempting to wipe out parliamentarism, which was dominated by party politics and which, owing to the absence of a required majority, was incapable of making decisions. Of these totalitarian forces it is important to mention Carl Schmitt's *decisionism*, which prepared the ground for fascism in some regards. His antiparliamentarianism, even today, has many advocates from among the ranks of those who are dissatisfied with the small-mindedness, the avarice, and the impotence of parliaments and their members. In Schmitt's view, an efficient, decisive dictator is what people want because nothing can be *decided* in parliament's liberal debating forum.[26] "Liberalism, with its contradictions and compromises, existed...only in that short interim period in which it was possible to answer the question 'Christ or Barabbas?' with a proposal to adjourn or appoint a commission of investigation."[27]

The dissatisfaction with parliament, largely in keeping with Schmitt's ideas, led to the nonconvocation of parliament in Nazi Germany, while fascist Italy put forward a corporate alternative. In the corporate system a legislative body continues to exist but not on the basis of popular representation. It consists of the delegates of the various businesses and vocations. The businesses made the regulations largely themselves. The rationale behind this rather pathetic idea, which continues to recur even today, is that the person engaged in a given line of business is an expert

[25] V. I. Lenin, *The State and Revolution* (London: Penguin books, 1992), 42 (quoting Marx).

[26] It is certain that there are abnormal, extreme, and crisis situations where immediate, extraparliamentary decisions are necessary. But this may be controlled constitutionally (for example, when and for as long as this situation lasts). As opposed to Schmitt's dictatorship, the aim of the constitutional state in cases of emergency is to render the crisis situations manageable and to make sure that constitutionalism prevails. The *per se* problem with the Weimar Constitution was not that the *Reichspresident*, in a state of emergency, could pass decrees with statutory force countersigned by the prime minister. After all, this helped establish stabilization after World War I. What actually presented a problem was that the law, regulating the *Reichpresident*'s rights to the last detail, as required by Art. 48 of the Weimar constitution, was never drafted.

[27] Carl Schmitt, *Political Theology: Four Chapters on the Concept of Sovereignty* (Cambridge, Mass.: MIT Press, 1988), 62.

in this area, thus he is the best judge of the kinds of regulations that are needed. The principle underpinning the practice of the drafting of regulations by experts is the classical case of a person trying to have his cake and eat it. In self-regulation it is not expertise that will prevail but the most brutal group interest, cloaked in the guise of professional "truth."

As a reaction to the antiparliamentary sentiments of dictatorships, the constitutional states, after 1945, returned to parliamentary systems, but this time they attempted to address the previous impotence and division and strove to *rationalize* parliament. The following sections focus on this rationalized machinery.

4.2. THE STRUCTURE AND OPERATION OF PARLIAMENT

4.2.1 Parliament as an Institution

(a) Continuity

Parliament is the fundamental institution of a constitutional system not merely because members are popularly elected. An equally important feature is that the institution of the legislature–putting aside establishment and legitimization–exists independently of all external forces and other state institutions. The constitution declares that it must hold sessions in a given place and for a given period of time. The period cannot be too short, and if it fails to do its work, it has to be convened because no other institution may assume its duties and responsibilities (taxation, budget, legislation, and special, or extraordinary, governmental activities). And if some other institution did assume legislative responsibilities, its measures would be null and void. Provisions in the constitution ensure parliament's independent existence. Where such rules do not exist, it is impossible to speak of parliamentary constitutionalism.

Originally, the *continuous existence* of the legislature was sanctioned by constitutional conventions, British parliamentary practice, and other political traditions. Convention required the king to convene parliament annually, if necessary, to listen to complaints and because of the urgent dispatch of business. There were no rules calling for the annual convening of a *new* body. If the ruler found the convening of parliament unnecessary, he could go as far as not convening it. The most the Glorious Revolution could achieve was the pledge that a new parliament would be convened every three years, if within this period a parliament had not been convened.

Modern parliaments are permanent institutions that, from time to time, are partly or completely "renewed," and they are in session for a given period of time. This means that the representatives, being the constituent members of parliament, have to meet almost daily and be prepared to make decisions. If parliament dissolves itself or is dissolved, a new parliament must be convened within the time stipulated in the constitution. The institution cannot just "die" or disappear. Constitutions usually include prescriptions on the procedures according to which parliaments are convened and have to hold sessions. The Dutch Constitution, since 1983, stipulates that the Parliament be in continuous session during its term in office. In other states, more traditional solutions are applied, namely, parliament has to be convened within a few weeks after elections. The annual sessions begin on a given date and last until a fixed date.[28] A modern constitutional parliament does not depend on the executive to convene its sessions and define its agenda. Constitutions include provisions for the automatic convening of their parliaments. If the monarch, the president, or any other high-ranking official who is responsible for convening parliament should fail to carry out this duty, the parliament may convene itself.

As for *dissolving* parliament, various practices exist. The minimum modern constitutionalism requires is that, after the dissolution, parliament be automatically reelected within a short period of time and that the new parliament convene. If it is the president of the republic or the monarch who fixes the date of the election, he has little discretion.

The importance of the continuous and autonomous existence of parliament as an institution is best understood if we recall what can happen without such precaution. If the ruler is able to convene and dissolve parliament at his whim and if it depends on him to determine

[28] For example, according to the Hungarian Constitution, a new parliament must be convened three months after the mandate of the previous one expires or if it dissolves itself or is dissolved. The president convenes the new parliament to hold its opening session thirty days after elections, at the latest.

when sessions are held, then the kinds of substantive powers the parliament has are practically irrelevant. The constitutions of the antiparliamentary dictatorships of state-socialism stipulated a minimum number of session days of undetermined length for the parliament–which was otherwise granted most of the classical powers of liberal parliaments–and expressly objected to a parliament in continuous session because the members would then drift away and be alienated from the workers whom they were elected to represent. The short-lived practice of the Hungarian "socialist rule-of-law state" of February 1989 required a minimum of four "sessions." On average, a socialist parliament was in session for eight days a year, which was long enough for its puppet-members to recite the current panegyrics. There was even time to lift their hands or press the buttons when voting for the bills submitted in honor of socialist legality.[29]

(b) Terms of the mandate

The continuous functioning and renewal of parliament ensure its existence as an institution. Renewal and periodic elections are part of parliament's democratic legitimacy and bear relation to certain pragmatic ideas concerning checks and limits to power. Periodic elections are necessary as this is how the majority expresses its current will. It is not clear, however, why the terms in office for the elected members of parliament are two, three, four, five, and six years. These can be found in the American (1787), Swiss (1848), Hungarian (pre-October 1989), British (1911, in the Parliament Act), and American (1787, in the paragraph referring to the Senate) constitutions. In Eng-

[29] The duties of communist parliaments were pretty limited as they had to delegate their legislative functions to an even more trustworthy party institution, like the Presidential Council in the People's Republic of Hungary. It is not as if laws were overwhelmingly important in the people's democracies. Attempts by the socialists to establish "law-governed" states led in Hungary, in 1987, to an exclusive listing of legislative matters. Legislation by the Presidium satisfied socialist legality's easily satiable thirst for orderliness and hierarchy among the sources of law.

Tsarist Russia and the Soviet Union were incapable of even establishing a norm hierarchy, and post-Soviet Russia inherited this deformity.

The socialists' abuse of parliamentary sessions demonstrates the constitutional importance of the technical rules concerning parliamentary operations (how many days, from what date until when, and the like).

land, prior to 1911, elections did not have to be held for seven years, though in the nineteenth century there was only one parliament that remained in office for seven years, between 1867 and 1873, when Gladstone was the prime minister.

The reason for periodic renewal is this. If members of parliament are elected for life and no control by citizens is exercised over them, their power would be near absolute. Perpetuity would result in rampaging self-interest. Compulsory renewal is an internal restriction on power, and the stronger the democratic value judgment of the voters–the more the voters have to be taken into consideration–the more parliaments must apply "internal" restrictions. Parliamentary elections serve the renewed expression of the people's will only in part; they are perhaps more useful as a means of control and of maintaining a relationship between public opinion and parliament.

The term in office of the members of parliament are determined in terms of the self-limitation of government. The greater parliament's power is and the more difficult it is to counteract it by the other branches, the more important it is to introduce a shorter period for the term in office. The British House of Commons with its originally seven-, then five-year, term, follows a different logic. Here, respect for public opinion would require parliament to react immediately to changes in public opinion.[30] Until the beginning of the twentieth century, a British prime minister opted to "go to the country" (call early elections) for any major policy changes rather than break his election promises or act without the voters' approval. When reform of the House of Lords became necessary in 1910, Lloyd George held elections despite having a freshly elected new parliament and a strong majority in the House of Commons, which would have enabled him to carry out the constitutional reform. On the other hand, once new elections confirmed his plan, the House of Lords acquiesced.

Owing to democratic considerations (resulting from the desire to let the people's will prevail), in Philadelphia, in 1787, the drafters of the constitution almost sanctioned a lower house that would have had to be

[30] A well-functioning British government awaits by-election results with bated breath. It amends its policies to fall in line with popular demand because defeat at this stage, and especially the loss of a ruling-party constituency, is perceived as the whole country's criticism of the government's policy.

renewed every year. "When annual renewal is blocked, tyranny begins."[31] (In those days, in certain states, like Pennsylvania, elections were held annually at least.)

Practical considerations and the Philadelphia delegates' fear of popular rule led them to agree on a two-year term for the House. The representatives, they argued, had to be given time to familiarize themselves with the requirements of their office. The formulation and discussion of legislative proposals could not be accomplished in one year.

Continental traditions usually favor a four-year term in office.[32] It must again be emphasized that this cannot be taken as a standard model because in some places this is the only occasion during the four-year period when people can express their will, and there are no other branches to counteract parliament. Four years in a dynamically changing world may be too long, especially if the party elite have no sensitivity for the public's sentiments. Parliament will fail to be in touch with the mood of the people, and its democratic legitimization will be wasted. More frequent elections do not necessarily destabilize; on the contrary, if the dates of regular renewals are of considerable distance from each other, demand for direct democratic solutions and the likelihood of destabilizing popular initiatives increase. Longer terms have their own advocates. According to "competent government groups," time is required for the realization of an economic policy. In addition, a government has the "right" to benefit from the successes of its policies in (re)election. Success, however, cannot come about in two or three years. This, to be sure, is typically the government's problem, and it is not a constitutional argument. That frequent elections require the government to spend more money than is necessary is irrelevant, because there are ways to spend less on elections (including limiting the amount to be spent constitutionally).

Unicameral postcommunist parliaments, like that of Hungary, Slovakia, and Bulgaria, where the power of the legislative branch faces few formal checks and balances, are ripe for the American solution, namely, biannual renewal. Renewal every three years would be enough, if there

[31] Quoted in *The Federalist Papers* No. 53: Madison, 330.

[32] Referring to Europe in this context may be rather misleading, because in many places the structure is federal, and there are elections during the four-year period at the regional (provincial) level. In many issues the provincial legislature has the power to make decisions.

were another legislative house and president with some limited powers, though not directly elected. Of course, the chances of this happening in Hungary or in the other postcommunist unicameral systems are slim because the professional politicians who are involved in the legislative process have no desire to have their work frequently evaluated. But both limiting power and democratic legitimization require the shortening of the term in office of the members of parliament.

(c) Dissolution

A parliamentary body may cease to function before the end of its term, and under certain conditions it can dissolve itself or be dissolved. The relevant constitutional regulations provide room for a number of solutions. Generally, in a parliamentary system where the ministers lose the confidence of parliament (a vote of confidence is lost), it can be dissolved. Often this is a matter of tradition, and if dissolution is a possibility at all, the final decision may rest with the executive. The majority of the day or the majority-party leadership may wish to form a new government, or it may decide to go to the country, that is, it may ask the head of state (president or king) to officially dissolve the parliament and call new elections. How dissolution opportunities are used–if this is a matter of choice at all–is again a matter of political tradition. In Holland, where the system is built on wide-scale consensus building through political bargaining, since 1815 the monarch has dissolved the lower house eleven times and the upper house three. Tradition or the constitution may set limits to dissolution (probably linked to popular sovereignty); as a rule parliament cannot be twice dissolved for the same reason. (In the Netherlands this tradition has prevailed since 1868, while the Weimar Constitution explicitly mentions this point in Article 25.).

As *raison d'État* interpreted by party politicians has a say in the workings of parliament, there is need for a lot of space for flexibility, maneuvering, and bargaining (a larger space than would follow from the need for constitutional definition). Consequently, the rules of dissolution are rather flexible.

It is constitutionally acceptable both that the elected body itself decides as to dissolution or that it can be dissolved only by someone else (including the executive power), or it cannot be dissolved at all. In eighteenth-century England, the monarch had the right to dissolve the parliament whenever he wanted. In reaction, the U.S. approach is the complete reverse of this practice. Congress cannot be dissolved (not by itself or by any other person), and it is elected for a determined period. Modern English parliamentarism, in theory, rests on the assumption that both the executive and the legislative powers have the right to "dissolve" each other. Dissolution and the vote of no-confidence threatens the position of the people in the "other" power, and this is how the system of checks and balances becomes complete. In the case of separation in the U.S., the powers cannot affect each other's existence. The German Basic Law knows no opportunity for the *Bundestag* to dissolve itself; with the complicity of all the members, in 1982 it managed nevertheless to do so.[33]

The regulations in the Dutch Constitution are exactly the reverse, namely, the king (that is, the government) could dissolve the parliament without any restrictions. Since 1958, however, Dutch public opinion holds that the government has no right (to initiate) dissolution. If the Dutch government could dissolve the parliament, this in practice would mean the party with a relative majority in the second house and which participates in the government would be entitled to do so. Instead, all the parties in the legislature, or at least all the majority parties, must give support before the government can ask the king to act.

In 1989, the Hungarian Constitution sanctioned the right of Parliament to dissolve itself.[34] The president may dissolve the body within twelve months if the government is voted out in Parliament or no government can be formed (the government and its program is rejected) within forty days.[35]

[33] As the Federal Assembly, in accordance with the agreement of the parties, did not nominate a new chancellor in place of the chancellor who was voted out, President Carstens called new elections. The Constitutional Court found this to be in keeping with the Basic Law (62 BVerfGE 1 (1984)) because, although it went against the Constitution to force an election by abusing the provisions of constructive no-confidence, the consensus of the branches of power rendered revision by the Constitutional Court impossible in a political issue. The text of a constitution is not omnipotent, even in the eyes of its guardians, especially if the entire political elite agree on an anticonstitutional interpretation.

[34] This is a typical development in the transition to democracy. Parliament insisted on all powers of autonomy as a reaction to communist party rule, which relied on the executive.

[35] A president running for reelection by Parliament, may dissolve the Parliament, which is not likely to reelect him after a given number of no-confidence motions. It must be noted that the Constitution does not say after what period of time after the last

The initial excessive importance attributed to parliament brought about a whole range of problems in the postcommunist Eastern European states because of the sometimes inevitable unpopular measures taken by, and the internal weakness of, the institution. In the newly independent republics of the former Soviet Union, the parliaments are divided, paralyzed, and chaotic, as if attempting to demonstrate in practice the Marxist-Leninist tenet of the impotence of "Western parliamentarism." Disillusionment came to a head when the building of the Russian Parliament was bombarded. In response to the dissatisfaction, parliament's powers were restricted in a number of constitutions. The presidents of many post-Soviet republics were granted almost unlimited power to dissolve their parliaments. The often and worldwide heard explanation was that it was unacceptable that discord and sloth paralyze the life of the country, especially in "hard times like these." If the members of parliament do not work for their pay, they must be fired. The great example followed in matters pertaining to presidential dissolution powers is that of the Fifth French Republic, where the president of the republic, after some consultations, may call new elections whenever he wishes. When discussing the powers of the executive, we will see that the right to dissolve parliament may not necessarily motivate members to work harder, but it may indeed force them to be more disciplined in voting.

The above dissolution models fit into constitutionalism, provided a new parliament is formed within a given deadline and none of the powers become dominant (something the French solution comes close to doing, but this power, since de Gaulle, has not in practice been taken advantage of, to the detriment of the parliamentary majority). What is more, all constitutions have to take efficiency and governability into consideration. Efficiency in a given context may refer to sanctions pertaining to the dissolution of parliament, although there has not yet been a sanction that has stimulated reluctant and divided parliaments to work together.

---

no-confidence motion the president may exercise this right. And the combined application of the British and German models is not appropriate, either in theory or in practice. If the British model is applied, it depends on the government or the parliament whether, in the event of a no-confidence motion, it gives itself another chance or turns to the country. In addition, it is incomprehensible on what grounds the president, elected by parliament, restricts the existence of the parliament on which his reelection depends.

The fact that parliament may be dissolved involves undeniable dangers to constitutionalism. In the Weimar Republic in 1932, Hindenburg repeatedly dissolved the parliament, and in the ensuing interim, he governed the country with presidential decrees. These dissolutions contributed to the process that led to Hitler's rule. Constitutional considerations would then require the dissolution of parliament to be subjected to specific conditions. In a rule-of-law state the laws are predictable, in other words, it is important to define, if possible, in concrete terms, when parliament can be dissolved. If such limits restrict self-dissolution, it would affect parliament's sovereignty; however, if the right of dissolution by another branch becomes subject to specific nondiscretionary conditions, parliament's position improves.

4.2.2. The Conditions of Free Debate and Decisionmaking

(a) Caligula's horses: the personal rights and immunities of members

The fundamental rules of parliamentarism mainly concern the members and the functioning of parliament. The Petition of Rights of 1629 ensured members of the freedom of speech in the English Parliament. This, as the petition states, means that members are not answerable for what passes in the Commons.[36] This rule is the first constitutional guarantee of free speech in history. In certain states the members' immunity is taken to apply to all statements made in connection with their work, regardless of where the statement was made (for example, in France).

According to British practice, which became widely adopted by the eighteenth century, members of parliament could only be arrested in exceptional cases and only when caught red-handed. Legal proceedings were launched only if parliament itself gave permission (waived immunity).[37] Without immunity, of course, the executive power could have

[36] According to Art. 9 of the Bill of Rights of 1689, "the freedom of speech, and debates or proceedings in Parliament ought not to be impeached or questioned in any court or place out of Parliament." Freedom of speech is restricted to parliament under the Danish, Irish, Japanese, and Dutch constitutions.

[37] In some countries parliament may refuse to allow proceedings against a member of parliament even upon the request of the member concerned when the member hopes to be acquitted in court.

simply arrested the opposition. Hence comes the fundamental importance of this institution in an age when parliament or a group of its members regularly fell into conflict with the king. It was because of similar experiences that parliament was so keen on being the only institution that has the right to judge its members. In many states parliament makes decisions concerning immunity, that is, whether legal proceedings can be initiated against a member (whether the member can be arrested). This is parliament's competence over its members. (Sometimes immunity is referred to as a prerogative.)[38] Rules protecting members may be turned against them, however. Representatives cannot be dismissed or excluded, except as in the U.S., for "disorderly behavior," which is interpreted as including immorality, with the concurrence of two-thirds of the respective House. For disciplinary reasons the member's right to appear and vote in parliament may be temporarily restricted or suspended (even this raises constitutional issues).[39]

Unfortunately, the parliamentary majority may exploit immunity to keep the opposition members on a short leash or, alternatively, to get rid of them. In Hungary, in 1946–47, the parliamentary middle-class majority, succumbing to secret, and later public, blackmail, first waived immunity of opposition members (accepting false charges leveled by the communist police, that is, the executive) and then of its own members on the grounds of trumped-up allegations. In the end, after its numbers had been drastically reduced, the terrorized middle-class majority simply gave up its fight.[40]

[38] In case of *flagrante delicto* (being apprehended in the very act of committing a crime), generally speaking, no special authorization is necessary. According to the Anglo–American tradition, the member is exempt from arrest during sessions.

In some of the Commonwealth states that follow British traditions, it is not the court but the parliament that may rule in impeachment cases. (In principle, in accordance with the above approach, journalists who make offensive comments against parliament can be called to account by it.)

[39] According to the Italian House Rules, Art. 60 (2), a member may be barred from entering the chamber from two to fifteen days. The French concept is very similar.

[40] From 1946 to 1948, the Hungarian communists sliced up the Parliament, salami style, according to the good old French recipe. This is how Robespierre and his party came to power during the French Revolution. The uncertainty surrounding the immunity of representatives–the fact that they could be extradited to their enemies–first helped and then later caused the sad end of the Jacobins. Salami tactics seem to be universal. On November 3, 1913, the final version of the Chinese Constitution was

According to contemporary practice adopted in many states, a member's *right to speak* depends on the faction leaders. In principle, the British parliamentary practice (Standing Orders) still considers parliament the primary forum for open debate between the majority and opposition. Consequently, special pains are taken to let the speaker of the opposition know the issues to be raised in parliament, so as to give him time to prepare. At the same time, the right of the members of the party in office, in this respect, is considerably restricted. The members have to draw lots to decide who wins the chance to speak in connection with the proposal at hand. The opposition does not submit bills.

The party is all; *the individual is nothing*. This is the final point reached today in the history of what was intended to be the most democratic political institution. No matter how important the members may seem in light of their immunity, privileges, prerogatives, and activities, they are at most replaceable cogs in the wheel of the legislative process. Sometimes they act as a piece of grit trying to obstruct the movement of the other wheels. Contrary to all eighteenth-century myths about the popular mandate of individual representatives, in reality the members cannot make individual decisions. Only the faction as a body may decide. The reason why the members have rights at all is to enable the legislative machinery to continue working. Laws are made by parliament not its members. The members and the body work against each other, which may turn into acute controversy when it comes to the right to submit bills, determine the agenda, question ministers, and debate, instances when personal participation and initiatives are considered crucial.

There is something heartwarming in the romantic heroism of the lonely member of parliament and in the individual responsibility of the members. Endre Bajcsy-Zsilinszky was the only one to speak out against the Germans in the Hungarian Parliament, thereby saving the whole nation's face. What would have happened if not a single protest had been made? The protest did not make Parliament take action, and the masses did not take to the streets either. Nevertheless, it counts for something that one person dared tell the truth. The same applies to

---

submitted to the National Assembly, which was elected on April 8 of the same year. By this time, seven months after the first session of the Assembly, the application of the "salami-cutting" method had left an insufficient number of assembly members to vote for the constitution. The members of the original majority were extradited, one-by-one, to the police authorities on conspiracy charges.

differences in opinion. But this person could not save Parliament's honor. Even in issues of morality, it is the opinion of the body and the majority that counts. The opposition may be taken into consideration as a faceless phalanx but hardly ever the individual.

It is not the individual who is entitled to speak in parliament and to submit proposals but the majority and the opposition or the factions; parliament's chivalry is directed at the opposition. This explains why the individual member's right to debate is restricted. (The number of times a member may speak in parliament and the duration is limited in modern parliaments.)

Undoubtedly a number of constitutions, by emphasizing the traditional delegate's role, explicitly include the member's right to submit bills.[41] But standing orders efficiently curb this right, for instance, by declaring that individual bills need not be included in the agenda if they are not supported by one of the committees (the bills do not even need to be sent to a committee if the plenum has not accepted them). Parliament is the cabinet's lawmaking factory, an assembly line producing statutes, at least when it enjoys a stable majority. Where there is no majority, parliament is just like a broken record. In the U.S. Congress, however, where the powers are separate and eighteenth-century traditions are honored, individual bills play a more prominent role than in the states on the Continent, or in the ones that follow more recent British practices, because party discipline is less important in the U.S. system. But according to the rules of procedure in Congress, the opinion of the committees is decisive. A proposal dies without the support of a competent committee.

The German Basic Law goes even further in that it makes the existence of parties a crucial criteria for democracy to prevail. The Basic Law, on the realistic principle that proposals not supported by any party are doomed to failure and consume precious time, gives the members' right to put forward proposals an ominous twist by saying that motions must come from the Federal Assembly (*aus der Mitte*), which means that 10 percent of the members need to support it, according to the house

[41] If each member represents a specific constituency, it is understandable that opinions can differ. But it is mostly just a form of seeking publicity if a member of a party submits an individual bill to the plenum. If only the appointed party mouthpiece blares, instead of the publicity-seeking, stepping-out-of-line party members, there are fewer misunderstandings.

rules. This, in practice, prevents smaller parties from submitting proposals.[42]

Members claim that they must give account to their voters, and if they cannot prove that they personally acted in the voters' interest, they break their promise and lose the trust that earned them their mandates. This is a standard argument in favor of delegates' rights. In the case of unbound mandates, it is difficult to justify, in reference to the above concerns of responsibility, the members' individual rights. In addition, their reelection in most systems depends on whether they are members of a popular party and whether their party nominates them as candidates. If these two conditions exist the members can hope to share in the fate of Caligula's horses.

(b) Openness in parliament

If parliament is the place of debate, of political education, of the shaping of public opinion, indeed, of forming the general will through debates, then the rules of parliamentary procedure should facilitate debate and public reasoning. The rules pertaining to debate and decision making can rarely be found in constitutions, the exception being the right to interpellate and question, in other words, the obligation of the executive to answer members of parliament's questions.[43] The provisions in the constitution mostly refer to matters such as the number of readings a bill must be given before it can be put to a vote. This is the "institutionalization" of circumspection.

Additional arrangements for debate follow from the constitution's organizational provisions pertaining to the structure of parliament. The rules of parliamentary debate can be found in the house rules (standing orders) and the traditions prevailing in parliament.

The provisions on open debate and the house rules concerning the press have inevitably opened up parliamentary debates to the public, and debates have become the center of attention. To be sure, this has fundamentally transformed parliamentarism.

[42] Similarly, in Japan the support of twenty members (in budget proposals the support of fifty members) has to be won before individual proposals can come before the legislature.

[43] Question time in parliament and interpellation are instruments to supervise the executive and, as such, cannot be looked upon as the intellectual instruments of parliamentary debate and examination only. See Chapter 5.

Before 1834 it was forbidden to take notes in the gallery of the English Parliament. To bypass these restrictions, the *Morning Chronicle* employed a man who could recount a sixteen column speech, word for word.[44]

In theory, open parliamentary debates made it possible to judge the behavior of members and to use this information to control the reelection of a member. How members vote has been made public in the English Commons since 1836 and in France since 1885.

Openness has its price. Roll call made it possible to identify and deport the delegates of the French Convention that voted in favor of Louis XVI's execution.

With parliamentary sessions made public, new vistas opened before parliaments. The "responsibility" of the members toward their voters became more practical, and, consequently, the purpose of debates became less facilitative of a shared understanding of matters and convincing fellow members, but increasingly parliamentary behavior aimed at influencing public opinion and the constituencies of the respective members.[45]

When parliament's function and legitimacy changed again–in the age of party politics and efficient state government–the rules of procedure could be adapted to new parliamentary functions without significant amendment of the constitution. The objective, by way of *rationalizing* the assembly-line parliament, was to restrict the members' chances of taking advantage of speaking in parliament and to restrict parliamentary debate and speeches.

4.2.3. PARLIAMENT'S SELF-DETERMINATION

(a) House Rules

A jealously guarded privilege of parliamentary operations is that no other government institution be allowed to interfere in parliament's

[44] Jürgen Habermas, *The Structural Transformation of the Public Sphere: An Inquiry into a Category of Bourgeois Society* (London: Polity Press, 1989). In the Hungarian Parliament of the Reform Age (the first half of the nineteenth century), law students, who were present as apprentices, divided the speeches among themselves so as to be able to better recall them.

[45] See above, for the downside in party politics and the age of mass media.

business.[46] It is a basic principle that parliament should decide its own rules of procedure, or it makes use of its traditions (precedents).

The adoption of parliamentary rules does not require the participation of any outside institution. Neither presidential signature nor royal assent is required and the courts cannot investigate the regulations nor the application of the internal procedures. Courts have no jurisdiction in parliament's internal affairs. The German Constitutional Court Act explicitly forbids the examination of the parliament's house rules, bar those cases when they refer to fundamental constitutional rights.[47] Parliamentary procedures may be reviewed if the adopted resolution concerns the rights of the members acting as a state institution.

The importance of a principle becomes visible when the principle is violated. The French Constitution of 1958 deviated from this principle, prescribing the approval of the Constitution Council as the condition of the validity of the house rules.[48]

The principle that parliament should have autonomy over its own affairs makes perfect sense. But to what extent is it possible to realize this autonomy if practice works on assumptions that do not coincide with those on which the principle is based? What happens if parliament functions without taking the house rules into consideration, if the majority disregards procedural requirements? If there is no quorum and the legislature still votes, or if there are irregularities surrounding the vote, for instance, if there is a multiple vote, what happens then? What if a complaint is launched that is then duly investigated by the parliament, and a majority comes to the conclusion that nothing irregular has happened and that the law was not breached? Would such approval of the procedure aid in correcting the problems concerning it?[49]

[46] In addition to the majority rule, constitutions mostly contain rules pertaining to internal functions, where there is a probability of a conflict of competence among the two chambers and if the conflict cannot be easily solved by the two chambers.

[47] Third-party (nonmember) rights traditionally restrict parliamentary immunity. See *Stockdale v. Hansard* (1839, 9. A.& E. I).

[48] CC 59–2. For example, the house rules that would have limited the duration of the speeches of the members of government were rejected as unconstitutional. The provision of the Constitution requiring such mandatory review was intended by de Gaulle to curtail the autonomy of legislation that he feared.

[49] Self-determination may validate parliament's self-degradation. Let us suppose that a qualified majority is necessary for a law's passage. The president of the legislature says a law has been passed although there was no qualified majority. In the ensuing dispute

As opposed to the principle of self-determination, another principle requires that no one be the judge in matters concerning himself.

From this point of view the authority of the French Constitutional Council to review legislative procedures and house rules is not really inconceivable. As long as a constitutional principle is behind the controlling procedure, the solution may be qualified as constitutional. However, one should clearly distinguish between the making of internal rules (nonreviewable) and the application of rules of procedure in parliament's own deliberations.

The constitutional guarantee of parliamentarism–the independent existence of parliament–has made it compulsory for parliaments to be *formed* without any outside intervention. Consequently, nineteenth-century constitutions prescribe in relative detail how parliaments *themselves* are to certify the mandate of elected members. As electoral systems have been transformed and as professional technical staffs supervised by public bodies (in reality, parties) are responsible for counting the ballots, and as electoral systems are not described in constitutions, parliaments have partly resigned their privileges and have allowed various courts to settle election disputes.

House rules, in some cases, are collected in thick volumes. In general, however, parliament functions by observing only a few principles. It is the exceptions and the procedural details that fill the thick volumes. The principles seek answers to the following fundamental questions: What proportion of support is necessary for decision making? What is the organizational form of parliamentary work? To what extent does everything need to be open to the public? And who is the subject of the parliamentary procedures?

(b) Passing laws in parliament

The answer to the first question can be found in constitutions and, accordingly, parliament passes resolutions based on the *majority principle*. In this respect, parliament functions according to democratic prescriptions because, as a result of the equality principle of democracies, all

---

on validity, a simple majority is all that is required because it is an issue concerning procedure. A simple majority would not be enough if we have to observe the rule that says the rule to be applied in the case of procedural decisions should be just as stringent as the conditions pertaining to the decisions under examination.

votes are of equal worth, and the majority in number is decisive. In reality, however, the house rules–the functioning of parliament and the organization, excluding appointment-related and legislative decisions–frequently deviate from its principle in favor of proportionality and the protection of minorities. The decision on the number of members present required to pass laws is left by some constitutions, like the Weimar one, to parliament, as it is an issue of internal autonomy (Art. 32). Others, like the Hungarian Constitution of 1989 (Art. 26), state that 50 percent of the total number of members is necessary for a quorum and prescribe the *yes* vote of the majority of members present to pass laws. The Belgian Constitution requires 50 percent of *all* the members, plus one vote (*absolute majority*), while in appointment matters the majority of the members present can make a decision.

In certain cases the constitutions or laws require a qualified majority when electing certain officers or deciding specific issues and when laws are passed or amended. It is disputed whether a law, in the absence of a definite constitutional provision, can require a qualified majority for cases when the given law itself is to be modified. Conversely, is it constitutional if a law permits a minority to declare it null and void?[50]

The principle of parliamentary majority raises the issue of how constitutional the legislature is. Is it possible to decide *everything* with a prescribed parliamentary majority?

The majority principle has been present in parliament from the very beginning. The lords in parliament (out of mutual interest) considered each other brothers and equals. Parliamentary "democracy" thus preceded the "majority-through-election" principle, which is understood to satisfy the logic of popular sovereignty. As a matter of fact, majoritarianism is not an inevitable feature of parliamentarism. For instance, the Polish *liberum veto*, from a logical point of view, quite correctly required complete unity in voting. The destabilizing experiences concerning complete unity contribute, however, to a pragmatic justification of the majority principle.

[50] In early 1995, the U.S. Congress declared that a three-fifths majority was necessary to pass any law raising taxes. Constitutional objections (namely, that a simple majority was enough to pass a law) were refuted with the argument that this was only a procedural rule (a quasi house rule).

On event of a qualified majority, clarifying the terms of a quorum is necessary.

It does not follow from the practice of decision making in parliament that certain issues cannot be withdrawn from parliament's authority or that the majority rule cannot be replaced by a qualified-majority requirement. Where there is a supermajority requirement it is irrelevant from the perspective of the majority principle, the number by which 50 percent of the votes has to be exceeded, but it does matter considerably to the minority.[51]

(c) *Qualified majority*

The requirement of a qualified majority (supermajority) seems to aid in the protection of minorities.[52]

Others consider the institution of a qualified majority a terrible arrangement.[53] This is certainly a frequently heard complaint in government circles. But anything that is considered unpleasant for the government creates a presumption in favor of its constitutional value. A qualified majority in a decision-making system that lacks sufficient checks and balances is the only means by which the rule of the majority

[51] Theoretical arguments can be marshaled supporting the necessity of making decisions with an absolute majority. But it is still an open question how the vote of the members present but abstaining should be counted. The government majority is required to make a greater effort if the strictest definition of majority applies. This would mean that a law would only be passed if the majority of the elected members voted for it. The French Constitution applies the reverse of this rule to strengthen the government's position. A motion of censure against the government is successful only if 50 percent of all the members of parliament vote for it (that is, against the government).

If the less-stringent meaning of "majority" were to apply, given the actual absenteeism of members, it would help preserve the ability of parliament to function. The condition for the aforementioned to occur would be a strict absolute majority in certain cases (for example, no-confidence, or, perhaps, granting confidence to a newly formed government or adoption of the government's program). Furthermore, a law passed according to the stringent approach may determine other cases when an absolute majority would be necessary. Such arrangement, as is true of all strict majority rules, would increase the pressure to find consensus. This could be of social value, so long as it does not threaten to paralyze the government.

[52] The qualified majority contradicts the formal-majority principle because it gives the minority a veto right against the majority. If a two-thirds majority is necessary for a decision to be accepted, the votes between 50 percent plus one and two-thirds carry greater weight than do the other votes. It is possible to argue in response that before the vote, all votes are equal, so equality has not been violated.

[53] This is the prevailing view in Hungary among governing politicians regarding the Constitution of 1989.

can be restricted. Westminster-type parliamentarism, not made palatable by traditions, led to autocratic majority rule in some of the former British colonies that adopted British parliamentarism.[54] One should respect the means with which one can avoid the fate of former colonies in Africa, where the British majoritarian tradition helped to legitimize dictatorships. The two-thirds majority rule does not favor the parliamentary minority only. The issues requiring a two-thirds majority vote favorably influence the position of minority social groups and actually protect minorities. Parliamentary oppositions, by definition, have to oppose government initiatives, including those directed against minority groups.

The supermajority rule restricting classical majority parliamentarism emerged at the dawn of modern constitutionalism to protect the basic institutions of the constitutional system. Article V of the U.S. Constitution requires a two-thirds majority of both houses of Congress to propose amendments to the Constitution. The framers of the Belgian Constitution of 1831 were afraid of a future royalist majority in parliament supporting the king's antiparliamentary activities. To prevent such a majority the constitution provides that a two-thirds majority vote in both houses is necessary to allow the king to become the ruler of another country (Art. 62). Since then, in several states a special qualified majority came to be required for the passage of laws in certain important legislative matters. In bicameral systems this solution, understandably, is less frequently resorted to or deemed necessary. In these instances, as French practice would have it, important issues are regulated by what is termed *organic* law. Organic laws require the agreement of the other legislative house; in the absence of such agreement, an absolute or quali-

[54] Lijphart considers Westminster-type parliamentarism advantageous for homogeneous societies, describing it in the following terms:(1) concentration of executive power–one party and bare-majority cabinets, (2) fusion of power and cabinet dominance, (3) asymmetric bicameralism, (4) two-party system, (5) one-dimensional party system, (6) plurality system of elections, (7) unitary and centralized government, (8) unwritten constitution and parliamentary sovereignty, and (9) exclusively representative democracy. Arend Lijphart, *Democracies: Patterns of Majoritarian and Consensus Government in Twenty-One Countries* (New Haven: Yale University Press, 1984), 4–9.

Unicameral postcommunist parliamentary systems come nearer to this ideal than to the consociational one.

fied majority of the house of representatives (in France, the National Assembly) is necessary.[55]

4.2.4. Collective Participants

(a) Committees: grounds for existence and entitlement

Classical parliament meant one huge physical space in the parliament building where all the members gathered. Members increased in number, while the size of the hall did not necessarily increase. In the House of Commons in England, the number of seats does not correspond to the number of members. Following the Nazi bombardment of Westminster, Churchill insisted that parliament's building be restored without alterations, and a political tradition was preserved.

The anointed forum for forming opinions, clarifying views, and debate, bar the time of votes, perhaps interpellations, and important political announcements, is almost always empty. The members give their speeches to vacant rows of seats and, at most, send their messages to the public at large. Only their most trusted friends listen to them live. Parliamentary work is carried on but nearly exclusively in committees.

Parliaments are bodies with large memberships.[56] As the state and law's role in social engineering increased, parliaments were forced to develop into complex organizations, enabling them to handle complex

[55] According to the French Constitution (Art. 46), organic laws require mandatory, prior Constitution Council review. The laws on the courts, Constitution Council procedures, and finances belong to the area of organic law.

The German Basic Law does not mention the concept; however, with laws that provide for execution by the Land administrations, consensus with the Federal Council is necessary before the law can be passed. In Germany today, this procedure is followed in about 60 percent of the federal legislation.

[56] The size of a given country has only a slight relationship with the number of members in its parliament. Perhaps the largest legislative body in history was the 2,250-delegate Soviet Congress of the People's Deputies. The British House of Lords has 1,200 members, while the House of Commons, 650. The Italian lower house has 630 members, while the French and German lower houses have roughly 500 and 600 members, respectively. The Hungarian Parliament, with its 386 members, seems conspicuously crowded in comparison with the Austrian (183), the Australian (125), the Czech (200) and the Dutch (150) houses of representatives, even though these are bicameral institutions. (All figures are approximates.)

and large-scale issues. The state was assigned welfare matters, and the relationships to be regulated have grown increasingly complex. The time allocated to parliamentary debate and decision making has been limited. In the case of an unstable government, several session days are lost while it is under formation. Supervising government's activities takes time, too. One of the most important means of supervision is the one-hour or whole-day "question time" and political debate. The division of labor is unavoidable, and for expertise to prevail, work must transpire in small groups, that is, in committees.

This begs the question: Is the *delegation of the powers of the plenum constitutional*? At the dawn of modern constitutional systems confusion ruled supreme. At its first session in 1789, the French National Assembly ordered that debates be held in committees, which would then put forward proposals. A few days later, however, they came to a different conclusion, saying that the nation was only represented by the plenum, so only what was said at the plenum should be taken into consideration. As a compromise, they finally agreed on weekly plenary sessions for debate. The French Constitution of 1791, adopting this principle, declared that the legislature as a body was the institution of national representation. At the same time, however, the Constitution authorized the National Assembly to form itself into a committee of the whole at any time.

Dissatisfaction with the number of empty speeches in parliament and efficiency considerations led to the increasing importance of committee work.[57] For simple physical reasons the work of committees is less public, consequently, they are more difficult to supervise because, according to constitutional provisions, they do not need to sit publicly. Paradoxically, because of the lesser importance of publicity and because of the semipublic nature of their work, the committees have managed to preserve something from the original value of parliamentary debates. Here projecting a favorable public image is of lesser significance, so it is not done. Woodrow Wilson wrote that "it is not far from the truth to say the Congress in session is Congress on public exhibition, whilst

[57] If we exclude the subcommittees in the U.S. Congress, the Mexican Parliament is the institution with the largest number of standing committees: more than fifty. In response to earlier experiences with a multicommittee legislature, the French Constitution of 1958 (Art. 43) limits the number of standing committees to six. Philip Laundy, *Parliaments in the Modern World* (Dartmouth: Gower, 1989), 120.

Congress in its committee-rooms is Congress at work."[58] The permanent committees make the work of the full sessions easier, letting them devote more time to political debate and the supervision of the government. To be sure, these debates are less concerned with the bills that will determine fundamental political issues. Based on British parliamentary traditions, some still have reservations concerning debates that are not conducted in front of a full plenum.

Over time, committees were gradually granted constitutional recognition and special rights of procedure. In the Weimar Constitution, committees were given the power to order the chancellor and the Imperial Diet to appear before them (Art. 33). The committees have prerogatives in connection with the submission and handling of bills, and the house rules, in some states, allow expedited treatment for bills originating in committee.

The committees' opinions in strong party systems usually reflect quiet agreements among the parties or the impossibility of an agreement ever being reached. After a committee has hammered out an agreement, there is no point in arguing over concrete issues. This explains why committee opinions are given preferential treatment and plenary sessions are relegated to the background.

In the relationship between parliament and its committees, the issue of delegating legislative powers tests the meaning of constitutionalism. In a party system, as the committees are comprised of members reflecting the composition of the plenum,[59] debates are among those who are best qualified to participate in them, and parliament is expected to pass numerous laws quickly, the temptation that the constitution would delegate legislative powers to parliamentary committees is great.[60] After all, if in some systems the executive power can assume the role of the legislative power, too, and if in all systems the executive power is entitled to regulate the independent executive, the above delegation may qualify as a pardonable transgression. In the Italian House of Representatives the president of the house may submit a proposal to this end, but

[58] Woodrow Wilson, *Congressional Government: A Study in American Politics* (Gloucester, Mass.: P. Smith, 1973), 69.

[59] In the British Parliament some of the committees are headed by the opposition, similar to Hungarian practice. In the U.S., all committee chairs are appointed from among the members of the majority party.

[60] The Italian Constitution explicitly allows this (Art. 72).

if 10 percent of the representatives or the cabinet object, it is the plenum that passes the law.

Paradoxically, parliament's supervisory role is specifically assumed by the parliamentary *inquiry committee*, which has been constitutionalized in the constitutions written in this century. In 1832, the English Parliament sent out a royal investigative committee to examine town administrations. The primary work of the committee was to collect information for legislative reform, so the independent experts in the committee played an important role.[61] The former British colonies that have adopted English parliamentary traditions have been successful in this form of information gathering before making decisions. *The method is appropriate for pushing back one-sided proposals coming from the public administration.* The work of fact-finding committees reveals the opinions of the various interest groups without their coming into contact with the actual decision makers. All in all, both in Continental and American practice, the standing parliamentary committees should partly assume the role of the royal investigative committee.[62] As these committees must deal with current legislative issues, too, and as the current legislature, generally short on time, processes the administration's proposals, the solution does not always yield positive results. This is true even if the fact-finding independent committees function efficiently, as they do in Germany and in the U.S., due to the checks and balances and strong lobbying.

The opportunity to learn of various points of view, independently, seems especially important in places where the national public bureaucracy has a dominant role in the preparation of laws. Postcommunist parliamentarism is increasingly becoming defenseless because, while politicians are enthusiastically advocating a Westminster-type parliament and dream of playing the roles that were common in last century's parliament–dreaming is easier than working–they do not want to acknowledge Westminster's other role, that of the diligent inquirer. (True, in nineteenth-century liberal Hungary, Prime Minister István

[61] The British standing committees often act as general fact finders. The House of Lords also has several investigative fact-finding committees and others that make political proposals.

[62] Interestingly enough, in the U.S. the independent committees are often established by the president, and sometimes the Congress sets up mixed committees in which the officers of the executive also participate.

Tisza's parliament did not copy this British parliamentary work ethic either, only the club room filled with cigar smoke.)

Investigative committees are aimed exclusively to satisfy the opposition's publicity demands, and they serve to directly supervise the work of the executive (for example, if scandals occur). In some cases investigative committees are set up at the request of a small minority.[63] Under ideal circumstances, half of the members of the investigative committee and/or its chair are members of the opposition. Given its political nature, any committee investigating concrete matters is clearly a parliamentary committee; it consists of members of parliament only.

It stands to reason that the *procedural* powers of investigative committees should be included in the constitution, as in the German Basic Law. (If we expect such committees to produce results, their procedural license should be similar to what is granted judges investigating criminal matters.) In addition, though not necessarily at the constitutional level, the subject matter and the duration of the investigation has to be clearly determined in the resolution setting up the committee. These are obvious requirements, except that the government majority may not be interested in logic. If an investigative committee has to be set up, the political interest of the majority loyal to the cabinet is that the committee investigate as little as possible and that the reliability of the information found should be highly questionable. Constitutionalism in politics helps make the obvious compulsory as, otherwise, what would follow from the politically obvious leads to the opposite of what would obviously be reasonable.

Whatever the findings of an investigative committee or its minority, only the parliamentary majority can remedy the irregularities found. A sure measure of parliamentary morality is whether the revealed problems and irregularities remain unresolved. Public opinion is supposed to take care of the rest.

[63] According to the Weimar Constitution (Art. 34), 20 percent of the members could request such committees, and a similar percentage is required in the Hungarian House Rules of 1994. The German Basic Law raised the limit to 25 percent, and the Belgian Constitution of 1831 allows either house the right to conduct investigations (Art. 40).

(b) Party factions

Besides the committees, the House Rules and some newer constitutions have placed other collective participants in prominent places.[64] These are the party factions, the parliamentary groups of the members pertaining to the same party. The party factions were granted procedural advantages at the expense of individual members (who are outside the factions). Long before modern parties existed, the members who voted alike and who acted in unison sat next to one another in parliament. In the nineteenth century, each of these groups functioned increasingly under the direction of an elected leader. But it is only in modern party systems that party factions have become decisive factors in parliamentary work.

The exceptions are not without their moral. In the United States, where there is no modern mass party with a permanent membership, the representatives, and especially the senators, have managed to preserve their independence to a great extent. They often vote against their "party line," or, in exchange for their vote, they require the party line (if one exists) to be modified. America is a relic of early electoral party politics and early parliamentarism. In parliamentary systems today, party factions can easily become the real actors in parliament.

[64] Several of the more recent constitutions, like the 1958 French or the Dutch as amended in 1983, do not want to recognize party factions, even though they undoubtedly play an important role in the life of parliament. The faction's role is significant despite the fact that sometimes party politicians breach party discipline and withdrawal from the faction cannot be penalized, which means a member opting out of the faction cannot lose his right to vote.

Party rule in parliament would be complete and parliament would really succumb to partisanship if the member expelled from a party faction, or who withdraws from it, were to subsequently lose his seat. This is the dream of party leaders. A not wholly self-interested explanation of this dream says it would ensure parliament's stability, something that has been so difficult to achieve in the second half of the twentieth century with special electoral provisions and various parliamentary techniques. Where the member is "voted" into parliament from the party list, the voters voted him "in" instead of Caligula's horse, so the member should either stay in the faction's stable or become a horse that can be traded.

The Hungarian House Rules of 1994, in view of the Constitution, could not go as far as this, but they "penalize" the member excluded from or leaving a faction by not allowing him to join any other faction for six months, making the person a legislative outcast.

On the whole, the rights of the factions and the committees, as well as other provisions in the house rules, restrict the rights of the individual members. The restrictions may correspond to express constitutional provisions and certainly have been approved by the members who voted for the house rules. But do they correspond to the ideal of constitutionalism? Is not parliamentarism breached if *relegating* the members becomes secondary to group formations? A preliminary to these questions is: To what extent is parliamentarism about the members? If the members were bound to one constituency, the restriction of the members' rights in favor of committees and factions, that is, the institutionalization of putting the member at the factions' mercy, would hardly be acceptable. As there is nowhere a binding mandate, this argument may be quickly refuted. Should not the subjects of parliamentary powers be the body of the whole (the plenum) and its subcommittees, especially in systems where the members get into parliament from party lists to satisfy the requirement of proportional representation?[65] This begs the question: Is not the member like a building block who primarily has functions only as part of a body, and these functions and, accordingly, rights exist only under these terms? If the person is not important, there are far-reaching implications. Proxy voting would be legitimate; in Europe today, delegating one's mandate to another member is a widespread practice in accordance with standing orders.

Where the faction is granted the right to speak on the floor–as well as other rights–the aim is to diminish the individuality of the members and their potential for breaking up the party faction. The solution strives to strengthen the efficiency of party representation in parliament.

All this is corroborated, for instance, by German parliamentary logic, which considers the parties constitutional institutions. The Basic Law, with an eye to the experience of Weimar, acknowledged that parliament was the scene of party activities and not the activities of individuals. The

[65] In Austria (*Bundesrat*), Portugal, Spain, Brazil, and in a number of other South American countries, there is a "closed-list" or "proportional-representation" system applied in one or both houses of the legislature. In Japan (in the House of Councilors, the upper house) and Paraguay, the system is not fully proportionate, thereby favoring the larger parties.

In some states (Holland, Italy, Israel, and Belgium) certain preferences are incorporated into the "party-list" system. In some of the Scandinavian countries the majority of the party seats are allocated proportionately, according to the party list, while compensatory seats are distributed among the smaller parties. See Laundy, 14–22.

Basic Law strives to reconcile this reality with popular representation.[66] The parties are the instruments through which the public can express their will primarily through elections.

> The expression of the people's will coincides with forming the state's will only if the people, as the constitutional or creative organ, exercise state authority through elections. Political parties...constitute intermediate links between the individual and the state...instrument's by which the citizen's will can be put into effect even between elections; they are the "mouthpiece" of the people...In a modern mass democracy...[the state] could not hold elections without political parties...[67]

Consequently, parties are not only given constitutional protection but become the participants of the parliamentary state with recognized functions. Thus the parties, or *at least their election campaigns*, can be funded from the budget without any constitutional misgivings.[68]

(c) The opposition

The constitutional dialogue in parliament does not assume the equal right of members to speak in parliament and to submit proposals but is built upon respect for the rights of the opposition parties. To maintain a dialogue, the opposition has to be granted collective procedural rights in proportion with their numbers, and in some cases (especially in two-party systems), their procedural rights should equal those of the ma-

[66] The German model for the *open* recognition of the constitutional role of parties has so far not found much following. The French Constitution of 1958 (which perhaps accidentally emulates the solutions of the Weimar Constitution) does not mention party factions, though Art. 4 recognizes and guarantees the role of parties in the election system as "instrumental in the expression of the suffrage."

[67] 20 BVerfGE (1966). Quoted in Donald P. Kommers, *The Constitutional Jurisprudence of the Federal Republic of Germany* (Durham and London: Duke University Press, 1997), 204–208.

[68] The solution, nevertheless, resulted in numerous legal debates, partly because party budgets are constitutionally supervised and partly because numerous German Constitutional Court decisions have only partially clarified the extent of permitted funding. It is still not very clear which parties are entitled to funding.

The emerging postcommunist democracies use direct support. Such practice could be justified when democracy is "new or developing," yet the perpetuation of the party-funding system, which is approved by all the parties, is constitutionally questionable. The system still does not eliminate the dependence of parties on private creditors, neither does it separate the parties from the state. Thus the parties live off the state, thinking that elections but not constitutional principles are the only social tests they have to pass.

jority. This is supplemented by the house rules or traditions on committee memberships and seniority. In some cases, as in the United States, the winning party gets to chair all the committees.[69] In other places, like the Israeli *Knesset*, the positions are allocated to correspond with the distribution of power in parliament. The Hungarian Standing Orders of 1994 were even more generous to the opposition in allocating positions. The Germans allocate debate time in parliament based on the number of members a given faction has.[70]

To be able to approach the parliamentary minority issue in a manner that is acceptable to the minority and which is constitutional, it is important to let parliament function as a forum for debate. There is no dialogue if the opposition is not granted the opportunity to speak and if anyone can be silenced by a majority vote. In the dialogue, the opposition is just as important as the majority; they are both in the same situation so they should be granted the same rights. The same does not apply to the individual members of the opposition, whose right to speak can be restricted without much ado, similar to the way the rights of the individual members of the majority are restricted.

When the committees are set up or the rules of debate are laid down, the opposition, that is, a minority of the members, is often granted additional rights. So it seems as if the house rules or the traditions breach the equality of rights. Why should a minority be granted advantages? This objection misses the whole point. In reality it is not the equal weight of the votes that is being discussed here, no matter how important this might otherwise be. What is being discussed *ex post*, after the elections, is that there is a majority–defined in any manner–standing opposite a minority. The rights granted to the two groups formed under similar conditions, assuming they were formed lawfully, remain, however, unequal. *After* the decision has been made, the original proportionality disappears; the difference in numbers is lost to the dif-

[69] In certain committees the opposition and the ruling faction may count on an equal number of places, even in the United States (especially if the committee deals with issues of immunity and, perhaps, in some of the investigative committees).

[70] In many places the house rules are extremely strict in their allocation of time and, in certain situations, the allocation of seats on the committees. In contrast, the traditions of the British Parliament are rather lax; time is allocated as agreed "through the usual channels" between the parliamentary parties. This allows for shortening the length of debate on the second reading of a bill to one day.

ference in quality. The majority gets all; the minority nothing. However, as the minority in parliament is not a transitional occurrence but a permanent situation as well as an institution, in other words, there will always be those who are in the minority (quite often the members of today's majority), and as the minority is necessary for parliamentary dialogue, according to the democratic rules of the game, they need to be granted *additional rights* to restore the balance in the dialogue.[71]

The (government) majority and the opposition represent different qualities, and to balance these differences, the opposition may be granted additional rights. Since the position of the two groups is not equal, they cannot be handled in a similar manner, but this will not change their relations in actual decision making.[72]

The inflexible "majority principle" advocates the contrary. The majority and the minority, as their positions are unequal, may be handled differently.[73]

4.3. UNICAMERAL *VERSUS* BICAMERAL SYSTEMS

The feudal multicameral system originally reflected the divisions among the feudal estates. This model, in modern, federal, popular representative systems, was easily incorporated into constitutional traditions.

[71] This does not affect the legal equality of the minority members (opposition). For instance, the minority representative groups are also entitled to take advantage of collective services (in proportion to their membership). Committee positions may be allocated proportionately with the number of seats, but this is a rather complicated issue. The equality argument suddenly ceases to promote mechanical allocation. In this respect the same standards are not applied to the opposition as they are to the majority.

[72] The parliamentary minorities' need for procedural rights is easier to understand in connection with the educational requirements of, for instance, two different language communities. If the education is uniform with equal-access rights, then it would be education in the majority language. If the two language groups were granted equal benefits in their respective schools, these would not be enough for the education of the minority in a number of cases because their costs are higher. Once we recognize the right of the minority to study in its own mother tongue, this means as well that we recognize the "unequal" additional expenses of achieving the objective.

[73] Cf. the views of Judge Kerans in *Mahe v. R. 33 C.R.R.* 239 (1987). "As the 'majority' and the 'minority' positions are dissimilar, they may be treated differently. If this were not so, the majority rule would be anticonstitutional."

But in the United States, for instance, it was not merely the need for the representation of the member states that brought about the establishment of the Senate. The framers of the Constitution were rightly suspicious of the unrestricted democracy that had nothing to counteract it and that would prevail in a unicameral representative system. Hence with the additional need for a second chamber, Madison sought to improve a further shortcoming of the House of Representatives, too. By making the Senate a stable institution, he sought to counteract the inexperience of the representatives brought to the fore by the short period between elections.

According to the original U.S. model, the Senate was comprised of the "quasi" delegates of the member states in the federation, in other words, it was the organ of representation of the member states. Since 1913, the residents of each state, regardless of its size, directly elect two senators.

The Swiss Constitution of 1848 comes close to the original American model. The cantons each delegate an equal number of representatives to the Canton Council. Conversely, since 1848 German tradition supports the delegation of representatives to the Federal Council by the cabinets of the member states (in 1848, half of the representatives were delegated by the government and half by the legislature). The number of delegates sent by each member state has nothing to do with the state's size.

The advocates of checks and balances in nonfederal states look enviously upon federal systems where duplication is a structural necessity. Federal bicameralism may be considered a mixed blessing, yet it is something that balances and restricts *inside* parliament. But in the case of monolithic state structures, the duplication of parliament brings forth theoretically unanswerable questions regarding popular sovereignty. Which of the two houses will represent the people's will? At times the second house is elected indirectly, which weakens its popular legitimization.[74] In this manner, however, it has fewer reasons to demand powers for itself to counteract the directly elected chamber.

[74] In the Commonwealth states that follow British traditions, it is not uncommon to find a second house with appointed members. In Canada, appointment to the Senate is performed by the sitting prime minister, consequently, the Senate–though formally it has almost the same rights as the elected House of Representatives–restricts itself in exercising its powers. In Jamaica, the prime minister appoints the majority of senators, while the leader of the opposition decides who should take the minority seats.

In feudal representative systems, the feudal estates met in separate bodies.[75] The French Revolution put an end to this practice. The French Constitution of 1791 (Tit. III, par. 1) institutionalized a unicameral system because the *nation was united* and the citizens had equal rights.[76] If the two assemblies agree, the second chamber is unnecessary; if they disagree, the second one is obnoxious. These arguments are logical, but wisdom, in opposition to logic, would have required a second house to ease political conflicts and the chaos of the transitional period. In later and wiser ages, where logic was not so important, politicians kept returning to the bicameral system. John Stuart Mill argued that giving one chamber too great a power would make it complacent.

In nonfederal states a special form of bicameralism evolved from the English parliamentary system that until this very day, preserved feudal privileges. To have a bicameral parliament in a unitary state seems almost the rule. The reason for the continued existence of senates may be found in the pragmatism of historic traditions and interests. In places where the existing upper house has a say in the making of any new constitutional order, it could hardly be expected that it will vote for its

[75] In the earliest English parliament there was no such separation. Cf. Albert Frederick Pollard, *The Evolution of Parliament* (London–New York: Longmans, Green, 1920). The most powerful lords were granted special privileges by the king, and they also demanded that they be given the right to participate in government. Thus their position was fundamentally different from that of the other members of the nobility. At the close of the fourteenth century, the delegates of towns had a separate meeting place from that of the knights. It was this physical separation–and the shared interest behind it–that enabled these two bodies to each have a separate existence.

[76] There are, however, republican considerations going against unicameral representation. The Bolivian Constitution of 1826, which was based on popular representation, advocated a tricameral legislature. The third chamber, called the Censor's Chamber, was established to supervise the executive. The Constitution of 1826 was in effect for only one year, but its three chambers and life-term president are not a novelty. As Simon Bolivar's personal creation, it had great influence on the South American continent. It pointed out the dilemmas facing liberal statesmen when the constitution made it their duty to let the people's will prevail where the people, in the politicians' views, lacked political maturity.

A record five chambers were created by Josip Tito in the Yugoslav Constitution of 1974. The interest not appearing here is not worth mentioning. That the system did not work was the idea.

own abolition.[77] The parliamentary reform of 1911, during the course of which the House of Lords was threatened with abolition if it was excessively obstructive, only complied with traditions because the British Constitution was so very flexible.[78] In other places such an "interpretation" of traditions would be termed revolutionary.

The "organic" process of preserving the second house is well demonstrated by the Dutch–Belgian example. According to the Belgian Constitution of 1831, members are chosen by the same constituency as the senators. The electoral district of the senators equals with the provinces, but they do not represent the provinces. Senators were elected for eight years, and in those times, one had to be very well off to become a senator. Since 1848, in the Netherlands the members of the first chamber are elected in the provinces, similarly to the Belgian Senate, but they are elected directly, so the difference in the composition of the two houses in the Netherlands is the result of the differences among the constituencies only. Traditionally the powers of the two chambers were almost identical. Thus sometimes the idea of abolishing the duplication of powers comes up. The first chamber (the "upper house"), however, has developed its specific constitutional function, namely, it acts to balance the workings of the second chamber, the legitimization of which is more direct.

The preservation of the upper house through reform is a typical nineteenth-century phenomenon. The advantage of this solution was that it enabled politicians to democratize the earlier institutions without causing any radical upheaval. The originally–for reasons of principle–unicameral French parliament became bicameral after 1875 as the price of a compromise that was struck to have the republican system accepted.

[77] The upper house of the Czechoslovak Federal Parliament agreed to the separation of the two member republics only after they were given a guarantee that the republics would, for at least one term, establish senates where the former delegates hoped they would be given a place. The promise was included in the Czech Constitution, but elections were not held until 1997.

[78] Since the 1830s, supporters of the House of Lords have argued that it functions to the advantage of the principle of representation because it only obstructs a bill sent up from the House of Commons when the public does not wholeheartedly want the new law. In other respects the recommendations from the House of Lords provide ideas for further consideration. Today, when the House of Lords has practically no power to speak of, this may be more true than in the nineteenth century.

In 1875, the republicans were reluctant to accept (due to the previously mentioned objections of principle) the institution of the Senate advocated by the royalists. Gambetta, however, later qualified the second chamber as "the founding principle of all parliamentary governments" because–also due to the circumspection resulting from the method of its selection–it counteracted all hasty decisions made by the representatives (the National Assembly).[79]

Denmark (1954) and Sweden (1971) abolished the second chamber because they considered it an institution that could not be reconciled with democratic equality.[80] Owing to historical traditions, they were less afraid of the abuse of power, and in both, social democratic values are very strong. It is paradoxical that it was monarchies which took this step.

The constitutional acceptability of the second chamber cannot today be disputed even in nonfederal states. The division of parliament helps to counteract the power of the legislature and–similarly to multiple reading–may contribute to prudence in parliamentary deliberation. It may prevent rash decisions from being made. Even following the reform of 1911, the House of Lords could delay the legislative process by two years, except in cases of money bills.

Bicameralism helps diminish the dominance of parties, especially if different electoral systems are used to elect the members of the two houses.[81] The term in office of the members in the two houses should be different, so the dominance of one of the parties in one house may be

[79] Cf. James Bryce, *Studies in History and Jurisprudence* (New York: Oxford University Press, 1901), 239.

[80] Unicameral systems exist in Europe: in Finland, Greece, Portugal, Hungary, Slovakia, Bulgaria, the Baltic states, and Slovenia. Israel (because of social-democratic influences at the state's founding) has always had a unicameral system. New Zealand abolished its second chamber in 1950. It seems the unicameral system is more widespread in some of the smaller states. But China also has a unicameral system, while in the Caribbean countries, which have small populations, a (appointed) second chamber functions.

Norway and Iceland divide their representatives into two chambers after a single election.

[81] The most often used senate electoral models are election by the electoral assemblies of given territorial units or the election in constituencies (e.g., regions) that are different from the constituencies voting for the lower house. In certain cases the rules pertaining to the election of senators may differ, too: the legal voting-age limit might be higher, or with partial (staggered) rotation, the senators may serve longer terms.

counteracted by a different kind of party dominance, which, even in federal states, is the objective of the counteracting division of the two houses.[82]

Parliament is comprised of the representatives of the people, but in a bicameral system neither body can pronounce itself to be the exclusive trustee of the people's sovereignty. The downside? The procedure is drawn out, and the division may in certain cases paralyze the legislative process, depending on the powers of the second chamber.

The question is, therefore: Where does the relationship between the two houses stand? It goes without saying that the relationship changes, depending on what the electoral legitimization of the bodies is and on whether one has a federal system in mind or simply the duplication of the legislative function. In most federal systems the federal assembly's position equals the other chamber only in matters concerning the members of the federation (for example, the German Federal Council). The U.S. Senate, however, because it was institutionalized also to moderate the activities of the House of Representatives, has completely equal powers (and in some matters, like foreign policy, greater powers) with the House.

If we look at the 1831 Belgian and the 1848 Dutch parliamentary models (and the impact of the English model can easily be detected here), the divisive systems formally assume the equality of both houses, with the condition that the budget may be submitted only to the lower house.

In the Third French Republic the two houses were equal, on paper. But the Senate could not revise the budget, only accept or reject it. As a repercussion, in the Fourth Republic, the organ that was then called the Council could object to the National Assembly's resolution only if it queried the constitutionalism of the legislature. In an effort to counteract (break) the unyielding power of the National Assembly, de Gaulle granted the Senate almost equal powers. The two houses of the Italian Parliament enjoy equal powers. Although the text of the Dutch Constitution would suggest that the two houses are nearly of equal

[82] The Irish Constitution was drafted in an age when corporatism was quite attractive. As a consequence, the Irish Constitution, quite uniquely, allows for the direct appearance of social interest groups in the Senate. Some of the senators are appointed by the prime minister, but the majority are elected by the Electoral Council comprised of members of parliament, members of the local governments, and appointed senators.

power, in parliamentary practice, however, the first chamber (the house formerly of the nobility) is primarily engaged in supervising the legislature and the executive. It sometimes rejects a bill approved by the other house, and in this event no law can be passed because there are no regulations to resolve such controversies. The first chamber does not have a say in the composition of the Dutch government; it is the second chamber that has the right to hold no-confidence votes. As the composition of the government falls in line with the party divisions of the second chamber–the division in the first chamber tends to deviate from this–the first chamber is more independent of the government. Thus the original parliamentary function of public control may continue to exist, whereas in other countries it has been rendered rather formal by party domination in parliament. Since, according to the constitution, submission of bills is the prerogative of the second chamber, the first chamber may exercise quasi-constitutional supervision.[83]

4.4. THE LEGISLATIVE PROCESS

4.4.1. PRIMARY LEGISLATION

Though the original Latin name *parliamentum* refers to "speech," in parliaments not only views are exchanged, but here action is also taken. In some systems the parliament forms and supervises the government, it is involved in politics, and it strives to direct the politics of the country, or elect or appoint officers. In other systems none of these are done, or they do them differently. But what is common in all parliaments is that they draft the primary–the most important–legal statutes and *function as the legislative branch*.

In classical parliamentary systems, original legislation is the exclusive power of parliament. There are newer models, however, where parliament occasionally shares this function with other organs. In France, since 1958 the cabinet (council of ministers) has had the right of original

[83] This is perhaps why demands for constitutional court reviews in the Netherlands are so infrequent.

legislation in matters not reserved to Parliament by the Constitution of 1958. Even among the specified parliamentary-legislative subject matters concerned primarily with fundamental rights and institutions, there are subjects to which parliament may give only guidelines.

Most constitutions simply state that parliament is responsible for legislation. Sometimes there are additional references that let the reader know which laws will apply to all state organs and citizens.[84] The delegation of the legislative powers to the elected (popular representative) body is fundamental to democracy because, in this way, citizens can create laws for *themselves*, even if indirectly.

Parliament's actual legislative function is a matter of principle in terms of constitutionalism. Since the French Revolution, a number of constitutions define the regulation and restriction of fundamental constitutional rights as an exclusive parliamentary power, arguing it is the executive that is most likely to violate human rights.[85] In certain cases fundamental rights may be regulated only if there is a qualified legislative majority.

In itself, parliament's exclusive power to pass laws says very little about its role in determining what is to be included in the law. On the one hand, the constitution may restrict the legislator's freedom in choosing legislative domains. On the other hand, it may prescribe that

[84] In federal systems the issues decided by the federal legislature and those by the member states' legislatures are listed in relative detail. It seems to be a general rule that in cases where federal law applies, it is also supreme. A characteristic constitutional limitation of federal laws is that they must be necessary for the federation to be able to fulfill its role. The American Constitution stipulates that the federal legislature can pass laws exclusively on matters enumerated in the Constitution.

The German Basic Law stipulates that legislation is exclusively the federation's responsibility in those matters specifically listed. In other specified matters, both the federation and the *Länder* may have legislative powers (Art. 72 (2)). The latter are "concurrent" legislative matters, including practically the whole of economic legislation. In matters not specifically mentioned, the *Länder* have exclusive legislative rights (similarly, in theory, to the American member states' rights). In concurrent legislative matters, at least in theory, the federation has legislative powers only if specific conditions are met, for example, if a matter cannot be effectively regulated by the legislation of individual

Länder, or the maintenance of legal and economic unity calls for federal legislation. The German Constitutional Court has always been of the opinion that the federal legislature is in an appropriate position to determine whether these conditions exist.

[85] For the reasons and the related problems, see Chapter 8.

a given issue be settled entirely and exclusively by the law passed by parliament. In places where the constitutional court is strong, the observance of these constitutional provisions is continuously monitored.

Civil rights and liberties are the most frequent obstacles of the legislature's sovereign lawmaking authority. Some of the limits are to be found in the concept of unalienable rights. Further, it is possible to interpret eighteenth-century constitutional theory, which influenced the American Founding Fathers, in a manner that the state may only enact laws in cases where there is an explicit constitutional authorization, leaving all other matters to the realm of liberty. This libertarian concept is clearly visible in the works of Adam Smith. In his opinion the legislative process (an action of the state) should only apply to a small circle of issues (the enforcement of contracts, public services, like building roads and public safety, and defense matters). The tasks and the mission of the contemporary welfare state, however, are much more complex. Arguing that society cannot exist without the state exercising its regulatory function and providing its services, governmental regulation is deemed necessary in practically all areas of life. At most, the fundamental rights expressly stated in the constitution and the explicit constitutional prohibitions on legislation are what need to be taken into consideration.

Naturally, if the inviolability of human rights is taken seriously or it is believed that the state has only as many rights as the people transferred to it in a contract, the legislature would not have the authority to pass statutes in all matters. (Rousseau's general-will theory disregards the principle of limited power and puts the population at the mercy of the legislator to whom all power has been delegated.)

Liberty, today, if it does not become a specific fundamental right, means the state may only interfere with liberty if for some reason or other its functioning makes this necessary. So liberty cannot be restricted arbitrarily without some constitutionally acceptable reason.

The legislature has also to take into consideration the other constitutionally guaranteed competencies and powers of the other branches of government. In federal systems in particular, the member states' legislative powers must be observed in federal legislation. As indicated earlier, in the United States federal legislation has to be either grounded in an enumerated power or at least *necessary* to achieve the enumerated objectives of the Union.

Considerable freedom of legislation results from the power to spend. *The government spends the taxpayers' money on what it wants.* The liberal ideas that are so intimately connected to constitutionalism require the state to be neutral. The liberal approach stands against the state supporting any group or special interest when allocating public funds; neutrality in spending, however, was never raised to a principle of constitutionalism. Even the most sacred right of Americans, that of free speech, does not set limits on the state in spending legislation. The U.S. Congress constitutionally violates the principle of viewpoint and content neutrality when it grants appropriations for publications that have won the legislators' momentary support. The government can selectively fund activities that reflect one or another particular viewpoint; this is simply not considered by the U.S. Supreme Court as viewpoint-based discrimination.[86]

Regarding the legislature's general freedom, the German approach is similar to the U.S. one. Despite the constitutional restrictions in the German Basic Law, in 1953, the Constitutional Court, after certain hesitation, decided that the legislature was free to determine the need for spending and that this could not be subject to judicial review.[87] If there were to be any constitutional control, it would focus on the *equality* of the funding and not on the necessity or the objective of the funding. The Hungarian Constitutional Court, too, rejects the examination of the adequacy of the instruments chosen by the legislature. Whether a chosen measure is appropriate is a matter within the legislature's discretion. Judicial review comes into play only if there is any question of a violation of a fundamental right or if the legislature abuses its discretionary powers. This comes close to the rule-of-law prohibition regarding *abuse de droit* (abuse

[86] *Rust v. Sullivan*, 500 U.S. 173 (1991). The U.S. Supreme Court upheld the law that stipulated as a condition for hospitals receiving federal support that they *not mention* any services they may offer for women seeking abortions.

The constitutional criteria of German and Hungarian abortion regulations is that the attention of the woman seeking an abortion *be made aware* of the negative effects of such a procedure. This is done to protect the rights of the fetus and not because of legislative liberty in matters concerning spending power. However, when the German Constitutional Court ruled that covering the direct costs of an abortion from social-security funds was unconstitutional, it prohibited the use of the budget for activities that violate a fundamental right (the right to life). In a constitutional state, in order to protect fundamental rights it is appropriate to restrict the freedom of the legislature.

[87] 2 BVerfGE 213, 224 (1953).

of right) applied to French administrative decisions as a means of legal supervision.

Sometimes the indirect limits used in judicial review against arbitrary legislation–together with the application of the principles of a rule-of-law state–may prove to be truly effective substantive control. This applies to spending and even to taxation. In theory the power to tax might be the legislature's most uncontrolled power. In addition, this activity is founded on the notion that the legislature is constitutionally authorized to disregard ownership rights. After all, a tax is a form of expropriation without compensation, where not even the public purpose for which the tax was collected need be given. The basic principle of parliamentarism requires only the participation of taxpayers through their representatives authorizing the legislature to impose taxes, that is, to expropriate without compensation. The imposition of taxes and the use of the taxes collected are, in theory, a matter of government politics and within the sphere of legislative freedom, except for the procedural restrictions. But the obstacles resulting from the nature of the law are still in effect. By nature the law must be general, that is, generally applicable. A public duty (tax, or "contribution") that affects only a small group may be deemed unconstitutional because the law is not general.[88] Furthermore, a levy (contributions) or an exemption may be declared unconstitutional if it is deemed to violate equality, if it is discriminatory.[89]

All these legislative restrictions are exceptions or peripheral conditions stemming from the general limits to the legislature as a branch of power. They result from the constitutional doctrine that finds only limited government acceptable. Beyond this general control, constitutional courts have limited authority over the legislature's freedom to regulate because a more extended review power would not be compatible with the courts' constitutional role, as they have no mandate to legislate. The courts are involved in protecting the rule of law and the

[88] A German statute that institutionalized a home-building contribution (levy) was found to be unconstitutional. The whole population would have been required to pay this contribution, but only those who were building their own homes would have benefited from it (67 BVerfGE 256, 274–80 (1984)). If the levy had been imposed on only one group it would have made the law constitutional, because it would have been economic legislation where the Court is not expected to investigate necessity.

[89] 55 BVerfGE 274, 302–304 (1980); *Norwood v. Baker*, 172 U.S. 296 (1898).

principles of constitutionalism in the legislative process; and the products of legislation do not require an examination of the necessity and expediency of laws. All steps in this direction increase the danger of turning the administration of justice into a political process. Judges should not be involved in politics and should not take a stand on any party policy. The extent to which it is possible to avoid this is another matter.

Although most constitutions define legislation as the formal responsibility of parliaments, the content of the legislative process is partly determined by the administrative bureaucracy under the supervision and influence of the executive.[90] This could undermine the independence of the legislative function on a "technical" level and, along with it, the balance among the branches of power. This is especially so in Westminster-type systems, particularly if the specific parliamentary ethic, so decisive in Germany for instance, is missing. Without a proper professional ethos in parliament, the legislative body exercises, at most, a supervisory function; in legislative matters many parliaments seem to function as a voting machine acting on party orders.

One of the main risks of Westminster-type systems is that the cabinet makes parliament the source of its own unrestricted and hidden legislative power, in violation of checks and balances. Here general *authorization* laws play the role of the rotten fig leaf, hence the importance of parliament's real power to determine substantively the legislative process.

Dissatisfaction with the legislature, among other things, was what undermined the authority of the Weimar Republic and the Fourth French Republic. These constitutional systems failed, among others, because the parliamentary legislature could not properly control and manage the administration.

The separation of the branches of power cannot help against the increasing influence of the executive in legislative matters. The executive has the right to propose laws in semipresidential and South American presidential systems. Even in the United States the president has the

[90] In parliamentary systems cabinets have special legislative-initiative power. Beyond special priority rules, the rules may provide for voting procedures that work in favor of cabinet proposals. The government's proposals, at the government's request and in certain cases without parliament's approval, are given priority. Besides procedure, both expertise and predominant interest are on the cabinet's side.

opportunity to put his proposals into effect, especially if he and the congressional majority belong to the same party. In the U.S., between 1890 and 1942, 20 percent of the ninety most important laws were proposed by the president, and a further 30 percent were proposed by the president and Congress together.

The changes of the legislative branch to influence the contents of laws are perhaps more a function of the party structure than of the form of government. In the U.S., party discipline is "underdeveloped," and the executive branch traditionally is looked upon with distrust and animosity because of the separation of powers. In the *consensus-seeking* parliamentary political systems, the opposition's support is primarily sought, with varying results, through coordination in parliamentary committees. The concessions make the draft laws different from the proposals of the executive power. Experts, who are independent of the executive, may play a key role in these committees. The weight of the proposals (amendments) put forward by parliamentary committees is enhanced if they are presented as expert opinions, because professional hearings and expert opinions are considered to have prestige. This lends to the prestige of bills, for instance, in Germany, and this is what makes parliament's appearing as a central factor in the legislative process acceptable to the civil-service administration.[91]

4.4.2. Delegation of the Legislative Function

Constitutionalism (the separation of powers) requires that there be a specific body (government organ) possessing authority over legislation. It follows that the executive power could not regulate legislative issues of merit through its decrees. By the same token, the officer of the executive power (the administrative officer applying the law) should not be free to assess a given situation according to his discretion. Constitutions, however, do not often broach this issue. The sheer amount of executive lawmaking indicates the importance of the question. In England, in

[91] In the German Parliament, cabinet drafts reflect the outcomes of the public (ministerial) administration's previous struggles. The ministers try to recoup something from their earlier proposals in the committee debates, which further enhances the role of the committees in lawmaking.

1890, only 106 government decrees (cabinet orders) were passed. Since then, the state administration's authority has been extended to include a much wider circle of social issues. Thus the number of decrees proposed by the various departments of the executive has risen to several thousand annually.

This process, in light of increased state intervention and the growing number of state services, is unavoidable; it does not follow that the executive should itself determine the substance of regulations. There is a danger of transgressing the borders of constitutionalism if substantive, or fundamental, issues are decided by executive decrees. This practice divests parliament of its constitutional role, namely, legislation, and concentrates the determination and execution of state duties in one branch of power.[92]

How far-reaching the executive may go, at least in certain areas, in determining matters of primary importance without being restricted by courts, and how thin the line dividing legislation and policy was a problem. In 1934, the U.S. Congress approved a joint resolution pertaining to the Chaco conflict which provided that

> if the President finds that the prohibition of the sales of arms and munitions of war in the United States to those countries now engaged in armed conflict in the Chaco may contribute to the reestablishment of peace between those countries, and if [he] makes proclamation to the effect, it shall be unlawful to sell [any] arms...[until] otherwise ordered by the President or by Congress.[93]

[92] During a state of emergency it is possible to merge the branches of power for a transitory period, and fundamental rights can be restricted by the executive. According to Schmitt's weighty half-truth, the sovereign is the one who declares a state of emergency ("state of exception"). See Carl Schmitt, *Die Diktatur* (München–Leipzig: Duncker and Humblot, 1921), 194. This is especially true if the organ declaring the state of emergency and exercising the power in the situation is the same, in other words, if the executive declares a state of emergency enabling itself to exercise power. In the event of a state of emergency, the power to legislate is constitutionally delegated. But in states that take constitutionalism seriously, the extraordinary powers are not exercised by one organ but by a mixed body instead. The rights that can be suspended and the extent of such suspension are determined in advance, and the approval of an organ independent of the organ exercising the special powers is sought prior to the declaration or confirmation of the state of emergency. See, for instance, the German and Hungarian constitutions.

[93] Chaco is a circa 100,000 sq.-mile area in the middle of South America, under the jurisdiction of Argentina, Bolivia, and Paraguay.

In other words, the president, in the interest of peace, may prohibit the sale of arms but may grant exemptions to his prohibition, also in the interest of peace. More simply, in the interest of peace the president may issue regulations on the sale of arms at his discretion.[94]

The Supreme Court held that had the president exercised (original) legislative powers under this authorization, it would be unconstitutional. This was not the case, however, because the legislature, by saying "in the interest of peace," indicated the policy to be followed, and the rest came under the executive's constitutional authority over foreign-policy issues. True, the legislature provided guidance on the level of principle because it would have been a different guidance to say the president has to regulate arms exports in accordance with the country's trade (especially arms trade) and security interests. In reality, however, the president can interpret the resolution's language as he pleases. It is unlikely that his decisions will be contested in court on the grounds of impracticability. It follows that the law does not include any restriction in merit or guidance. So the authorization, in reality, is the delegation of Congress's legislative prerogatives. The issue here was related to foreign policy, traditionally the domain of the executive.[95] The U.S. Supreme Court is stricter if it finds that the executive legislation is without any delegation on a matter pertaining to congressional powers. During the Korean War the president issued an executive order directing the secretary of commerce to take possession of the majority of U.S. steel mills.[96] The

[94] *United States v. Curtiss-Wright Export Corp.*, 299 U.S. 304 (1936).

[95] In some European states attempts are made to keep foreign policy under parliament's control, although, within certain limits it also falls under the executive's direction. The need for control is especially strong if foreign policy affects the armed forces. Recently the German Constitutional Court ruled that parliamentary approval was necessary for sending armed troops abroad on a peace mission. The Basic Law contains nothing that would serve as a basis for this decision, which represents a middle-of-the-road opinion between the government majority party's and the opposition's points of view.

[96] There was the threat of a strike in the steel mills. In the president's view, a work stoppage would have endangered the military effort. By introducing seizure orders and subordinating the steel mills to direct government control, it was possible to avert the strikes, which would not have been possible in privately run plants. *Youngstown Sheet & Tube Co. v. Sawyer*, 343 U.S. 579 (1952).

This example demonstrates the advantages and disadvantages of the absence in the American Constitution of a constitutional provision on the state of emergency. The

order was declared to be an unconstitutional violation of Congress's legislative privileges. The decision affected private property, which is a matter within the exclusive lawmaking powers of Congress. The president had no legitimate grounds to exercise such regulatory powers.

If the executive controls parliament's decisions through party rule and party discipline, it can extort statutes that would give it practically a free hand, and it would not even be formally responsible for the decisions made because, as is the practice in English law, it would be making decisions as authorized at its own discretion. The legislature would also be exempt from responsibility, arguing that it has constitutionally authorized the executive to settle the matter appropriately; at this point its responsibilities come to an end. Paradoxically, authorizing the executive not only strengthens the legislative power of the cabinet under party influence but also the legislative powers of the state bureaucracy, which is either resistant to party rule or represents other nonparty demands and interests. This could bring about a unique kind of checks and balances, which could not have been anticipated on the basis of constitutional considerations.

What could be used to counter the delegation and carving out of "original" executive legislative powers on purely rule-of-law considerations? If parliament delegates to the executive the power to determine the content of the law, this may violate the principle of its own constitutional responsibilities (although they are always somewhat obscure). At the same time, however, such delegation can be derived from the supremacy of parliament and its unlimited legislative power. The separation of the branches of power in itself does not answer the problem of whether the power to legislate can be delegated. The U.S. Constitution requires the president to ensure that the laws be faithfully executed,

advantage is that judicial control is always possible in all measures, including control over the nature of a state of emergency-like situation. The disadvantage is that there are indeed situations when special state of emergency-type regulations are needed. In this case the president argued that the Korean "theater of war" extended to the American continent in terms of arms supplies. This can be a dangerous argument because it is then up to the president to determine what concerns war and what does not, and he may on these grounds restrict the right of public assembly or free speech. This occurred during Word War I, when the U.S. intervened in the Russian Civil War. In these cases, however, it was the prosecution and the judiciary that extended the parameters of the "theater of war," resulting in the restriction of rights in the United States.

which implies executive lawmaking power. Besides this, the president has the power of original legislation to be able to exercise his constitutional responsibilities. Further, he and the designated organs of the executive may issue orders if the law explicitly permits them. For example, the Administrator of the Environmental Protection Agency is instructed by various laws to enact the necessary regulations to attain environmental objectives in the law and to ensure that statutes are enforced with the result, for instance, that fish will return to designated rivers in five years' time.

Presidential orders enacted in the exercise of constitutionally mandated presidential duties cannot be controlled by the Congress because of the separation of powers.[97] Ensuring the constitutionality of such executive orders is the judiciary's responsibility in cases when third-party interests are affected by the alleged illegality of an order.

How seriously the nondelegation doctrine is taken will depend on constitutional relations, the fears concerning the executive power, and the strength and self-perception of the executive power itself.

In the absence of a contrary constitutional provision, it is difficult to challenge parliament's discretionary right to authorize an organ that was granted regulatory powers by the constitution to assume parliament's responsibilities. The legislature may argue that, notwithstanding the delegation in terms of constitutionalism, it still has the means to control the executive, and if executive orders turn defective, it can always pass corrective laws instead. This may not be sufficient, but no miracle can be expected from the judicial review of statutes either. The judge is fighting a losing battle if he wants to restrict the executive's legally granted freedom to regulate. The judge is in no position to dispose over funds which would be necessary for an arrangement that would be legal and constitutional in his mind.

An extreme example of legislative authorization, or delegated legislation, is the German Authorization Act of 1933, which gave Hitler,

[97] In an effort to keep the executive and its legislative function under control the Congress has introduced a series of special measures. It has created regulatory bodies, like the Federal Communications Commission (FCC), which is responsible to Congress and not to the president. Paradoxically, these bodies are at the same time administrative, quasi-judicial, and regulatory organs. Another efficient technique for congressional control of the executive are "sunset" laws. Except renewal by Congress, such acts expire on specific dates in compliance with the authorization in the law.

technically, unrestricted power. The act states: "besides following the *legislative procedures* stipulated in the Constitution of the Reich, the Reich's government is also entitled to pass laws." By letting laws be changed by orders, the law gave the executive a blank check and allowed it to use it to cover any "expenses" incurred. The knife of delegation that fatally stabbed democracy in the back was created from a provision in the democratic Weimar Constitution which delegated authority to the executive to manage crises. Under "normal" conditions, the provision worked reasonably well; it turned fatal in crisis.

The jurisprudence of "developed socialism" was perhaps slightly less forthright than that of Nazi Germany because this legislative function, which enabled the derogation of laws, was delegated to a special parliamentary body–in Hungary, the Presidential Council (Presidium). After delegating the power to legislate, parliament's supervisory function ceased. Parliament, if it is still in session, may at most revoke the delegation by passing a law. This could not have happened in Nazi Germany, and it would have been impossible to imagine it ever occurring in the socialist states, even if parliaments were convened at regular intervals.

After returning to the rule of law, the radical response to crisis situations deriving from total legislative delegation would have been to return to Rousseau's classical theory and to prohibit all original decree-making power. Accordingly, the executive would be responsible only for the details of execution. But even this would not be a miracle cure. It is difficult to determine where the boundary between "details" and "delegation" is drawn. It would be nearly impossible to physically regulate all the technical details of a matter in a law. Or if parliament were "able" to do this by voting for the administrative measures necessary for implementation together with the law proper, there would be no possibility for continuous adaptation. For instance, if parliament were responsible for determining all official prices when prices need to be regulated, there would never be a current regulation on prices.

As to the obligations and penalties directly affecting the public, the rule of law requires that the conditions of delegation be clear cut, and the addressees to whom or what the lower-level order applies must be indicated in the delegation order.[98] In addition, all this is a necessity in a

[98] For instance, if it is not clear who the addressees of the decree made by the organ with the delegated legislative powers are, the German Constitutional Court will declare

constitutional system to protect rights, as basic rights can be limited only in a law. Moreover, the *regulating* of rights implies the danger of restriction, hence the need for all fundamental rights to be regulated by *statute*.

In the Basic Law, the Germans tried to head off the tragic Weimar mistake by introducing strict rules to restrict the *delegation* of legislative powers (Art. 80 (1)). The executive may be empowered by statute to enact statutory orders that have to be observed by all organs and citizens. But the content, purpose, and scope must be specified in the delegating act itself.[99] Ancient legal principles establish that the institution with delegated power cannot delegate this power to another institution.

---

the decree null and void as unconstitutional. When taxes were imposed on "vertically integrated" companies, originally the law authorized the executive power to introduce some form of compensation for those who had been disadvantageously affected. The Court ruled it could not be accepted in a rule-of-law state that such an important concept ("vertically integrated company") not be defined. The Germans do not demand, however, that laws on delegation be as specific as possible.

The need for certainty in definition leads to the issue of determining penalties in decrees. It is a general requirement of a rule-of-law system that, where liberty is to be restricted, regardless of how the deprivation is defined, it can only be applicable by an act of parliament. As this is interpreted in Germany, the frames of criminal law may only be supplanted by parliamentary statute (78 BVerfGE 374 (1988)). A person who commits an economic crime will be imprisoned only under the Penal Code, if the act itself violated a statute. For instance, if someone issues a counterfeit draft and this violates the prescriptions in a decree on drafts, the person responsible cannot be imprisoned for issuing a counterfeit draft. If someone exceeds the speed limit, however, he cannot protest against the imposition of a fine, despite the fact that the speed limit is regulated in a decree issued under statutory authorization. The legal source chosen cannot be objected to here because the sanction has nothing to do with the restriction of liberty. (Problems arise if the fine is commuted to a prison sentence.)

The Americans are more "generous" in their definition of punishment. The Supreme Court declared it constitutional when Congress created a commission authorized to promulgate binding sentencing guidelines (*Mistretta v. United States*, 488 U.S. 361 (1989)). The decision was passionately disputed. The law under review gave only broad guidelines on the various categories of offenses and on the assessment of the characteristic features of those found guilty.

[99] The Italian Constitution has, in addition, a condition on time (Art. 76). The delegation must be for a limited period only. Moreover, in exceptional cases of necessity and urgency, when the government on its own responsibility issues provisional measures having the force of law, they must be immediately submitted to Parliament. If Parliament does not approve the measures within sixty days, they are deemed null and void from the date of issue (Art. 77).

The Basic Law, however, grants this special power, as long as subdelegation is specifically authorized by the delegating act.

The French Constitution (Art. 38) enables delegation of legislative powers only for a fixed period of time. Besides the temporal restrictions, statutory orders (*ordonnance*) issued by the government (cabinet) under delegated legislative powers must be submitted to Parliament before the date set by the enabling act. The French Constitution stipulates approval of the government's program as the condition for delegation. German constitutional practice tends increasingly to accept it as sufficient if the enabling statute offers a definite program for the decree maker. In England, certain decrees (orders) must be presented to an appropriate committee in Parliament. After presentation, however, there is no possibility for supervision in merit, owing to the scarcity of resources. Thus the examination of decrees is a formality, but the members do (may) read them and may raise unpleasant questions in Parliament that may lead, ultimately, to the questioning of a minister's responsibility. This procedure prompts departmental "legislators" to exercise "beneficial self-censorship."

The German Constitutional Court considers the limits on delegation as a means to divide the branches of power in a system of checks and balances. Limited delegation might be more important in a system of checks and balances than in a system where the branches of power are separate and where the relationships among them are more distant and the potential for the executive to be granted legislative power is smaller. To be more precise, the absence of the nondelegation doctrine is more dangerous in a system of checks and balances. If such a doctrine is not followed, the legislature may evade its constitutional function; the executive may assume the role of the legislature without having to assume responsibility for its decisions; and the law may lose its predictability.

Parliament is the institution with the greatest responsibility for the people's will. But if legislative power can be delegated, representative bodies will not be the only institutions making the most important socio-political decisions. The principle of democracy is violated by the executive's uncontrollable legislation.[100]

Of course, the requirement of bounded and limited delegation may have reasonable practical limits. A usual form of delegation is when the

[100] See the *Kalkar* case, 49 BVerfGE 89, 126 (1978).

executive is authorized to carry out a given statutory objective by observing professional practices and in accordance with the scientific precepts of the day. Such general clauses are upheld as constitutional, even if the law aims to protect a fundamental right. In connection with the Kalkar nuclear power plant, the German Constitutional Court ruled that, "the legislature is obligated to make...all crucial decisions in fundamental normative areas, especially in those cases where basic rights become subject to governmental regulation."[101] However, it was constitutional when the legislature left it to the executive to determine in an order what would satisfy the requirement of sufficient rights protection.

In keeping with the logic of the *Kalkar* case, those advocating efficient administration strongly oppose a strict legislative control over the executive. Prior to the introduction of the New Deal, strict conditions governed delegation in the U.S. After 1935, to enable the executive to handle crisis situations, the legislature liberalized the restrictions on delegation.[102]

After initial resistance, the Supreme Court decided it was acceptable to grant the executive a vaguely defined authorization that would only refer to the objectives (scope) to be achieved. It was left to the executive to issue orders determining the means with which to realize its objectives and meet obligations. A "sweeping delegation of legislative authority" is unconstitutional, but a statute is constitutional that directs the secretary of labor to "set the standard which most adequately assures, to the extent feasible, on the basis of the best available evidence, that no employee will suffer material impairment of health" if they

[101] 49 BVerfGE 89, 127 (1978). Quoted in Kommers, 139. The Atomic Energy Act provided that a nuclear installation license can be issued only if the applicant "takes every necessary precaution in the light of existing scientific knowledge and technology to prevent damage resulting from the construction and operation of the installation." The scientifically "necessary knowledge" is "an indefinite legal term," nevertheless, its use is constitutional because the need to adapt to scientific and technical changes must be granted. The term allows for the definition of clear meaning in view of current legal and social-professional practice.

[102] Conversely, the classical European solution is to grant special delegation in cases of emergency. Here the edictal legislation based on the constitution itself prevails. For this to occur, however, a state of emergency must be declared, and parliament has the right to determine the end of the state of emergency.

regularly work with certain dangerous materials.[103] Like in the German nuclear safety case, the drift of the statute is clear. It requires some form of strict protection of health by taking into consideration the available scientific information.

Delegation, even in the above case, at least according to the court, is not so complete and open as it seems. The procedural *due process* principle in the U.S. Constitution still binds the delegated legislative power. Thus it is unconstitutional to pass autocratic regulations, even if there are no specific guidelines in the law. Those concerned must be given a chance to take part in the drafting of regulations, and state agencies must prove that their draft regulations correspond to statutory prescriptions.[104]

Notwithstanding the deferentialism, the differences in the German and American methods of restricting delegation are considerable. In the system where the branches of power are separated and the executive has original popular-democratic legitimacy, it is understandable that the constitution grants him original power. So the need to delegate legislative rights is less stringent, at least in certain areas. In a system of checks and balances the delegation of legislative powers is made constitutionally possible, at least it is not prohibited, and there is nothing standing in the way of delegation; but by doing this, parliament avoids having to perform its primary constitutional function. Owing to the nature of Continental courts, the willingness to delegate cannot be counteracted by the adoption of elements from the American practice of judicial review.

[103] *Industrial Union Department v. American Petroleum Institute*, 448 U.S. 607 (1979). "The term 'occupational safety and standard' means a standard which requires conditions or the adoption...of methods reasonably necessary or appropriate to provide safe and healthful employment and places of employment." 84 Stat. 1591, 29 U.S.C. § 652 (8).

Justice Rhenquist's concurring opinion argued that the law violated the doctrine of nondelegation because the political decision is left to the executive and because it does not give straightforward guidance (an "intelligible principle").

[104] The executive regulator has to prove that it has taken the available information into consideration when drafting work-safety regulations.

The American courts, as opposed to their British counterparts, go to great lengths to control the decision making of the administration. Though they do not undertake to review the outcome of the weighing of facts, they require proof that all relevant points and facts have been taken into consideration.

In the emerging postcommunist constitutional systems, from time to time the institutionalization of nearly unrestrained delegation is openly demanded. Politicians argue that changes in the economy and the need to overcome pressing economic difficulties require the state to respond immediately, and only the executive can handle such problems. In Poland and Russia, politicians strove to facilitate economic reforms by institutionalizing legally binding presidential decrees. In Estonia, in 1992, when a similar enabling draft was rejected, the prime minister resigned. It is worth considering whether there are any forms of *interim* delegation that are able to link an efficient, quick response with parliament's participation or at least with some form of subsequent parliamentary control. In these systems, however, the stringent constitutional restriction of delegation is especially important because of the communist legal traditions, which favored delegation. Constitutional traditions and conventions are nonexistent and slow to emerge. The postcommunist executive power, due to constitutional arrangements, is already too strong (as opposed to parliament), and its power is enhanced by the party system. The courts do not volunteer to undertake substantive supervision over administrative legislation, and postcommunist constitutional principles do not include the participatory control of delegated legislative drafting. Of course, public participation in regulation could be institutionalized, but it would most probably only strengthen neocorporatist influences. Moreover, these dangers cannot be counteracted by a statute that excludes delegation in connection with basic rights.[105]

105 The Hungarian Constitutional Court has already differentiated between "secondary" regulation and original regulation of important substantive issues of a basic right. The question now is whether it is possible to enact executive decrees to "regulate" secondary issues of basic rights.

Chapter 5

THE EXECUTIVE POWER

The autocracy of the executive
power will come about.
Thomas Jefferson

5.1. THE DISCRETE CHARM OF EFFICIENCY

The term *executive power* is hugely misleading. It conjures up an image whereby the executive seems simply an instrument in the hands of a supreme and single power. In the United States, where the branches of power are separated, in theory each branch has exclusive authority in its own domain. In parliamentary systems, the relationship between the legislative and executive branches is more fluid, including the worrying situation when it is the tail that wags the dog, that is, the executive, or the government (as the core of the executive is called on the Continent), dictates to the parliament. In some states there is no dog, only its tail, in which case the government does not even bother to ask the parliament what kind of policy it should follow.

When examining the relationship of the branches of power, one can see in modern constitutional systems that the heads of the executive, or at least some of them, are in a way dependent on the legislative branch. This dependence may simply be the result of the need for the executive to observe and execute the laws, too. The budget also restricts the executive. In the event of a possible violation of the constitution, it is the parliament's duty to call those responsible to account, or at a minimum, legislation initiates impeachment. But the legislative branch does not determine in all cases who will head the executive and for how long.

Misunderstandings begin with the definition of concepts. What kind of institutions should be listed under the heading "executive power"? Constitutional law usually deals with the *head* of the executive, and this is potentially misleading. It may create the impression that the executive power is a fortress in which the leader does whatever he wants. Constitutions deal mostly with the executive departments that are connected with the legislature. The principle underpinning this approach is that the legislature will tell the executive what to do and will also determine which of the executive's departments are responsible for executing and finalizing any law's provisions. Everything beyond this is an internal executive matter. The constitution restricts the executive only by considerations of legality and basic rights. All the rest, in theory, is within the executive's exclusive domain, including unrestricted subordination and unlimited freedom in designing organization. The exceptions, however, are important and worthy of consideration. The German Basic Law, bar a few exceptions, does not permit the federal executive to become an administrative power (the *Länder* execute public administration). In other places and times (like in nineteenth-century Britain), local self-governments had the authority to restrict the administrative-organizational activities of the national executive.

The executive branch is important as an institution because it has a monopoly on coercion, and it is an organization that controls physical resources. The questions surrounding it forever remain the same: How much freedom does the executive have to dispose of these resources? To what extent does the head of the executive have the authority to withdraw them? All in all, under what conditions does the chief executive exercise direction and control over the entire executive branch?

Constitutionalism requires that constitutional principles prevail in the internal relationships of the executive branch, especially if these principles affect accountability and constitutional control. The indispensable conditions of accountability are transparency, the restriction of government secrecy, judicial review of administrative resolutions, and the state's obligation to pay damages for violations of rights and the law. The rule-of-law element of constitutionalism must extend over the executive's operations and its internal relations, and it must abide under the rule of law. The extent to which the rule of law actually pervades the executive, that is, there is a set of organizations directed or influenced by expediency and state interest, is another matter.

Traditionally the absence of democratic decision making characterized the executive branch. In the organizational form of the executive, that is, in the public administration hierarchy, sub- and superordination with military-like chains of command were omnipresent. Thus it seemed sufficient to parliaments to deal with the head of the executive: it was assumed that he, within the framework of the law, could and would impose his unrestrained will on the administration, transmitting the mandate coming from the legislature. The subordinate departments did not require any further democratic legitimization. The head of the executive had the right to appoint and discipline, and to influence decisions (again within the boundaries of law, that is, by respecting the prohibition on the withdrawal of authority) and the need to comply with the political *trend* (loyalty within the limits of respecting the neutrality of the public service).[1] The executive branch's administrative arms, contrary to that of parliament, at most would be linked to the indirect or direct democratic legitimization at the highest level.

The executive branch is not ordinarily, and perhaps never, organized in a democratic and deliberative way. It staunchly opposes majoritarianism in decision making. Here debate would threaten efficiency. The various branches of government function according to different principles and follow different considerations. This is a complementary functional argument–already used by Montesquieu–in favor of the separation of the branches of power. The deliberative administrative decision making (for example, ministerial colleges) of the French and Russian revolutions resulted in decision-making paralysis.[2]

5.2. WHO OR WHAT IS THE HEAD OF THE EXECUTIVE?

5.2.1. Kings and Presidents

When defining the executive power, constitutions deal with the leader of the executive and his relationship with the legislature.

[1] The provisions guaranteeing the neutrality of public service are missing from most constitutions. Until the twentieth century, public administration and civil servants were not constitutional topics.

[2] These dysfunctional collective decision-making arrangements originate primarily from the central power's overwhelming fear of losing its autocratic power, because if it is a single person who can make unchecked decisions at given administrative levels, then the heads of departments (ministers, for example) would have uncontrollable power against the autocratic ruler or executive leader.

In a constitutional monarchy, it goes without saying that the ruler himself is the executive power, and the monarchy is constitutional primarily because the ruler's ministers are responsible to parliament for executing the king's orders (better to say, orders are void unless and until a minister countersigns them). The ruler and his ministers often conferred, but cabinet decision making and the government as a collective entity became permanent fixtures only after a slow and long evolution. In America, the king's place was taken by the president of the republic, elected for a fixed period of time, and there is no (collective) executive body. The "ministries" (departments) are headed by "secretaries" and "administrators" who are appointed by the president and can be dismissed at any time. These leaders head their departments, independently, by grace of presidential confidence, which lasts for two years on average, shorter than a European minister's term.

Europe followed a different route. By the time the republican form of government solidified, parliament's supremacy vis-à-vis the king had been considerably consolidated. Thus in the countries that "switched" to the republican form of state, there was a weak monarch to be replaced. Consequently, in the Third French Republic (1875), against the wishes of the royalists, the authority of the parliamentary elected president of the republic was considerably restricted. The prime minister and his ministers directed the executive branch, all of whom the Parliament supervised. This form of government was gradually established in the parliamentary monarchies, too (Great Britain, Belgium, the Netherlands, and the Scandinavian monarchies). In monarchies the principle of confidence did not traditionally come into play. The ministers chosen by the king were his servants and counselors, who exercised countersignature and were responsible to parliament (under criminal law). In no other respect was there any connection between the executive and the legislative branches. The king could not be called to account, even in cases when the law was breached. This explains why ministerial responsibility was crucial when constitutional regimes were first established.

In countries where the monarchy was relatively strong before a republic was declared, matters were more complicated. When the German Empire collapsed, in 1918, many politicians suggested the adoption of the U.S. presidential model. Max Weber was in favor of a directly elected president who would have the right to appeal to the people, call elections, consult and dissolve parliament without a minister countersigning the order, and who could be recalled by a referendum requested by at least 10 percent of the voters. Although the independent authority of the directly elected president was not included in the Weimar Constitution, the president's role was determined with the powers of the dethroned emperor in mind.[3]

The competing popular legitimacies of a directly elected president and a representative parliament, on the one hand, is a contribution to the separation of powers, yet it may undermine the foundations of constitutionalism. Dual power destabilizes, as was the case in Russia in 1993 or even when there was a "dual power" in 1917, before the complete communist takeover in the October Revolution. The popularly elected savior who relies on the people disregards parliamentary constitutionalism. This contingency, however, did not occur to Weber, but it was discussed in the works of the German law professor Carl Schmitt, who used Weber's thinking as a point of departure for his own offensive.[4] Schmitt turned Weber's plebiscitary-charismatic presidential power against the impotent parliament, not by building the president's power on the constitution but, instead, on the president's *direct connection with the people.* According to Schmitt, the presidential election, demonstrating the unity of the people, is more important than frequent parliamentary elections, which merely reproduce the division of party bureaucracies.[5] The president as the head of the whole nation is a *neutral power* and, at the same time, a political leader. The president is responsible for the political integration of the people and not to parliament.

Originally parliament was the scene of the "people's independent representatives coming to an agreement in open negotiations" and "where party interests were transformed into a will above parties." Later on, parliament became that place where pluralistic power sharing among organized social groups occurred. The president of the republic protected the constitution from the parties' pluralistic self-interests, so he became the "protector," not as the Weimar Constitution prescribed but in the spirit of the German people's constitutional unity and totality.[6]

[3] Similar ideas come to the fore when a dictator seeks legitimacy (e.g., in Hungary during Admiral Horthy's governorship, from 1919 to 1944).

[4] As Schmitt became a Nazi in 1933 without any fundamental modification of his ideas, one may regard his ideas as leading to, or enabling, a totalitarian practice.

[5] Carl Schmitt, *Verfassungslehre* (München–Leipzig: Dunckler and Humblot, 1928), 50.

[6] Carl Schmitt, *Der Hüter der Verfassung* (Tübingen: J.C.B. Mohr 1931), 89, 159.

This view does not, and cannot, fit into constitutionalism. If the president protects and embodies something "absolute" and some kind of popular totality, if his power is independent and enduring, if he himself becomes *the* unified power, it is impossible to speak of constitutionalism as the negation of the totalization of power.

A "constitutionalism" that identifies itself with a single leader poses a real threat. It is dangerous just as all simple solutions are: it easily seduces public opinion.[7] In de Gaulle's model the president is given more power than in Weber's, because in the French Constitution of 1958 some of Parliament's traditional legislative powers pertain to the government (the executive). The legislature in France was placed under the supervision of the Constitutional Council, which in the early years after 1958 was under de Gaulle's control. What is more, he did not hesitate to use the referendum against the Constitution. He went to the outer limits of constitutionalism, but he remained within its boundaries by respecting and enforcing popular sovereignty (what Weber required from the plebistic-charismatic president). When he lost his power over the voters in 1969, he resigned (as he did also in 1946). His successors did not attempt to exercise charismatic power but were satisfied with a more traditional parliamentary system, all the more so because, by that time, parliamentary party discipline had become stronger and they did not need to–and probably could not–turn to the people for support against parliamentary anarchy or for power. In the French Parliament, power relations reflect popular power relations relatively faithfully, yet these do not endanger governability. Nevertheless, dual executive power continued to remain operative, at least in the sense that the president could intervene in certain activities of the executive branch, or he could assert a leading role in certain affairs. In the French model, the same executive body may, in effect, have two independent legitimized leaders; the directly elected president may strive to direct foreign policy similarly to the government, which operates as authorized by Parliament.[8] But in theory the responsibilities of the executive power may be divided in a

[7] "A false notion which is clear and precise will always have more power in the world than a true principle which is obscure or involved." Alexis de Tocqueville, Democracy in America (New York: Vintage Books, 1945), 172.

[8] A 1992 amendment to the Polish Constitution states that the ministries of defence and foreign affairs are to be headed by a person in the president's confidence, because the president has special responsibilities in these areas.

manner so as to determine which responsibilities fall to the president (the king) and which to the government. While the president as the head of state is directly elected and certain executive functions, especially those activities that embrace the whole nation and are in theory above party politics, come under the personal direction of the head of state, other functions (partly overlapping or parallel activities) belong under the government's authority. The whole government or its members are appointed by the head of state, but in keeping with the principle of parliamentarism, they cannot function without Parliament's confidence.

In view of the popularly elected president's actual legal status and his relationship with the executive branch, his statesman-like personal qualities and charisma have a bearing on his role beyond what is written in the constitution. Where constitutionalism is guided by a historically motivated fear of charismatic leaders or less charismatic but powerful dictators, the president will deliver only ceremonial speeches, like in Hungary or Germany today. Parliament elects the president, and his duties extend, at most, to special occasions.

Following the collapse of fascism, anticharismatic sentiments prevailed, and in theory, it is this conviction that should guide posttotalitarian regimes everywhere.[9] But some of the postcommunist constitutions, for instance, were written under conditions of deep socioeconomic duress; such emergencies beg for a dictator. The idea of a providential president is still haunting. It resurfaced in de Gaulle's concept of the presidency, which determined the Constitution of the Fifth Republic, and it had its impact on Boris Yeltsin's constitution of 1993. One-man rule was attractive where constitutional "renewal" was dictated by the personal ambitions of former communist leaders who turned into "democratic" leaders. From *perestroika* onwards it appeared as if the presidential system would preserve the power privileges of the communist party or its leaders. In addition, as the parliaments elected after 1989 were divided and impotent, presidentialism became increasingly attractive.[10] This explains why the postwar anticharis-

[9] What diminishes the Weimar model's attraction is that with its inadequate regulations on the state of emergency, President Hindenburg was able to dissolve the helpless and excessively and fatally divided Parliament and govern the country with his own chancellor (prime minister), who did not enjoy the Parliament's support. Technically, Hitler's access to power was made possible in this way.

[10] The debates during the transition process after 1989 focused on whether to have a weak, relatively strong, or strong president. The main problem with this division is not

matic trend, which was alien to one-man rule, was reversed. The result is often a compromise for which there is no solution: constitutions may leave legislative-executive relations unsettled, contributing to future clashes and uncertainties.

In most of the former Soviet republics, constitutional changes have increasingly strengthened the position of the head of the dual executive (Russia, Kazakhstan, Georgia, and Belarus). The presidential authority in the Polish Constitution of 1989 was determined by the Communists who hoped that, in its new form, they could continue to govern. (Similar attempts, although unsuccessful, were made in Hungary, too). Owing to the division of the Parliament, democratized presidential power continued to exist in Poland, leaving the scene open for possible charismatic leadership. Notwithstanding attempts to the contrary, the Polish Constitution of 1996 settled for restricted presidential powers. This duality probably gave rise to the kind of incidental solution seen in Bulgaria. The Bulgarian Constitution of 1991 invests the president, who has almost no formal power, with the legitimacy of a directly elected president for a five-year term. In reality, the increased legitimacy strengthens the president's role in protecting constitutionalism, and as such, it is neither superfluous nor destabilizing. In fact, the popularly elected president had the necessary legitimacy to solve the political crisis that occurred in 1997. He who can speak in the name of the people but cannot act is in no position to damage the system of checks and balances.

5.2.2. Governments and Prime Ministers

Up to this point we have discussed the executive as a separate branch, which is typically headed by one person. In parliamentary systems, however, the government (council of ministers) heads the executive, al-

---

in its simplistic formalism. What seems to be forgotten here is that this division looks only at one element of the constitutional order and fails to consider that presidential power can be interpreted only in terms of the separation of powers, whereas the separation was excluded by strong parliamentary legitimistic demand and parliamentary legislation. A "relatively strong" or "strong" president in a parliamentary system, functioning *without* the separation of the branches of power, may disrupt the internal structure of the executive branch and make the threat of the development of a *parallel* executive branch imminent.

though it is formally dependent on parliament. Parliamentary government is a special combination of a single-individual and a collective leadership, though purely collective leadership frequently occurs, too. There is a tradition of directorate, and in a number of states, the government itself is a collective body in which the prime minister is only the first among equals and the government makes its decisions by majority or by consensus, or the ministers make decisions on their own and assume responsibility for the specific tasks they oversee.

The following four relationships between the prime minister and the government are typical and can be discerned (the actual solutions and practices can be found somewhere among the various models).

(1) Parliament elects the prime minister, and he chooses the ministers who will work with him. Parliament does not confirm the ministers in their positions (although appointment by the president does present a minimum of control). In England, a select group of ministers form the cabinet, and the prime minister decides who among his ministers will become its members. The government's political positions are determined by the prime minister. The ministers direct the work of the ministries and are responsible for what they do. But the government's decisions are only collective in form, as it is the prime minister's will that dominates. If the ministers chosen by the prime minister do not support his policies, he may replace them with ministers who will. As a matter of form, however, the prime minister's decisions cannot take the place of the government's decisions. This means that the prime minister cannot issue an order instead of the government because he has not been explicitly and specifically authorized. Usually it is the government that resolves conflicts among ministers, but in certain cases the prime minister may intervene, and his word is decisive.[11]

(2) The prime minister is simply the first among equals. Parliament elects all members of the government as a whole. In some models the government may be voted down only as a whole, while in others the

[11] The German Basic Law (Art. 65) reads: "[t]he Federal Chancellor shall determine and be responsible for general policy guidelines. Within the limits set by these guidelines each Federal Minister shall run his department independently and on his own responsibility. The Federal Government shall settle differences of opinion between Federal Ministers. The Federal Chancellor shall preside over the conduct of Federal Government affairs in accordance with rules of procedure adopted by it and approved by the Federal President."

ministers may be voted out individually. The prime minister has an important role in preparing the meetings of the government, but the government makes decisions like a real collective body.[12] The prime minister cannot issue orders to his ministers in this instance, but what he can do is ensure that collective decisions are properly executed.

(3) After the collapse of the French monarchy, in 1792, Condorcet suggested that citizens directly elect a seven-member national executive committee. But this model assumes the separation of the branches of power. Or, perhaps not? The Swiss (in Art. 95 of their federal Constitution) have preserved elements of the French directorate model. A seven-member federal council heads the Swiss Confederation and is the supreme executive organ. Parliament elects the members of the directorate, but they are not answerable to it. There is no *confidence issue* nor recall of members, though they are responsible for making sure that the political line advocated by the parliament prevails. The members of the council are elected individually for a four-year term and have designated responsibilities. They may be reelected. Since 1848, the council has been continuously in session because the councillors' mandates do not expire at the same time.[13]

12 The Bulgarian Constitution is very strict about the candidate of the largest parliamentary faction being the candidate for prime minister. The prime minister selects his ministers and the parliament votes for the government, consisting of the already hand-picked ministers.

13 The composition of the Federal Council reflects the various regional, political, and religious divisions as none of the parliamentary parties are in a position to elect–with a majority vote–their own people to run the executive. Council members have to reach a consensus on decisions, and the chairmanship changes annually.

It might be worth considering that for systems where the president is elected by parliament, it would be better to elect a three-member presidency in which the members are continuously renewed (the first member's mandate would expire in three years, while the third member's in nine). The limited powers of such a politically balanced body, as opposed to parliament, are more legitimized than those of a president elected with a single majority and who, because of his reelection hopes, becomes rather defenseless in his last year in office. The members of the body would assume the representative role of the head of state, taking turns every year. The decisions in merit would be made with a majority vote or, in some cases, unanimously.

Of course, if the parliament has a second house with restricted authority, whose consent is yet necessary for the president's discretionary decisions to be effective, the collective head of state is less important.

(4) In semipresidential systems the president of the council (prime minister) is *generally* nominated or appointed by the president of the republic, while the members of the government are appointed or relieved by the president of the republic on the prime minister's recommendation. Parliament can express its no-confidence in the government, but this may lead to its own dissolution. The president of the republic may chair government sessions.

5.3. THE PREROGATIVES OF THE EXECUTIVE POWER[14]

5.3.1. The Prerogatives in Opposition to Parliament

Nineteenth-century liberal constitutions left several royal prerogatives untouched; the new executive branch, that is, the government legitimized by parliamentary vote of confidence, gradually assumed these prerogatives. From among the prerogatives it is worth mentioning the submission of bills (something unknown to systems where the branches of government are separated) and the sanctioning and promulgation of laws. In this regard, too, the executive derived certain powers from royal prerogatives. For a law to come into effect it had to be signed by the king and countersigned by one of his ministers. Even if we disregard this mostly formal ritual, there is a muddle surrounding parliament's and the U.S. Congress's exclusive legislative right. Why is it that the executive may submit bills and may, in the end, even approve the outcome of the procedure, whereas legislative deliberation is left to be carried out by another independent organization?

What is more, in typical parliamentary systems the representatives of the executive almost always have constitutional prerogatives pertaining to participation in parliamentary debates. The ministers may be present and are entitled to speak at parliamentary sessions and meetings of par-

[14] The government's position may be strengthened if, in a bicameral system like in France, it can act as an arbitrator in disputes between the two houses of the legislature. It is then in a position to decide whether to put aside bills on which the members do not agree. This is quite troubling from the perspective of parliamentarism; however, the German Basic Law, by establishing a mediation committee, precludes this event.

liamentary committees. Parliamentary rules give them the right to speak without requiring that they wait their turn.

Nevertheless, modern constitutions–for fear of parliamentary instability and at the same time overwhelmed by government efficiency concerns–have gone beyond these traditional prerogatives. Seen from a slightly different perspective, governmental practices attempted to reinterpret traditional institutions in the spirit of efficiency. It was not easy. When seeking to increase the government's executive power, certain difficulties arise from having to satisfy opposing requirements. On the one hand, in a parliamentary system the government depends on the parliament; otherwise the parliament cannot exercise its control. On the other hand, the increased importance of state services require the government and state to be efficient, and this requires administrative independence and *stability*. Political responsibility and its manifestation, that is, the institution of no-confidence–often corresponding to the members' job aspirations and their personal or party interests–may undermine government's continuous work.[15]

[15] Between 1875 and 1914 the Third French Republic witnessed forty-eight governments, for an average of nine months and twenty-two days. The Fourth Republic managed an even more negative record. In twelve years there were twenty-two prime ministers, and each government was in power for an average of six months. In the Fifth Republic, governments have managed to survive for an average of two-and-a-half years. Italy, since the 1946 Constitution, has been living in the notorious condition of constant government crisis.

Between 1867 and 1918 there were twenty prime ministers in the Austro-Hungarian monarchy. On average this means a two-year term in office, a relatively good indication of stability. From 1875 to 1890, Kálmán Tisza was prime minister without interruption, though after each election he slightly reshuffled his cabinet. The pre-1918 system emulates the stability of the British parliamentary system inasmuch as the changes in prime ministers occurred frequently because the prime minister refused to follow his party's political line. Kálmán Tisza, for example, won the 1890 election; however, the loss of votes was so significant that it seriously affected his political standing within the Liberal Party. Tisza formally resigned on a symbolic issue. (The monarch refused to sign a law that would have allowed Lajos Kossuth, the leader of the anti-Hapsburg revolution of 1848, to keep his Hungarian citizenship.) Tisza's successor, Gyula Szapáry, resigned because, dissenting from other leaders of his party, he did not approve of the compulsory civil registry of marriages. In most cases government crises were resolved without having to call new elections.

5.3.2. Protecting The Government: The Vote Of No-Confidence Made Difficult

In a parliamentary system the government's existence hinges on parliament. If the parliament is unstable, this dependence threatens to leave the executive without a leader, which, in turn, endangers the smooth functioning of the state. To strengthen the government, and through it the position of the executive power, attempts have been made–particularly after World War II–to render more difficult the abuse of the vote of confidence. Government stability improved dramatically as a result. The German Basic Law institutionalized the motion of *constructive* no-confidence. For a no-confidence issue to be raised in Parliament, 10 percent of the members have to support the motion, and the chancellor must resign only if the majority of members have declared their no-confidence and have come to an agreement on a new chancellor. If there is a multiparty opposition, the election of a new chancellor is more difficult than simply voting out the current chancellor and forcing new elections to be called.[16] Obviously the makers of the Basic Law considered the government's (and the parliament's) stability of utmost importance. Fear of government paralysis prompts the Basic Law to allow the federal president, if the Federal Assembly rejects a law together with a no-confidence vote and if the Federal Assembly is not dissolved, to declare a legislative state of emergency–for six months–if he has the Federal Council's approval. This means that government proposals rejected by the Federal Assembly become laws, provided the Federal Council approves them.[17]

[16] In Germany, the no-confidence motion failed in 1972, but was successful in 1982. The chancellor may also request a no-confidence vote (like the Social Democrat Chancellor Helmut Schmidt, in 1982, because he wanted to force his reluctant Free Democrat allies to support his antiunemployment policies) so as to strengthen the ruling party alliance. In some cases the confidence vote is applied to force early elections. If the government is denied confidence and there is no new chancellor, the parliament *may* be dissolved at the president's discretion (see Chapter 4).

[17] This solution, bound by many restrictions, supplants the system in the Weimar Constitution. In Weimar, after a state of emergency was declared–and the grounds for such declaration were never clear–the constitution enabled the president together with the government, which was not necessarily supported by the parliament, to legislate through decrees.

The constructive vote of no-confidence, which in Hungary was introduced by a 1990 amendment to discipline the then-coalition partners, restricts, in theory, parliament's influence over the government.[18]

The Constitution of the Fifth French Republic shows an even more dramatic deviation from the classical model of governmental responsibility. De Gaulle's constitution took away some of the parliamentarians' legislative rights and turned the institution of no-confidence–and the parliament-government relationship–inside out. The Fifth Republic, in this respect, also rejects the earlier, unsuccessful parliamentarism. Voting on the acceptance of the government's program is more the weapon of the sitting government than an exercise in governmental responsibility to parliament. The French government uses it if its policies become controversial in the eyes of the public. Article 49 (3) of the French Constitution states that the issue of confidence can be linked to given bills. If the government declares the bill to be a confidence issue, if it "pledges its responsibility" on "the vote of a text," the bill becomes law without a vote, provided 10 percent of the MPs do not submit a motion of censure. In forty-eight hours–during which the government may call upon its supporters–a vote is held. In this vote on censure the abstentions are not counted, and an absolute majority is necessary for censure.[19] No government has yet been ousted with this system. A bill can become a law even though the majority voted against it or–as in half of the cases–no vote was held. The pledge of responsibility to a text was

[18] The Hungarian Constitution includes very stringent rules that serve government stability; however, the rules are somewhat inconsistent. At least 20 percent of the members have to sign the no-confidence motion. In this respect, the Constitution "protects the government" even more than do the French and German ones. At the same time, disregarding the possibility of being discredited in the eyes of the public, the no-confidence motion may be used for obstruction without any restrictions, meaning the same members can continuously put forward no-confidence motions. What is more, the Constitution considers a vote to be a confidence vote only if it follows a motion explicitly put forward as such (that is, either the proposal of 20 percent of the members or the government's own motion to call for a vote of confidence). The rejection of a bill or any other government proposal does not qualify as an indication of no-confidence, at least not explicitly.

[19] A representative who signs a censure initiative that fails to bring about the government's resignation cannot submit such a motion again during the parliament's same session. Supposing that government has at least a 51 percent majority, this means there can be at most four such motions put forward during a parliamentary session.

taken almost forty times in thirty-five years, particularly during the Socialist government of Michel Rocard. At that time the Socialists alone did not have a majority but the 1958 stabilizing device was advantageously applied against its coalition partner's defection. The application of this device is perhaps more successful in the foreseeable case, when the government with a majority has to discipline its own party members who, looking to their constituency, avoid association with any unpopular measures. These dissidents would obviously not want the government to be ousted.[20]

In light of the above-mentioned constitutional devices, it is no wonder that modern German and French governments stay so solidly in place.[21] Since 1958, in France a government has only once been ousted. This happened when the president, by way of punishment, dissolved the National Assembly for failing to obey his wishes. This stability, in view of the more than sixty motions of censure and given the ease in bringing down governments during previous regimes, is indeed remarkable.[22] In Germany, too, the withdrawal of a coalition partner led to the fall of the government only once. The Russian Constitution of 1993, "further developed" the institutions of the Fifth French Republic in the Weimar

[20] In Germany, after a no-confidence vote not followed by the establishment of a new government, the president may, *within a short deadline* (twenty-one days), dissolve the Federal Assembly (Art. 68). The three-week period is considered adequate for the parliament to find itself a government if it wants to stay. The French Constitution (Art. 49) requires the government to resign after being censured. The president of the republic may dissolve the National Assembly, but he can do so at any time, regardless of censure.

[21] Just like those superweapons that are designed to help avoid the mistakes of former commanders, these stabilizing devices hardly ever actually had to be tested. Political scientists claim that it is not so much the devices in the Constitution that led to the stability of the French Parliament and government in the Fifth Republic, as it was de Gaulle's popularity and, later, the transformation of the French party system, namely, the fragmentation process came to an end. In Germany, it is difficult to decide whether the stability is due to the bipolar party system and the possibility of forming coalitions or to the strong party structure that comes from the prescriptions of the Basic Law and the electoral system.

[22] In 1962, de Gaulle, bypassing the National Assembly, had the Constitution amended by a referendum and introduced direct presidential elections. In response, the incensed National Assembly, because they could not take measures against the president–as the supermajority necessary to impeach him was missing–overturned the government.

tradition. In principle, given the difficulties and dangers of nonconfidence, the conditions of government stability are assured. This gain is questionable, however, because an impotent presidential dictatorship seems to be emerging.[23]

Where the opposition between the legislature and the executive is strong, the vote of confidence is the ultimate instrument by which government may discipline its own supporters. That things should come to a head in this way can be attributed to the changes resulting from party discipline and, in general, party structure. There are states, however, where parties and parliaments are fragmented; nevertheless, they do not resort to the no-confidence device. In the fragmented Dutch multiparty system, where there is no clear majority, seeking compromise is of overall importance (consocial democracy). If a coalition government resigns, it is because of internal tensions in the cabinet. Should this happen, the government cannot call new elections without approval from the parliamentary parties and the parliamentary majority.[24]

All in all, the constitution has little to do with how parliament applies the institution of confidence to control the executive. In Holland, the last formal vote of confidence was held in 1939, and the budget was last rejected in 1919. But in Italy, where like in Holland there is no dominant party and there is no constitutional obstacle to putting forward motions of no-confidence, the confidence device is repeatedly used with "success."

[23] The Russian Constitution of 1993 provides that the president appoints the prime minister and, at the prime minister's recommendation, the government. Though a no-confidence motion may be put forward against the cabinet, the president is not bound by it. If no-confidence is repeatedly declared within three months, the president either relieves the government or dissolves the Duma (parliament). On event of the latter, the censured cabinet may continue in office; they do not even have to be sworn in anew. As the Duma cannot be dissolved for a year after its election, the president may have to govern with a government inimical to the parliament.

[24] Technically, the government must request that the monarch call new elections.

5.3.3. The Executive Submits Bills and "Fills in the Gaps" of Missing Legislation

Governments are normally entitled to submit bills. This is a right confirmed in constitutions but difficult to justify theoretically. If legislation is parliament's responsibility, it would follow from the separation of powers that parliament should exercise its authority over the whole of the legislative process. The French Constitution of 1791 (Tit. III, ch. 3, sec. 1, par. 1.1.) explicitly prohibited the king from submitting bills; the monarch could only recommend matters for consideration. However, if the modern government, which in principle is commanded by experts and does on occasion have an accepted program, were not to submit proposals, legislation would likely be (even) less efficient. In general, governments submit most of the bills that go on to be approved. The United States is again an exception because the president cannot formally submit proposals but has to win his party's support (if they are in the majority): here an influential party member will submit the bill.

For the government the submission of bills is just an opportunity. Real power would imply that the government can pull the proposal out from under the wheels of the parliament's bureaucracy or, if it has the ability, successfully avert parliament's attempts to amend it from the floor.[25]

Legislation of the Third and Fourth French Republics notoriously overhauled government proposals, including the budget proposal. Ministers and their officers were called upon to appear before the committees dealing with their proposals and were often forced to agree to all kinds of compromises. The supporters of government's legislative privileges argue that free-floating parliamentary legislative procedures result in inconsistent laws and private agreements, while the resulting incoherent budget and the related economic intervention following pork-barrel politics make the budget completely inappropriate. Meanwhile, the government continues to be responsible for something over which it has very little influence. This perhaps is the most serious internal contradiction of both the unstreamlined checks and balances and the separation-of-powers systems.[26]

[25] The executive power's legislation is discussed *supra*, in connection with delegated legislative powers.

[26] In the U.S., where the branches of power are separated, the acts of Congress that trigger spending cannot be controlled by the executive. Before the institutionalization of the (constitutionally controversial) line-item veto, the president had no power to counter this.

The legislature prescribes responsibilities to the executive, thus in parliamentary systems, in theory, the executive is answerable to the legislature, which need not supply the necessary instruments to the government, nor is it liable for failing to ensure them.

The above as well as other considerations of checks and balances led in modern constitutions to guarantees of government prerogatives, primarily in connection with the budget. These are supplemented, on request, by procedural preferences (order of voting, priority to urgent matters), which are the due of government proposals.[27] In states where the branches of power are separated–partly because of the inadequate functioning of the political system and partly because the legislative branch can sometimes become too rigid as a result of its separation–the executive's need to have decree power, which fills in the gaps of missing legislation, increases. In the South American presidential systems the term *decretismo* was coined to describe this phenomenon. In Brazil, under Fernando Collor de Mello's presidency, on average a new presidential decree of statutory power was issued every other day.[28]

5.3.4. THE BUDGET

The naked heart of the state can best be seen in the light of the constitutional provisions pertaining to the budget and finance. The Cadiz Constitution of 1812 is one of the earliest constitutions to stipulate the government's exclusive privilege to submit the proposed budget. Article 85 of the Weimar Constitution stated that the lower house of the parliament could raise expenses in the budget only if the Imperial Council

[27] As the Russian Constitution forgot to ensure the executive these privileges and as legislative procedure is determined by the Duma's House Rules, the executive has no prerogatives. This further damages not only the Russian executive's financial efficiency and rationality, but the Duma's legislative performance, too, which has already been undermined by the numerous and still-increasing number of factions and the individual members' unrestricted right to submit proposals.

[28] Giovanni Sartori, *Comparative Constitutional Engineering: An Inquiry into Structures, Incentives and Outcomes* (Baskingstone-Hampshire: New York University Press, 1994), 170. The Brazilian Constitution states that such decrees may be issued in case of "urgent need." Decrees must be confirmed by the legislature within thirty days. The president himself decides when such urgent need exists–it seems permanently–and he may extend the lifespan of a decree by thirty days at a time without additional conditions.

approved them, while the current Basic Law openly stipulates that the federal government's consent is needed for bills that increase the budget's expenditures or cut its revenues.[29] In France, it is not necessary to vote on the government's budget proposal as long as it is coupled with a motion of censure that is not resisted. It is probably no accident that fiscal constitutionalism or at least *a chapter on the budget* is practically missing from all postcommunist constitutions. They deem it enough to say, for example, "The Parliament shall determine the state expenditure and shall approve the budget and its execution" (Hungarian Constitution, Art. 19 (3) (d). Only the Romanian Constitution provides what should happen if there is no approved budget. The other constitutions do not seem to want to admit to this foreseeable event.

Of course, parliamentarism was traditionally much more concerned with revenues. Parliaments were established because without them the king (the executive) could not acquire any revenue. There is no modern budget without revenues based on taxes, and the imposition of taxes is parliament's special privilege. Indeed the executive is, in this area, formally without special privileges.

In Great Britain the government's special role in submitting the budget was, in effect, retained. In other states the constitution and other laws had to explicitly restrict the rights of expenditure initiative of the members of parliament. These rights were perceived to promote only destabilization and obstruction. Budget debates revealed the most irresponsible side of MPs. Forcing the state to spend money on popular projects and getting support from the budget for their constituencies are irresistible temptations to members, and, in view of their role, perhaps it would not really be appropriate if they actually resisted such tempta-

[29] It is no coincidence then that the German Basic Law has at least forty-six long paragraphs on this issue. The majority of the sections allocate tax authority between the federation and the provinces. Contrary to France, the German Basic Law does not give radical privileges to the government over the budget, consequently, it takes into account that the budget may not be accepted, so it includes provisions of appropriation that ensure the functioning of the state administration and its services within the framework of the previous budget. To provide security for the necessary emissions, the government is entitled to borrow the funds needed to sustain budget management. To protect the budget, the government's approval has to be sought when legislative proposals requiring additional funds are voted on. The German model does not require protection against the individual members' initiatives because they are not permitted to submit amendment proposals to the plenum.

tions. But if the constitution is to be characterized as the means of limiting those in power, this rule has to be applied to the members whose spending habits are not discerning. What most constitutions cannot keep in check and under control is government spending.

Government's supremacy in budget matters was taken to the utmost perhaps in England, partly because of provisions in the Standing Orders. Only the government is allowed to submit budget proposals, the draft budget being the exclusive secret of the Chancellor of the Exchequer. The members have very little time to study complex proposals. In this case, plenary sessions take the place of committee meetings, and the members may only make proposals on *reducing* the budget. The House of Lords, in practice, has little authority over money bills.[30]

The French Constitution of 1958 orders all acts pertaining to money matters, that is, financial acts, including acts on taxes, duties, and fees, to be debated at special sessions. It is the government's privilege to propose the budget. The proposals put forward by members cannot be aimed at reducing revenues or increasing expenditures. The executive enjoys complete supremacy in determining expenditures because its administration provides the data used in budget planning. France is rather exceptional in this regard. Parliament has to enact the budget act relatively quickly after the government submits its budget proposal (in France the parliament has to do so within seventy days, while in England the days of debate have been limited to less than thirty). In other states the budget proposal is given priority upon the government's request. If there is a delay in its passage, the traditional rule on spending is that it must be proportionate with the amount approved in the previous year's budget. If the budget proposal is rejected, the government resigns. The radically progovernment and proefficiency French Constitution provides that, "should Parliament fail to reach a decision within a time-limit of seventy days, the provisions of the bill may be enforced by ordonnance" (Art. 47). (In practice, in case of difficulties the budget is linked with a motion of censure and approved in this manner.)

Budget proposals are debated typically in two or three stages. In the first round, total revenues and expenditures are debated. This is decisive given the rules on restricted amendability of single expenditure items.

[30] C.J. Boulton et al., eds., *Erskine May's Treatise on the Law, Privileges, Proceedings and Usage of Parliament* (London: Butterworths, 1989), 733–734.

Yet it is something most representatives do not even grasp. In the second round the amounts are earmarked (itemized) for allocation, within the straightjacket of the general balance. Allocated amounts are kept separate to preserve the general balance.[31]

The individual ministries may decide themselves how to regroup the money allocated to them, while it is the finance minister who approves the reallocation of funds among the ministries (chapters in the budget). This is the area where the executive's freedom is unrestricted.

Parliamentary and external supervision of spending is only subsequent and focuses on whether the beneficiary acted legally and whether the spending was justified and useful. As parliament is unable to take on the responsibility of supervision, constitutions set up special organizations to assume this responsibility. These organizations usually function as parliamentary organs or as courts working in parliament's name (for example, the Audit Office in Hungary, the comptroller general appointed by the U.S. Congress, or the Audit Court in France).[32] In Britain, the Crown by law appoints the auditor. The auditor is independent of the executive, works like a court, and is accountable to Parliament.[33] It is not quite clear what happens in Britain if Parliament rejects the budget report. This, contrary to the budget, is not a confidence issue, even in England.

[31] The German Basic Law uses here a substantive approach. Expenses and revenues must be in balance. The constitutional principle of a balanced budget–a pet project of American politicians who are attempting its introduction by amending the U.S. Constitution–in itself does not say much because loans can be revenue and a government-influenced national, or even private, bank is likely to provide loans.

[32] Art. 32/C of the Hungarian Constitution fails to mention the independence of the Audit Office, and it is unclear on whether it carries out its inquiries at Parliament's special request.

[33] Experiences with the involvement of parliamentary committees in the preparation of the budget are rather disheartening. The British have put a stop to this practice all together. British traditions require the chairperson of the Audit Committee to be a member of the opposition. On the other hand, the powers of the U.S. Congress over executive departments originate in congressional control over budgeting.

5.4. THE MYTH OF RESPONSIBILITY

The executive power is a strange centaur. The lower part of its body is comprised of a bureaucracy, a public service administration, while the upper part is a party politician who possesses the *Staatsraison* thanks to the voters and parliament but above all the kingmakers of his party. The powerful lower part of its body makes this the strongest branch, with the greatest chance to achieve its objectives. Knowledge is accumulated in the professional expertise of the lower part; or at least the professional bureaucracy may claim that it has sufficient knowledge to run the country, and undeniably a great mass of information is at our centaur's disposal. Besides knowledge, the means of constraint, the right to command, the knot, the straitjacket, and tear gas are all at the disposal of our centaur. In postcommunist systems, understandably, this is the branch that presents the greatest danger to constitutionalism, perhaps not because of the potential expropriation of power, but because it simply and naturally tends to undermine constitutionalism and (citing the protection of constitutional order) it prevents democratic transparency and supervision with the claim that these are unfavorable for its efficient exercise of power.

The executive often uses the claim of ministerial responsibility as an argument in favor of its privileges. Since the ministers are responsible, they need unrestricted power to live up to their responsibilities. Government will be unable to realize its mission if members of parliament, by having a say in what the laws should contain, distort efficient executive programs. But one need not go as far as antiparliamentarism. What is important here is that the whole administrative structure be under the direction of the government and the prime minister heading it. The huge hydrocephalus of the party organization thus suddenly finds an ally, and, for the administrative organization, the leaders of the executive emerge as the protector. The patron, however, becomes so dependent on its protégé-servant that it will enforce the organization's interests through legislation.

But what is this ministerial responsibility? It sounds grand because it is humble. Responsible government is "the peculiar contribution of the British Constitution."[34] "Responsible ministers" was the battle cry of

[34] Ivor Jennings, *The British Constitution* (Cambridge: Cambridge University Press, 1962), 143.

the Belgian liberals in 1831; and in Hungary, in 1848, it was the most straightforward demand in the most heroic chapter of the fight for national identity.[35] The demand "responsible ministry" meant that somebody personally responsible be appointed alongside the king. The king's holy person could not be called to account.

Ministerial responsibility and accountability, frequently referred to in this age of party discipline, is a myth without any risks. (The effective expression of parliamentary no-confidence is seriously obstructed by constructive no-confidence and the fear of dissolution.) Dicey was convinced that ministerial solidarity could transform the principle of ministerial responsibility into collective responsibility, but even in Britain it is the *coup* inside the parties that ousts ministers and their governments. Nowadays, in Britain and in other states following the Westminster tradition, like Canada, ministers manage to remain in their positions, even if the administrative organizations formally under their control violate the law or make mistakes, provided the minister can claim no knowledge of the mistakes. This is the opposite of the original meaning of British ministerial responsibility. As a result, wily ministers strive to know as little as possible, arguing they have to trust their army of experts.

It seems grotesque to speak of responsibility if we compare the amount of governmental tasks with the possibilities of elected, national legislative bodies. The elected body is simply not in a position to exercise supervision over the whole of the administration, thus it has no grounds–except if the political line is violated by a minister or one of them engages in illegal activity–for impeachment. Perhaps it is not even desirable to exercise comprehensive control.

Responsibility is replaced with accountability, and accountability is a duty to give evasive answers to uncomfortable questions before the public. (Parliamentary question time is the most effective way to control or supervise government.) What remains of responsibility after this, perhaps, only helps to strengthen the prime minister's one-person rule. If, ultimately, it is the prime minister who is politically "responsible," the others

[35] A macabre conclusion to the 1848 Hungarian story and the sad introduction to ministerial responsibility was that the first Hungarian prime minister's responsibility was taken so "seriously" by the victorious counterrevolutionary, antiparliamentarian absolutism as to have him executed.

will be his subordinates who can be relieved at any time. Otherwise, how else could the prime minister perform his duties responsibly?

Or perhaps ministerial responsibility and the powers demanded in its name hide the fear of a coup within the party, which could oust the leaders if they cannot deliver the goodies their supporters in parliament ask for. The references to ministerial responsibility cannot admit to this. Instead there is the recurrent theme of the ministers' moral responsibility for the management of the commonwealth (a commendable sentiment on the whole) and the foreboding assumption that, on event of new elections, politicians will be called to account by the public, because the government, whose hands were bound, was unable to perform, so the population turned against it. All power to the government! So it can win the next election. And anyway, if one has been victorious in the struggle for power, why can that person not be given the power? These are attractive or at least comprehensible human reactions: alas! none of these vindications can be derived from the principles of constitutionalism. The person who has won the election has not won all future elections and cannot use his power to this end.

Nevertheless, the power over the administration, especially if it is exclusive, may lend one considerable authority, especially in societies where there is little experience regarding self-organization, resources are scarce, and where the state as the owner and primary service provider occupies key positions in society. Let us not forget that, for example, in postcolonial and postcommunist societies, the public administration controls key economic positions. As of 1995, at least 20 percent of all employed persons in Hungary are civil servants, and the state employs more than 50 percent of the work force.

In this situation, the administration comes to the government's aid with two "constitutional theories." The first says "the person who appoints is the one who relieves, too," while the other says "the government is responsible for the entire implementation procedure" of policies because the government heads the executive branch. (It is easy to see in the latter theory that the principle of the separation of powers is transplanted into alien ground, which may not necessarily be observed there either.) The two theories together–simultaneously with centralizing the administration–ensure that parliament does not directly influence or manage administration. The government and the chain of command subordinated to it are entitled to decide how administrative positions are to be filled. The person making the appointments has authority over the appointed in all respects, at least according to the above beliefs.

This rather rigid military system of appointment and removal has its own logic, and it makes some sense, at least where total subordination is needed.[36] Let's say it is of utmost importance in the desert. But here our concern is with constitutional systems that have some kind of balance among the branches of power. Here, in light of checks and balances, neither the right of appointment exercised jointly by the branches nor the allocation among the several branches by law of the power to control personnel is unconstitutional. Quite the contrary. Even if we accept that within the public administration–*if the law makes no exception*–the above assumption of nonseverability does make sense as a point of departure, there are certain positions in, and activities of, public administration where political dependence is not desirable. In the event the government can direct and even remove civil servants after their appointments, continuous political influence will prevail. If the person who appoints cannot remove individuals from their positions or if a given person can only be removed if another organ, for example, the court, finds that the law has been violated, the given organ becomes relatively independent of the administration, though within the framework of the law it can still be directed and remains responsible.

There is no constitutional prescription pertaining to the independence of the central bank. The decision on the central bank is determined by the features of the given stage of economic development. If, however, independence has come about, it would be a mistake to argue that the government cannot work responsibly because the independent central bank (that is, the bank's irremovable president) hinders the accomplishment of its plans and economic policies. This is exactly what constitutionalism is about here. The government (for good reasons) needs and can act "freely" only within the boundaries of given conditions and institutions. There are times when it must resign itself to relinquishing or sharing the right of appointment and removal.

[36] The principle of the system of appointment and removal does not apply if the appointment involves a different branch of power. The president recommends the prime minister to parliament but cannot remove him or take part in appointing a new one in a constructive no-confidence vote. The constitutional justices are elected by parliament, and in accordance with current laws, they cannot be recalled. In Hungary, only the Constitutional Court may exclude its own members.

It is the same idea of power limited by division which renders the principle that "all organizations of execution should be subordinated to the government" unfounded. (Even the French Constitution of 1958 binds the executive in public administration matters inasmuch as the government cannot invent a new type of institution. In many instances the German Basic Law requires the Federal Council to approve the government's decrees where it effects the public administration.) Constitutionalism delineates the boundaries of the playing field. Of course, a core autonomy for the executive has its own constitutional legitimacy. If actual administrative decisions are staked out by the parliament or its committees, this is obviously of doubtful constitutional value, because, among other things, it is uncertain whether legal redress can be granted in such cases.

The reservations in connection with the executive power's "constitutional theory" are not prompted by parliament's and its members' awed admiration. After all, parliamentary majorities enforce only political considerations and not principles of constitutionalism; they behave just like governments. But at least party politics will not be determined by a small "central committee" but will take shape as a result of constant communication with the opposition.[37]

5.5. THE INTERNAL DIVISION OF THE EXECUTIVE POWER

The separation of the branches of power cannot prevent the strengthening of the executive, which, in parliamentary systems, can threaten with a temporary dictatorship of the cabinet and the party behind it. This dictatorship can only be replaced and counteracted with the dictatorship of a new government with a different composition and political line. The mild dictatorship of today's cabinet is countered and replaced only by a future cabinet dictatorship. A British parliamentary committee sums up this phenomenon as follows:

[37] R. A. Butler, 609 HC Deb. 13 July 1959, col. 37 as quoted in Anthony H. Birch, "The Theory and Practice of Modern British Democracy," *The Changing Constitution*, eds. Jeffrey Jowell and Dawn Oliver (Oxford, Clarendon Press: 1985), 86.

> The essence of the problem...is that the balance of advantage between Parliament and Government in the day-to-day working of the Constitution is now weighted in favor of the Government to a degree which arouses widespread anxiety and is inimical to the proper working of our parliamentary democracy.[38]

A series of solutions–not frequently appearing in constitutions–were devised around the world in an effort to diminish executive dominance in the checks-and-balances system.[39] Some of the solutions were included in constitutions, but more often than not, they are difficult to reconcile with the traditional solutions that do not provide a satisfactory balance of power, and judicial review, too, is reluctant to take them on board.

The first method of division, which also appears in modern constitutions, is the *dual executive power*.[40] At times a nonpresidential president is much needed, but there is a constant danger. The parliamentary division may require someone to move the state machinery out of its stalemate; but before this can be done, it is important to define the stalemate clearly, in a manner that will help prevent abuse. Also there are state responsibilities that should not be influenced by political party divisions. The president may be responsible for controlling the independent, nonpartisan state organs. Finally, a president may play an important role in

[38] First Report from the Select Committee on Procedure (1977–78) HC 588 par. 1.5. quoted in Gavin Drewry, "Select Committees and Back-Bench Power," in Jowell and Oliver, eds., 136.

[39] Likewise, the U.S. Congress created congressional bodies (commissions) to have an organizational impact on executive matters.

[40] Dual executive power is primarily mentioned in connection with semipresidential systems, though it would perhaps be more appropriate to consider *dual leadership* in connection with these systems, as Jean Blondel suggests. According to Blondel, the "dual leadership system is a system where two, and only two, persons share the general matters of government formally, actually and consciously." Jean Blondel, "Dual Leadership in the Contemporary World: A Step Towards Executive and Regime Stability," in *Comparative Government and Politics: Essays in Honor of S.E. Finer*, eds. Dennis Kavanagh and Gillian Peele (London: Heinemann-Boulder: Westview Press, 1984), 75.

In the French semipresidential system, the president, using the duality from time to time to protect his own position, lets the prime minister do the day-to-day practical administrative work and take decisions, while he, as "the man of vision" becomes the king reigning from afar. In the cases discussed below in connection with dual executive power, this model is examined in the context of a parliamentary system and not primarily as a parallel power, but, instead, as a divided power.

safeguarding the constitution *against* the influence of a closely-knit parliament and government.

Max Weber was perhaps the first to formulate–during the preparatory work on the Weimar Constitution–a theory of *dual executive power* when, fearing the excessive power of the uncontrollable administrative bureaucracy, he drew the government under parliament's control (including the institution of the vote of no-confidence) but retained a specific function for the president. The primary function of the popularly elected president is to supervise the government bureaucracy and represent a policy that is independent of parliament, comprised mainly of party bureaucrats. The president does have some power against parliament because he is granted popular legitimacy through popular election. This demagogue-leader may govern the state as a statesman while enjoying popular support. If he loses popular support–this is equivalent to failure–he has to resign (in this respect Weber stays within a democratic framework). In this model there are two competing representatives even if the president only appears when there is a stalemate in parliament or when a crisis situation emerges.

The model was attacked from many sides (though in the Weimar Constitution the president became an independent political actor only because of the deficiencies in the state-of-emergency provisions). Criticism centered on the dangerous mix of responsibilities that duality can bring about.[41] The president may relegate the chancellor into the background in the eyes of the people, although his political responsibility is more direct.[42]

[41] See Wolfgang J. Mommsen, *Max Weber and German Politics: 1890–1920* (Chicago: The University of Chicago Press, 1987), 379. At the same time, Mommsen, who was one of the first to notice the connection between de Gaulle's Constitution of 1958 and Weber's theory, acknowledges that a different kind of assessment is also possible.

Though mixing and destabilization are significant objections and the tragic end of the Weimar Constitution, much due to presidential abuses, do not lend much to Weber's theory, it is possible to argue according to a different logic. In Weimar, the president would not have had to come to the fore if the chancellor and his government had performed better, if there had been a quorum in the parliament, and if real politicians had been the actors instead of rancorous party officials and bureaucrats bereft of charisma. Under the circumstances, the president's power was necessary to handle the stalemate setting in, which was the result of the parliament's and government's incompetence. Weimar failed not because of its constitution, or in spite of it, but because society was fatally divided among extremist totalitarian parties.

[42] In effect, the Hungarian Constitutional Court referred to the president's lack of

The executive power under dual leadership has another option that Weber did not emphasize but can definitely be found in the Weimar Constitution. This is not a simultaneous dual power, and it comes into effect primarily when the state is paralyzed, when a parliamentary stalemate renders the ordinary (government-run) executive unable to function or when an extraordinary crisis situation requires a temporary dictator. Of course, this "dictator" could be the prime minister, too. The president's claims to this position are supported by his direct and, therefore, broader popular legitimization, due to the mode of his election, his distance from party politics, and his "all-national" role. The prime minister cannot afford the luxury of distancing himself from party politics.[43]

---

political responsibility when it denied him powers against the prime minister (the government). The Hungarian president is elected by the parliament, but he is accountable only by impeachment.

[43] For theories on the balance of power "shifting" between the executive (the president of the republic) and parliament, see András Sajó, "Prelude to Future Constitutional Crises," (in Hungarian) 34 *Világosság* 7 (1993): 17–25. The constitutional system needs fine tuning to the result of the latest parliamentary election. If there is a strong parliamentary majority, the election can be considered as a referendum in support of strong parliamentarism. But if the majority in parliament is not strong enough to "remove" the president with, for instance, a qualified majority or to confirm him in his position with a sweeping majority, in other words, if there is no overwhelming majority in the electorate desiring strong parliamentarism within the framework of the constitutionally defined parliamentarism, then the president's authority needs to be extended until the following election to preserve, among other things, government stability. Notwithstanding the above, presidential authority needs to be extended in relation to the neutral powers and the powers to be depoliticized, even if there is strong parliamentary rule.

In 1994, Giovanni Sartori published his theory on a similar model called "*alternating presidentialism*." According to this theory, the parliamentary system continues in effect while it is functioning. If it ceases to function, the system changes over to the spare motor and moves into a presidential operation mode. If parliament, during its mandate (e.g., two years), is unable to form a government supported by the required majority, the system changes over to a strong presidential model for the remaining period, that is, after the first successful no-confidence motion. In the remaining period, the president governs the country with parliament's approval and with a government appointed by him and not politically responsible to parliament, like in the United States. The president and parliament remain in office for the same period of time. Parliament maintains its legislative function, but presidential initiatives are given priority and go through parliament quickly. If any of the president's proposals are rejected, in certain cases legislation by decree might be possible. See Sartori, 94.

If the president does not embody some mystical totality (the nation, the people, or the like) but is preoccupied with maintaining his constitutionally approved distance from those exercising day-to-day power, and if his duty is not to embody the people and to lead them but to watch over the constitution in defiance of the concrete will of the people, then the responsibilities that the constitution or the political forces momentarily interested in avoiding conflict would like to remove from every-day party politics and neutralize may be placed under his supervision but not his *direction*. In this regard the executive power may be formally divided and dual in the sense that not all of its bodies are under the authority of one leader, that is, under the "responsible" government. Contrary to Carl Schmitt's theory, the president, through his limited control over the neutral power, does not acquire additional power. Neutralization does not increase the president's power. He, personally, does not make decisions in concrete "matters" (bar cases of emergency). The president has no right of direction in areas that, by common agreement in given situations, should be the responsibility of independent individuals. Such independence of activity is expected–from among others–of the president of the central bank.[44]

As a second device, the legislature may also attempt to remove certain executive organs from under the authority of the head of the executive and let them function either formally under parliament's direct supervision or allow them complete independence after the appointment of the head of the organ has been made. In some cases it is not the legislature but tradition that makes these organs, formally under the executive, independent, or it is the legislature that isolates the organ exercising the executive function from the head of the executive. The French Council of State is an example of the former and the Hungarian public prosecution organizations of the latter.[45]

[44] Such independence, however, is not a fundamental constitutional requirement, and there are situations in which, and economic theories according to which, an independent position for the central bank is actually detrimental. Cf. Jon Elster, "Constitutional Courts and Central Banks: Suicide Prevention or Suicide Pact," 3 *East European Constitutional Review* 3–4 (1994): 66–71.

[45] The American independent counsel, who is responsible for investigating any alleged crime of the president, vice president and attorney general, is an executive function (investigation), established by legislation technically under the judical branch and recognized by the Supreme Court as constitutional. (See *Morrison v. Olson*, 487 U.S. 654 (1988); Scalia, J., dissenting.)

In all these cases, in theory the legislature creates executive organs and even interferes in executive functions because it wishes to run a depoliticized and totally independent organ. This is the obvious objective in mind when creating bodies that regulate the various mass communication systems and that are simultaneously authorized to make concrete decisions. French and the Polish legislators had this in mind when they created broadcasting councils, the members of which are appointed partly by the president and partly by the houses of parliament (separately). The members of the British Independent Television Commission and the Radio Authority are appointed by the responsible secretary, but as tradition would have it, the secretary cannot revoke the appointment upon his pleasure (although the secretary of state has the legal authorization to do so). In the United States, there are also numerous independent regulatory bodies created and elected by the legislative branch that make decisions in concrete matters (issue licenses, impose fines, or hold auctions). The principle has never been frowned on by the Supreme Court. In England, quasi-autonomous non-governmental organizations (*quango*) are created in a variety of manners, by law or by various orders of the executive. The BBC, for example, was established by royal charter in 1927. Its Board of Governors

> is nominally appointed by the Queen in Council, although the right effectively lies with the Prime Minister. Traditionally this appointment is preceded by an accord between the government and the opposition, as well as–at least prior to the Thatcher era–by contact with the BBC itself.[46]

Would it be desirable if parliament or one of its organs or committees consisting of members of parliament were to decide on which area of artistic activity should come in for subsidies? Nothing much can be expected from politicians' unbiased literary criticisms or from the political lobbying of artists more or less in desperate need of funds. But would it be better (primarily from a political point of view) if a pseudorepresentative person (or a pseudorepresentative body) of those in need of support were to allocate the funds? The solution following the above lines of neutrality would be to create an arts council comprised of experts that would be independent both of politics and the potential beneficiaries.

[46] Wolfgang Hoffmann-Riem, *Regulating Media* (New York–London: Guilford Press, 1996), 69.

Parliament could give guidelines in law as to the points to be taken into consideration (for example, works of art promoting "patriotic education," or "decadence," or the works of art of domestic or minority or female artists, and the like) when deciding how funds should be allocated. Constitutionalism in this case would mean making the organ exercising the "executive" function independent. Elements ensuring independence are, for instance, the body's ability to automatically renew itself, its financial independence, or the impossibility to blackmail members with reelection, meaning that the members either cannot be reelected or that they are appointed for life. Political realism leaves one to suspect both the independence and the actual chances of independent bodies. However, the same political realism may work for decision making by neutral bodies. The ruling political forces do not want to undermine their popularity by making what by some would be considered unpopular decisions; therefore, they may delegate power.

The *third way* to limit the executive is in effect not the division of the executive power but its restriction, partly along democratic principles. The law may provide that some executive organs are not created (established, appointed, and the like) by the head of the executive but by the people or community concerned (for example, those regulated). On the other hand, in the Netherlands or in Norway, and especially in the United States, the organs of the executive have to make decisions according to a fixed and open procedure where there are set principles concerning participation. This, to a considerable extent, counteracts the orders of the head of the executive, especially if there is appropriate judicial review to ensure that any decision that violates the rules of public participation is rendered invalid. Supervision and even control by participation are important in cases when the executive's responsibilities are assumed by an independent body, so as not to leave the body completely on its own. Thus the public itself exercises the supervisory function, and this is further strengthened by judicial review, at least in regard to the observation of the rules of participation in decision making.

Chapter 6

THE RULE-OF-LAW STATE AND ITS EXECUTORS

The judge...counts for almost nothing!
Montesquieu

6.1. RULE BY LAW AND THE RULE-OF-LAW STATE

Law plays a central role in making a state constitutional. In democracies legal regulations are intended to keep society together, allowing neither private nor state despotism to prevail. But we should be careful not to fall into extremes regarding law's potential. At best, legal regulations restrict the freedom of exercising power to a bearable measure. In effect they render all kinds of freedom endurable for others while they ensure our own freedom to an extent that is acceptable to others, but with which we may be frequently dissatisfied.

The general cohesive power of law, in its nondespotic and tyranny-restricting role, is termed in Anglo-American legal usage as the rule of law. The terms used on the Continent are *Rechtsstaat* and *état de droit*. These expressions refer to partly similar assumptions and legal prescriptions found in the various traditions referring to the state's structure, organization, and operations. The common idea in the various concepts is that the state's bodies act according to the *prescriptions of law*, and law is structured according to principles restricting arbitrariness.

In the last century, the rule of law in Great Britain, similar to the German *Rechtsstaat* and the French *état de droit*, established a restricted system of constitutionalism. To be sure, no constitutional system can exist without the rule of law. The relationship is intimate, and the existing constitutional systems are inseparable from the rule of law.

The rule of law makes sense of legislative activity. Locke held that the supreme power had to govern by *promulgated, established standing laws* known to the people.

> And whosoever has the legislative or supreme power of any commonwealth, is bound to govern by *established standing* laws, promulgated and known to the people and not by Extemporary Decrees; by *indifferent* and upright *judges* who are to decide controversies by those laws and to employ the force of the community at home only in the *execution of such laws* or abroad to prevent or redress foreign injuries and secure the community from inroads and invasion.[1]

The constitutional system added to this the separation of the specific organs with different, specific functions. Locke makes no mention of the possible need to separate the execution of laws from the legislature.

In Rousseau's model of democracy, the general supremacy of the legislature and, consequently, of laws is justified by the relationship between the legislature and the sovereign people. In a rule-of-law system the special relationship of the branches of power is guaranteed, and the executive observes the laws made by the legislature, without either one becoming superior or subordinated. Simply put, the law must be obeyed. This also means living under the rule of law and not the rule of men.

Accordingly, the French Constitution of 1791 is based on the rule-of-law principle of the supremacy of the law, hence the king (as a state organ) carries out his duties in subordination to the law. "There is no authority in France superior to that of the law; the king reigns only by it and it is only in the name of the law that he can demand obedience."[2]

The *arbitrary decisions of the state and its representatives* are banned. But in rule-of-law systems it is accepted practice for the executive to exercise discretionary powers, which means it has the freedom to decide.[3] It remains to be seen whether "free discretion" is not merely a linguistic game promoted by those potentates who seek to make autocracy palatable.

Executive power, that is, the president's power to make independent decisions, does not mean that in American constitutional practice the tradition is absent that ensures the legality of administrative behavior

[1] John Locke, "Second Treatise of Government," in *Two Treatises of Government* (Cambridge: Cambridge University Press, 1980), § 131.

[2] Tit. III, ch. 2, sec. 1, par. 3.

[3] In the United States, in the "case of all cases" (*Marbury v. Madison*, 5 U.S. (1 Cranch) 137 (1803)) Chief Justice Marshall argued that the head of the executive, the president, cannot be sued for exercising his discretion. This was President Nixon's argument, too, in the Watergate scandal, when he refused to hand over the compromising tape recordings to the special prosecutor and when, in response, the court subpoenaed him to get hold of the tapes.

and represses the abuse of executive privilege. The executive's freedom to exercise discretion is primarily restricted by procedural requirements based on the *due process* clause of the U.S. Constitution. For intellectual and practical reasons, the current European rule-of-law concept adapted many due-process elements. Due process suggests that the law should allow for the participation of those a decision affects. The people who are concerned in this *participatory* decision-making process have to be given an opportunity to air their views under equitable circumstances.[4] If a group is given social benefits, the members of the group have rights in connection with what happens to that benefit (but they do not have the right to receive more benefits). This rule of procedure and the possibility of redress–not necessarily a judicial one–reduce the authorities' arbitrariness.[5]

The rule of law, similar to constitutionalism, is not an absolute value. We need to see its limitations, otherwise it would be impossible to safeguard, even against its own misdemeanors. Though the rule of law–that is, the restriction of the will of the authorities, those that use force, and those that hand out benefits–safeguards citizens, at the same time it puts them at the mercy of government's impersonal and mechanical forms, which have come to replace autocracy. Strictly applied, the rule of law allows no consideration of equity or the human condition. Suffering, being handicapped, or all the other characteristics that cannot be meas-

[4] The U.S. Supreme Court safeguards this right when specific interests are concerned. As a legislative criterion, *due process* is based on the Fourteenth Amendment. The amendment provides that "no State shall make or enforce any law which shall abridge the privileges or immunities of citizens of the United States; nor shall any State deprive any person of life, liberty, or property, without due process of law..." (The term *due process* was used also in the Fifth Amendment, in 1791, originally, in a criminal-law context.) Though property, of which one cannot be deprived without due process, is taken in the broad meaning of the word (legal expectations, e.g., the expectation of further benefits are included in the term), the law that explicitely excludes future benefits related to legal expectations is not unconstitutional (*Board of Regents v. Roth*, 408 U.S. 564 (1972)). Denying the extension of a teacher's contract who was employed for a year is not unconstitutional, even if there are no further negotiations prior to the decision, provided there is a law permitting this lack of fair treatment. The one-year contract did not establish property-like expectations.

[5] British judges call this "natural justice." They appreciated its importance as early as the last century, arguing that God listened to Adam and Eve before banishing them from the Garden of Eden.

ured are not considered. The means are separated from the objectives, the procedure from the outcome. And, though consideration of the latter would be advantageous, the former prevails. It is not cooperation that is decisive but opposition and victory. This corresponds in many respects to the market-efficiency principle, and social values may be threatened because of it.[6] The rule of law, like constitutionalism, is neither an absolute category nor a static rule. The ages differ on where the line limiting state power is drawn and what the role of law is in drawing this line or indicating where the hardly visible boundaries are.

Constitutionalism can partly diminish the rule of law's one-sided inflexibility and its alienation from life, because it uses not only the legal means of restricting power and it carries substantive values (freedom). Constitutional and equitable elements may be incorporated into the rule of law itself when, for instance, the law provides procedural advantages to the disadvantaged (for example, special services for the disabled) to ensure their procedural rights. All this points to the element of equality in the rule of law and facilitates the realization of equality both in form and in content.

The will of the state has to be cloaked in a legal robe, that is, the law must apply to the organs of the state as well. What is more, the organs of the state may act only if authorized by the law's provisions, that is, *they are bound by the laws* not only because they have to apply what is in the law but also because they cannot act without proper statutory authorization. Constitutionalism can be measured by how unambiguous the rules concerning the activities of the state's organs are and by how much discretion and equity they are entitled to, especially if a particular organ deals with citizens' rights. But no matter how much the state's activities are bound by law, constitutional freedom is not the result. Where everything is done according to government prescriptions, the rigidity and predictable restrictions make life unbearable. Too many or too few legal prescriptions are annoying, and not only anarchists would disagree with minister of state Herr Goethe when he claimed that orderly oppression is better than unpredictability and disorder.

[6] Cf. M. Horwitz rev. of *Whigs and Hunters*, by E.P. Thompson, *Yale Law Review* 86 (1986): 561, 566. "[T]he rule of law undoubtedly restrains power, but it also prevents power's benevolent exercise. It creates formal equality–a not inconsiderable virtue–but it *promotes* substantive inequality...By promoting procedural justice it enables the shrewd, the calculating, and the wealthy to manipulate its forms to their own advantage."

If laws are to be predictable and have the capacity to restrict arbitrariness and anarchy, certain formal requirements must be satisfied. As it is unavoidable that several rules may apply to the same relationship of life, determining which rule to apply is required. This can be achieved if the rules are *hierarchical* and the hierarchy of the state's organs prevails.

In modern parliamentarism, the parliament is the distinguished legislative organ. Accordingly, the monarch had to work with the parliament when passing laws. As the monarch's privileges have gradually dwindled, the executive branch has been granted original legislative rights, although in theory, only in the monarch's shrinking domain of authority.[7] Rousseau linked the hierarchy of norms with the source of the law: the law made by the people, being the expression of the general will, is the supreme and, at the same time, exclusive original source of law. The supremacy of law became a constitutional requirement.

The *hierarchy of the sources of law* is the expression of state hierarchy. According to this principle, legal enactments are ranked, and the higher-ranking norm prevails over the one that is lower. The legislature may influence and define the executive power if its laws are of a higher standing than executive decrees and orders.[8]

So important is the hierarchy of the sources of law in the structure of all legal systems that even in Soviet legality it was a fundamental precept. Lenin was desperate to have people recognize that the law in the Kaluga Province could not be different from the law applied in Khazan. Despite its strong centralization, Soviet law was unable to solve this problem, and the Russian Constitution of 1993 still preserves this chaotic heritage.[9]

Four ancient legal maxims constitute part of the hierarchy of the sources of law: (1) a statute made at a later date will overrule the earlier one of the same hierarchical level, or, in other words, it is always the last order that prevails; (2) in the case of specific and general rules of equal

[7] According to current English law, the executive's privileges are restricted to foreign policy and the granting of pardons (Lord Parmoor, *A-G v. De Keyser's Royal Hotel* [1920] A.C. 508, 575–6).

[8] See delegated legislation in Chapter 4.

[9] The relationship of the law to an order of the president (*ukhaz*) is not clear. It seems that the president has original legislative power until the legislature makes a law pertaining to the given matter. It is unclear to what extent the national parliament may overrule legislation of the member states (the "subjects of the federation").

hierarchical level, the specific one is applied irrespective of the date; (3) the provisions cannot have retroactive effect because, otherwise, the provisions of law would not be binding at all (everything could be subsequently changed), and (4) laws have to be general, that is, they cannot refer to one particular person or case (the prohibition on the bill of attainder).[10]

The makers of the U.S. Constitution considered these principles so important that they included them in the Constitution itself, not as a fundamental right but as an obligation pertaining to the legislature. It is entirely another matter that the ban on retroactive effect (the *ex post facto* law prohibition) was restricted to apply only to criminal law in America ten years after the Constitution was adopted. The principle remains important in terms of its protection of fundamental rights as well as the legitimacy of law. If this were not so, the assumption that a rational person can observe the law only if it is possible to know it, or may feel obliged to observe the law only if he can see that in its generality the law applies to everyone, would not be valid.

In Germany, as early as the nineteenth century, the rule of law was a constitutional requirement that had to be met by the state administration. The Basic Law extended the rule of law and applied it to the legislature, too. True, Article 20 (3) of the Basic Law provides that the legislature is bound only by the constitutional order, while the rule of law (acting, according to the "state and law") imposes obligations on the administration (the executive), the administration of justice, and, according to Article 28, on the member states. But the conditions of rule-of-law statehood are extended to legislation through the interpretation of ratified laws. What is more, the Basic Law, similar to the U.S. Constitution, explicitly prescribes a number of rule-of-law precepts. Accordingly, freedom can be restricted only by law (in the case of special fundamental rights, the law must satisfy requirements of form and content). The Basic Law requires the institutionalization of procedures that give warning of future legal developments. (This again brings up the ban on retroactive effect, not as a fundamental

[10] In J. Raz's view, law has to be prospective, open, clear, and relatively stable. The passing of laws has to be governed by open, permanent, clear, and general rules. The independence of courts is to be guaranteed, the principles of natural justice have to be observed, the courts have to watch over the observance of these principles, and the discretionary powers of crime-prevention authorities must not obstruct the law. Joseph Raz, "The Rule of Law and its Virtue," *Law Quarterly Review* 93 (1977): 198.

right but as a prescription concerning the administration of justice.) The right to have a hearing must be guaranteed in the proceedings institutionalized by law. But most of the guarantees concerning procedural rights have been derived from the general principles of rule-of-law statehood (especially the right to legal defense). When fundamental rights are regulated, the principle of proportionality (*Verhältnismaessigkeit*) must be observed. The origins of this principle can be traced back to the rule of Frederick the Great. The *Allgemeines Landrecht* of Prussia (II. 17. § 10) prescribed that the execution of police (*Polizei*) rights should bring with it only those measures (that is, *only* the necessary ones) that aided in the preservation of peace, order, and safety.

The French describe this internal boundedness of the authorities, using the concept of *legality*. (Legality, here, has a special meaning and refers to the restriction of the state administration according to certain principles.)

For laws and regulations to be influential, an independent forum must provide that the state's activities comply with the provisions of law. Anyone who suffers a loss because the authorities failed to comply with the provisions of law is entitled to turn to the *ordinary courts* to seek compensation. The state may call to account–under criminal law–the officer violating the law. But the French understanding–in view of the separation of the branches of power–does not allow the courts to exercise control over the executive. The decision to determine whether legality has been observed and the provisions of law satisfied is left to the judgement of an independent body formally inside the executive, that is, the administration, the *Conseil d'État* (Council of State). The Germans have established a separate administrative court specifically for this purpose.

The nineteenth-century Victorian concept of the rule of law placed the legal authorization and restriction of the state at the center of attention. According to Albert Dicey, the supremacy of law includes at least three conceptions.

First, "no man is punishable, except for a distinct breach of law established in the ordinary legal manner before the ordinary courts of the land. In this sense the rule of law is contrasted with every system of government based on the exercise by persons in authority of wide, arbitrary, or discretionary powers of constraint."[11]

[11] Albert Venn Dicey, *Introduction to the Study of the Law of Constitution* (London and New York: Macmillan, 1959), 188.

Second, no man is above the law, but "every man, whatever be his rank or condition, is subject to the ordinary law of the realm and amenable to the jurisdiction of the ordinary tribunals...With *us* every official, from the Prime Minister down to a constable or collector of taxes, is under the same responsibility for every act done without legal justification as any other citizen."[12] The third feature was that the general principles of the constitution, like personal liberty, exist as a result of judicial decisions.

Dicey's precepts were adopted in many countries, and his concept became a creed similar to Montesquieu's a century earlier. The reason for his influence is the same. Like Montesquieu, Dicey gave a false characterization of the British system.[13]

As the state's welfare services expanded, the socialists–close to Keynes's precepts–wanted the state's discretionary authority extended and launched an attack on the myth created by Dicey concerning judicial control over the administration. Under a Labour Party majority, Parliament strove to prevent the courts with their aristocratic bias from conducting judicial review. As Labour wanted to give the state a more prominent role than did the Victorian Whigs (Liberals), the legislature's role in authorizing the central administration was strengthened on the grounds that the services provided should be determined by the minister at his discretion. Thus regulation, both in procedure and content, became the government's responsibility. The government to a certain extent, however, is controlled by quasi-independent judicial bodies that have more expertise than the courts. (First Bevan, the minister responsible for creating Britain's modern health service, considered these bodies more politically reliable than the courts, which, in his opinion, were preparing for political sabotage.)

The legal restriction of the administration has since then been attacked by many who argue that "legalism" in the restriction of the ad-

[12] Ibid., 193.

[13] For instance, until 1947, legal redress for damage caused by the state administration did not exist. Moreover, Dicey, with obstinacy, misinterpreted French administrative law. The French, already in the past century, were not interested in denying administrative responsibility. It is true that there was no review by ordinary courts, but the French had a system that institutionalized the revision of the authorities' decisions, which enabled a review that could take the administration's requirements into consideration.

ministration becomes pathological.[14] In the past decades, however, at least on the Continent, attention returned to Dicey's original idea (known much earlier and outside Britain, too) of the administration being legally bound. Definite rules must be introduced to restrict as much as possible the activities of state organs. This is not necessarily disadvantageous for the public administration, because it can be exempted from subsequent and unpredictable political and legal callings to account. More rigid legal regulation protects those applying the law, too. This rule-of-law (constitutional) restriction clashes with neocorporatist endeavors. Such aspirations would require the law to give the administration a free hand and room to bargain with the representatives of special interests, for example, employees in a conciliation committee on matters concerning employment or potential beneficiaries of industrial-development subsidies.

The rule of law in all models holds that legal redress may be sought when state activities violate the law. The decision must be declared invalid, perhaps compensation paid, the observance of the rights violated must be guaranteed, and the violated interest must be protected. This is an important point even if the law–in developed constitutional states, too–creates immunities for the government. The precept "the Queen can do no wrong" is still officially in force in Great Britain.[15] Even in 1968 the home secretary argued in the Race Relations Bill debate that the government had to be fully relieved of responsibility for illegal race discrimination, because it was enough if ministers were responsible in Parliament. If in the unlikely event one of the government's departments were found guilty of discrimination (on the basis of equity), compensation would be given *ex gratia*. The constitutional solution–ministerial responsibility–would have facilitated, here, the restriction of the rule of law. In this case, the government gave in to parliamentary pressure and granted standing for damages.

Without constitutionalism and the constitutional protection of the law, however, protection against despotism, purely on the basis of the

[14] R. Titmus, "Welfare Rights," *Political Quarterly* 42 (1971): 113.

[15] Until 1947, it was always a matter of the home secretary's unfailing goodwill that enabled legal proceedings to be initiated for compensation for damage caused by the administration. But it was impossible to sue the Crown for damages caused outside a contract, even if the above conditions were given. The officer personally responsible could be sued, but he was hardly in a position to pay damages.

rule of law, is limited. After all, the conditions of the rule of the law are met, also, if the legal boundedness of state organs is completely formal. The legislature may satisfy the conditions of the rule of law if it indicates which state organ is authorized to execute a broadly defined task at its discretion. The executive power is then free to establish any kind of organ it wishes. Indeed, in the absence of any constitutional restriction, with a regulatory provision it can regulate anything on which parliament has not passed a law. It can thus assume the role of an original legislator, in which instance no more barriers to restrain it will exist. As it would follow from the rule of law, even if the rules it makes bind the government–be it primary or secondary legislation–it can change them whenever it so desires. In this respect, perhaps only the nonretroactivity postulate of the rule of law will have limiting effects. In other words, the executive power does not apply new rules to matters that occurred before the change in law took place.

Constitutionalism attempts to restrict executive legislation in two ways. First, it may demand that all regulations originating from the state's executive organs be traceable back to acts of parliament, and perhaps it may require that only the legislature establish a state organ or, at least, a type of organ. Second, it may restrict the freedom of state organs to regulate themselves and, more to the point, third persons by not permitting secondary regulations–especially in issues relating to fundamental rights–or the right to regulate is subject to authorization, which itself has to satisfy certain conditions. For this system to work, examining the "adequacy" of government acts is required. Another condition is that these acts should also be contestable, and this implies judicial review. Ordinary judicial or constitutional control (partly prior) can do this only to a certain extent.

The European courts did not examine authorizing laws themselves. In the name of the *rule of law*, British courts still do not venture to prohibit the application of an act, even if the act will confer unrestricted authority and even if it includes a provision that the courts will invalidate, without any second thoughts, as one that is contrary to the rule of law (in this case, *natural justice*), if the rule is made by administrative legislation.[16]

[16] Accordingly, the courts found the secretary of state's order to exclude recourse to the judiciary against a decision of a statutory commission an unacceptable violation of natural justice in a case where the legislature left it up to the minister to regulate certain

According to rule-of-law principles, the products of the legislature, the laws, should always imply that the regulation by order is rational, equitable, nondiscriminatory, and permit judicial legal redress. Short these conditions, the courts may declare them null and void. Apparently this gives the courts a nearly unlimited opportunity for discretion, similar to the kind we want to avoid in lawmaking. In reality these categories mean that there is a truly delimited examination. In English law, for instance, the *rationality* of the minister making the order is *presumed*; the court, without any particular ado, accepts the minister's affidavit if he states that the relevant circumstances were taken into consideration before he made his decision, that is, he genuinely believed he had "reasonable cause."[17]

The rule of law implies judicial-supervisory control over the observance of the provisions of law. But what this means in light of what has been said thus far is only that whatever is in the law is to be observed. Even due process has such a narrow interpretation: for example, U.S. Chief Justice William Rhenquist is of such a view.

There is a broader, more magnanimous definition of the rule of law. In this view, judicial review is extended until the application of certain principles is satisfied, regardless of whether these principles were written into the applicable laws. In France, the demand concerning the content of norms is expressed in the concept of legality, which primarily controls the administration's orders and decisions. In the event of *detournement de pouvoir*, that is, the application of power contrary to delegated objectives, the administration's act is voided. In Britain, similarly, an executive authority's order that oversteps its authorization (*ultra vires*) is invalid. Of course, it is difficult to formally violate the standard British authorization, which, for instance, says that "(1)...a local authority shall have power...to provide sites where caravans may be brought. (2) Subject to the provisions of this section, a local authority shall have power to do

matters connected with nationalization abroad. However, explicit statutory provisions may exempt the decisions of authorities from review by the court of appeal. The expression "'exempt from the court's ordinary jurisdiction' should be taken in the restricted meaning, which, in my opinion, means that if a legal order can have two meanings, the meaning which preserves the court's ordinary authority should be adopted." *Anisminic Ltd. v. Foreign Compensation Commission* [1969] 2 A.C. 147, Lord Reid.

[17] *Liversidge v. Anderson* [1942] A.C. 206

anything appearing to them desirable in connection with the provision of such sites."[18]

Neither the French nor the German concept of the rule of law is satisfied by simply protecting the rationality and fairness of the administration's proceedings. As a result, in all the legal systems of the European Union, through the practice of the European Court of Justice, there is growing respect for the rule of law, which now receives constitutional force.[19] Consequently, the principles of constitutional rule-of-law statehood are best illustrated by the minimum requirements of European Community Law. The precepts of due process (equitable procedure) and natural justice can be found among the European Court's general legal principles. Accordingly, the authorities may take measures only if they are authorized to do so and can *justify* their proceedings. The person whose rights are affected by the proceedings must be given a chance to state his opinion (*audiatur et altera pars*) and to defend himself.

Equality is perhaps the most important element of legality, giving judges the greatest room to maneuver. Equality is a specific requirement of the modern legal system. If those affected by the rules were not considered equal in their regulation, the prescriptions could not be taken as general. The requirement of the generality of rules, which mandates that norms apply equally to all equals, enforces modern Western society's basic concept of man, namely, the equality of people. While feudal law considered people different, which entitled them to different rights, in modern society the assumption is that humans are equal, at least before the state and the law. Equality implies equal (that is, impartial) treatment by the authorities. Equality may be applied in law in specific spheres, but even if people are considered equal, they are different from one another.

[18] Caravan Sites and Control Development Act 1960 (c 62) Sect. 24. In 1961, a High Court judge found "that a statutory power authorizing the Commissioners of Customs and Excise to make regulations 'for any matter for which provision appears to them necessary for the purpose of giving effect to the Act' was too narrow to validate a regulation by which they gave themselves power to determine conclusively what amount of purchase tax was payable in individual cases." *Customs and Excise Commissioners v. Cure & Deely Ltd.* (1962) I.Q.B. 340. See Stanley A. De Smith, *Constitutional and Administrative Law*, (Harmondsworth, Engl.; Baltimore, Md.: Penguin Education, 1973), 350.

[19] As the member states of the European Union constitutionally subject themselves to Community Law, the principles of Community Law (including the principles recognized by the European Court) apply to the national laws, in accordance with the individual nations' constitutions.

The law has to put these differences into effect, too; it has to recognize the "badness" of the guilty and the "merits" of the hard working. From this the technical meaning of equality is derived: there are practical limits to treating people as equals. But as the German Basic Law so forcefully states, everyone has equal human dignity.

In strictly legal terms, that which is identical is treated equally. More precisely, those who are equal from the point of view of regulation, or are equally concerned in the same matter, are treated equally. Accordingly, the defense is entitled to (at least) as much protection as the prosecution. This does not solve the practical problem of legality, namely, in which areas equality should prevail.[20]

Legal provisions are forward looking; they regulate future relations. The prohibition on retroactive effect is derived from this. Hence the requirement of legal certainty and the protection of *acquired rights and legitimate expectations* can be derived from the same principle also.[21]

When looking at the validity of rules with retroactive effect, it is a condition that the retroactive effect be expressed. If the public is to trust the legal system it must know the law. The law recognizes this need for trust by protecting *acquired rights and legitimate expectations*.[22]

[20] A classical Common Market case of handling matters of the same class similarly is the *Isoglucose* case (SA Roquette Fréres v. Council [1982] ECR 3159). The Council, in order to reduce the oversupply of sugar, imposed an additional duty, called contribution, on isoglucose, a sweetener in competition with sugar. The additional duty would have made the production of isoglucose so expensive that it would not have been worth producing. In order to restore equality, the European Court of Justice abolished the payment of the additional duty with retroactive effect.

[21] Further recognized principles of the rule of law are that the parties must act in good faith, that the authorities must be fair, and that in the event of *force majeure*, those under obligation must be exempted. Proportionality, similar to equality, is important. It refers to the principle that burdens can be imposed on the members of society in proportion to their capabilities, where proportionality is understood in its Aristotelian sense. From another perspective, these burdens may be imposed on the individual in the public interest only to the extent that they are directly necessary for the achievement of a given objective.

[22] Under the Common Market's Common Agricultural Policy, for instance, the Commission of the European Community paid companies bonuses for making barley unfit for human consumption. On June 1, 1970, the European Community stopped paying the bonus. Deuka Company denaturalized the barley it bought in May, according to the instructions after June 1, because it was granted permission to denaturalize the barley on this date. After having done this, it applied for the bonus. The Court did not

6.2. THE ADMINISTRATION OF JUSTICE

The administration of justice seeks to provide impartial settlement of individual disputes in accordance with the rules made by others for granting redress for grievances. As such, it is the guarantor of the rule of law. The administration of justice is ambitious and a source of frequent disillusionment. It would be more accurate to call this branch of power and activity the administration of law.

Until the nineteenth century, legislation and the administration of justice were not markedly divided. An influential English legal maxim of the late Middle Ages held that judges could create law or at least "find" it. This principle and practice continued to prevail in England even when the legislature was separated in organization, form, and content from judicial lawmaking and began to develop its own legislative privilege.

Contrary to judge-made law, statutes enacted by parliament do not use past legal disputes to determine principles and rules to be followed in the future, but they strive to give general solutions to the political problems that may apply in the future.

The duality of judicial and parliamentary legislation was untenable for a number of reasons. By the time of the French Revolution, judges were perhaps the most despised members of society, next to henchmen. Though they were independent–too much so to some–from the other branches of government, this did not work to the advantage of the administration of justice. Judges used their independence to extort bribes. Arbitrariness resulted from corruption, and legal chaos thereby increased.

The French revolutionaries held that judges could not play a role in lawmaking because they in no way had anything to do with the general will. In an effort to ensure a monopolistic position for the legislature, judges and courts were restricted to merely *applying preexisting law*. In England, however, the role of judges was different. Positions could not be bought, and judges were either respected citizens, like justices of the peace, or they were members of the bar of some repute who were vouched for by their colleagues. Many judges in the U.S. were, and are, popularly elected. Thus Anglo–American legal thought could consider

---

invalidate the order but ruled that lawful expectations had to be protected, so the company was paid the bonus due (*Deuka Deutsche Kraftfutter GmbH B.J. Stolp v. Einfuhr- und Vorratsstelle für Getreide und Futtermittel* [1975] ECR 759).

the administration of justice as an independent branch counteracting the weight of the executive.

In constitutional systems the role of the administration of justice, as a branch of power, is assessed differently, according to historical experience. The French tradition simply disengages this activity from the other two branches, so, paradoxically, this comes closest to the ideal of pure separation. Conversely, the British and some that follow the German tradition let the judiciary control–within certain limits–the legality of the executive's operations. In the U.S., the judicial branch checks not only the executive but the legislative, too, inasmuch as from a constitutional point of view, it may overrule the legislature's acts and their enforcement in actual cases. What is common in all models is the agreement that the institution applying the law cannot be one with the institution making it, since it is unfeasible in practice and unacceptable in terms of impartiality. The legislature is far too politically biased. For the same reason, the executive is also inappropriate to render justice, though the overwhelming majority of legal conflicts are settled by executive organs and quasi-independent bodies that the executive established.

If the legal system is to function constitutionally (as it should in a rule-of-law governed state), the judiciary's impartiality is essential. The organizational conditions and the judges' independence must be institutionally guaranteed by the law. Montesquieu argued that the judiciary can meet this condition only if it is an *independent branch of power*.

> Nor is there liberty if the power of judging is not separate from legislative power and from executive power. If it were joined to legislative power, the power over the life and liberty of the citizens would be arbitrary, for the judge would be the legislator. If it were joined to executive power, the judge could have the force of an oppressor.[23]

Independence from the other branches means that actual court decisions cannot be influenced by the powers that be. Impartiality in this respect means much more, inasmuch as even the *semblance* of the judge's bias against any party in a given case must be ruled out institutionally. Interestingly enough–due to traditions and technical difficulties–separa-

[23] Charles Secondat, Baron de Montesquieu, *The Spirit of the Laws*, and ed. Anne M. Cohler, Basia Carolyn Miller, and Harold Samuel Stone (Cambridge: Cambridge University Press, 1992), XI. 6.

tion from other branches in terms of personnel appointments cannot always be perfect. In the U.S., state judges–with some statutory exceptions–are directly elected by the people for a given term, while the members of the Supreme Court are appointed by the head of the executive branch, the president, but first with the Senate's consent. The lower (circuit) federal courts are established by Congress as stipulated in the Constitution. In keeping with centuries-long congressional practice, the appointment process of lower federal judges is similar to that of the Supreme Court.

The British Parliament has preserved its traditional function of administering justice, and in theory, the House of Lords functions as a court, too. While administering justice, the law lords may, in theory, participate in legislation.

In Germany, where the system is based on the prevalence of career judges, the members of the Constitutional Court are elected by a joint committee composed of the executive (the ministers of justice of the provinces) and appointees of the legislature. In France, the legislative branch has no role in appointments, but the president chairs the High Council of the Judiciary, which deals with matters pertaining to the justices. The deputy chair of the council is the minister of justice and the members are appointed by the president from among the judiciary.

The complete separation and self-determination of the judiciary in the context of appointment and removal from office is best ensured in the Italian Constitution. It is perhaps no coincidence that there the judiciary became the strongest check on the legislative and executive branches and has become the means for political supervision, not through traditional constitutional adjudication but by initiating criminal proceedings against politicians.

After judges are appointed, the other branches cease to have any influence over the judiciary. Judges are subject only to the law, cannot receive orders, and can hold no other position in another branch of government. Judges are irremovable; they hold their offices (absent when they are elected by popular vote) during "good behavior" (or, perhaps, when they reach the age of retirement). Sometimes even their financial independence is guaranteed by a constitutional rule.[24]

[24] "Judges…shall, at stated Times, receive for their Services a Compensation, which shall not be diminished during their Continuance in Office." U.S. Constitution Art. III, sec. 1.

The administration of justice, however, is not an issue concerning only the relationship of the branches of government. It is of fundamental importance to the prevalence of citizens' rights (including constitutional fundamental rights). *It is only meaningful to speak of rights if there is a forum where a valid claim has a good chance of being enforced.* Good chance means fair treatment, that is, the chance that is assured by a procedure that follows the formal requirements of justice. Fairness is provided in at least two ways. First, it has to be guaranteed that disputes are decided by a court of justice (*the principle of forum*) and, second, that the court itself be fair (the principle of due process or lawful proceedings).

The following fundamental conditions of access to a forum may be highlighted in terms of their constitutional significance and importance in a constitutional state: only the court has the right to try criminal cases and pass a sentence restricting freedom; all rights are enforceable in court; and if a right is violated, it should be possible to be granted legal redress before an impartial forum.[25]

The right of access to court assumes that anyone can be sued, and no one is immune from the authority of the courts. In other words, as far as the application of law is concerned, everyone is equal. On the other hand, the principle of access to court assumes that anyone can be sued only in a court, which had jurisdiction to conduct the proceedings even before the proceedings commenced, and that no one can be deprived of such access. This is the right to a court of "natural" justice.

A logical extension of this rule is that *exceptional courts* cannot be established. That someone should have to stand before an exceptional court established *during* the litigation process is unthinkable under the

[25] The German Basic Law permits judicial redress against any violation by the *authorities* of the fundamental rights, otherwise, it is the law granting a right in question that includes provisions on legal redress (which for reasons of the rule of law means, almost without exception, at least judicial review at some level). Article 6 (1) of the European Convention for the Protection of Human Rights and Fundamental Freedoms provides, in the determination of civil rights or in case of criminal charge, for a fair and public hearing within a reasonable time by an impartial tribunal. Many of the Strasbourg cases deal with this article primarily because the "right to hearing" is interpreted as a right to judgment, and judgment is delayed everywhere, and also because "civil rights" are interpreted in a much broader sense, as opposed to domestic law, and ensure judicial review in cases where domestic law prescribes a quasi-judicial process for determining civil rights and obligations. Belgium, among others, was forced to amend several laws as a result.

rule of law. Exceptional courts are not courts separated according to the cases they specialize in–specialization may be useful for the protection of rights. If specialization requires special measures in connection with the procedure or composition of the court, even that may be acceptable. But it is impossible to have exceptional courts hearing cases that are similar in terms with other cases except the *personal quality* or objectives of the accused. It is highly likely that such special courts will violate the fundamental principles of judicial independence and fair proceedings. This is why courts-martial and special military courts are highly questionable in terms of constitutionalism. Courts-martial are not made more acceptable by the fact that even rule-of-law states, which are particularly keen on constitutionalism, insist on having them. The persistent and almost completely uncontested existence of exceptional courts shows that, even today, state security can still determine the limits of constitutionalism. Neither military (state) secrets,[26] nor the estate prerogatives of armed personnel ("only a soldier may judge a soldier") are adequate as arguments.[27] The relationship between a military tribunal and a court is similar to that of a military march to music. If judge advocates are formally integrated into the ordinary judiciary, as in Hungary–a move which is not to be belittled–what can happen at most is that the band will be conducted by Franz Lehar.

Extraordinary courts were traditionally the classical form of an unconstitutional restriction of rights. The despotic executive power will always find a handful who are ready to execute or divine its political wishes when they are providing decisions and sentences. The American revolutionaries were prompted by their unfavorable experiences (the abuse of courts by the British) to constitutionalize the *jury*. It was a jury that acquitted Peter Zenger, the publisher whose paper attacked a British governor.

[26] Issues concerning state secrets may arise at any trial, consequently, in such cases a closed hearing is held. On the other hand, if some departure from general solutions is required, it should be because of the nature of the case and not because of the person involved in the proceedings.

[27] As part of the fight against terrorism, in 1986, the French Parliament voted in the so-called Pasqua Act. Under the act, courts hearing all cases concerned with terrorist crimes were comprised exclusively of career judges to avoid any terrorist attacks on assessors. The Constitutional Council found nothing here unconstitutional as the terrorist defendants were not discriminated against on unreasonable grounds. The difference in the proceedings was due to the special nature of the crime.

According to law and in the opinion of the trial judge, Zenger committed seditious libel and should have been sentenced to jail.[28]

The impartial and independent court can get near the truth and facilitate the exercise of rights only if there is a possibility to justify the right-claim in the proceedings, and if the person involved in the proceedings is not hopelessly defenseless. This is why it is a constitutional requirement that, for rights enforcement in court, the constitution guarantees the rights of the parties or, in criminal proceedings, that of the accused, and that the fundamental guarantees protecting the accused be constitutionalized and enforced.[29] The German Constitutional Court derives other procedural rights (for example, the right to have a lawyer and translator) from the concept of the rule-of-law state and human dignity. The right to a hearing is also a definitive principle according to the European Court of Justice (Luxembourg). At the same time, like an encyclopedia on procedural law, the European Human Rights Convention lists the procedural rights in minute detail.

[28] The jury accepted the defense's arguments. Hamilton argued that the jury had the right to decide how true the facts presented and statements made were. In other words, they could decide whether the criticisms against the British governor were based on true facts or not. The British common law continued to criminalize government criticism. In the United States, under Adams's presidency, the Seditious Libel Act of 1798 was enacted, which criminalized government criticism, very much in the "British" tradition. If this was possible seven years after the First Amendment, then it is small surprise that most of the new governments elected after the collapse of communism in eastern Europe with a mandate of eliminating the remnants of the previous oppression, tried to introduce seditious libel laws against government criticism.

The jury was so important for Americans that the right to a trial by jury is not to be found in the Bill of Rights of 1791 with the other "added" rights, but instead it can be found already in Article III section 2 of the original Constitution.

[29] Constitutional language, in terms of the above, tends to differ. The French Constitution of 1791 merely states that no man can be accused, arrested, or detained, except in cases determined by law and according to the forms that it has prescribed. This, however, has to be read together with the Declaration of 1789, which mentions the protection of the innocent ("everyone should be considered innocent until proven guilty"). There is no mention of the trial itself in these early documents. The German Basic Law, which is by no means more explicit than the French, says it must be guaranteed that everyone receives a hearing (both in civil and in criminal cases).

Chapter 7

CONSTITUTIONAL ADJUDICATION

Whoever hath an absolute authority
to interpret any written or spoken laws
it is he who is truly the lawgiver
to all intents and purposes...
Bishop Hoadly's Sermon, preached in the
presence of His Majesty, 1717

7.1. WHO GUARDS THE GUARDIANS?

7.1.1. MADISON LOSES A CASE IN COURT AND GAINS AUTHORITY

Through constitutionalism's turbulent history the attempt to limit power has coexisted in a strangely tense relationship with the precepts of parliamentary sovereignty and legislative supremacy. Constitutionalism implies that the supremacy of the constitution and acts of parliament must harmonize with the constitution's provisions. But what happens if the legislature, paying no heed to the constitution's prescriptions, makes a law that clearly contradicts them? As only the legislature has the authority to make laws and as there is no power above the parliament as legislator, no one can overrule the legislature's unconstitutional laws. Who then *guards the constitution to insure its observance*?

Clearly the mutual control exercised through checks and balances of divided powers is inadequate. In a system of checks and balances, what can happen at most, is that when joint decision making is necessary one of the parties will accuse the other of being unconstitutional and refuse to cooperate. In countries where one of the branches in its competence makes decisions alone, the other branches may use legal or political sanctions, for instance, no-confidence votes, dissolution, or impeachment coupled with recall (like impeachment against the president). But none of these provides a satisfactory solution to unconstitutional provisions–particularly acts of parliament–because they remain applicable despite other possible constitutional laws or political sanctions.

Additionally, it does not inspire confidence if one or another of the state organs or branches of power, which exercises power or makes decisions based on its original power, is appointed the constitution's guardian. This is so because (a) it will not provide any protection against its own decisions, and (b) such an authorization to the given organ will grant it additional powers vis-à-vis the other branches, which could upset the balance of power. What is more, no matter which organ is appointed guardian of the constitution, it will surely run headlong into the doctrine of legislative supremacy.

One can naturally assume that the executive branch will not heed unconstitutional laws, and judges will not apply them. The former could lead to anarchy because the executive could at any time come to the idea that any law can be dismissed as unconstitutional. Legal security is again threatened if judges are not allowed to apply a law that is thought to be unconstitutional because they may differ over which laws they consider to be so. What is more, the various legal systems and constitutional percepts attribute different roles to the administration of justice. In the classical French model, judges are made to apply the laws and not to review them. The British understanding is undoubtedly less rigid because the common-law tradition draws on medieval practice and expects judges to apply the "constitution." In any given case, the law–the sovereign will–could be rejected on constitutional grounds.

Traditionally, the examination of the constitutional nature of laws was determined by how one viewed the judges' role. On the American continent, in colonial times, the justices usually applied the specific colony's constitution and the British constitutional tradition in opposition to the local legislature. In this respect, they observed common-law practices dating from before the Glorious Revolution of 1688.[1]

This tradition was probably the point of departure for the drafters of the American Constitution. Hamilton says:

[1] In the *Bonham Case* the court found: "it transpired from legal books that in many cases parliamentary laws were controlled by common law and at times nullified them because if a law goes against ordinary law and reason, or it is disagreeable, or it cannot be executed, it falls under common law and under common law such a law is null and void." In *Dr. Bonham's Case*, 8 Co. Rep. 113.b. 114.a., "it appears to have been a commonplace as late as the seventeenth century that statutes which were contrary to the reason of the common law were invalid." Sir D.L. Keir and F.M. Lawson, *Cases in Constitutional Law* (Oxford: Clarendon Press, 1979), 1.

> A constitution is, in fact, and must be regarded by the judges as, a fundamental law. It therefore belongs to them to ascertain its meaning as well as the meaning of any particular act proceeding from the legislative body. If there should happen to be an irreconcilable variance between the two...the Constitution ought to be preferred to the statute...
>
> Nor does this conclusion by any means suppose a superiority of the judicial to the legislative power. It only supposes...that where the will of the legislature, declared in its statutes, stands in opposition to that of the people declared in the Constitution, the judges ought to be governed by the latter rather than the former.[2]

Nevertheless, the U.S. Constitution was already more than twenty-five years old when the Supreme Court found a federal law unconstitutional.[3] This case, in all its dramatic detail, highlighted practically all the later disputes regarding constitutional adjudication, the conflicts over the constitution's protection and republican democracy, as well as the establishment of their reasonably harmonious relationship.[4]

The Federalists lost the 1801 elections, and Jefferson became president. Jefferson, who was the American ambassador to Paris during the French Revolution, firmly believed that all governments devolved into corruption and tyranny within a short space of time, a belief supported by his experiences in France. As Rousseau's admirer, Jefferson believed in letting people express their will freely in all issues and in the working of the general will, which should be given the chance to prevail against the elected government. This enraged opponent of all forms of tyranny became the leader of a country that was established with his active participation fifteen years before his election. At the time of establishment, the idea was that, in this new country, the rule of law should prevail instead of the rule of men. With good reason, Jefferson distrusted the courts, including the Supreme Court, which was responsible for restricting the people's will by restricting the–supposedly impartial–legislature.[5]

[2] *The Federalist Papers* No. 78: Hamilton (New York: Mentor Book, 1961), 467–468.

[3] *Marbury v. Madison* 5 U.S. (1 Cranch) 137 (1803).

[4] Hereafter, I follow Page Smith, *The Constitution: A Documentary and Narrative History* (New York: Morrow Quill Paperbacks, 1980).

[5] Even in 1818, when Jefferson was no longer president, he was outraged when the law in the Dartmouth College case, which was made by freely elected New Hampshire representatives to amend the school's original founding charter, was nullified. The Court's decision was made with the "protection of property rights" in mind. Jefferson saw the Court's aristocratic tendencies in this ruling and probably not without reason.

It is little wonder that Jefferson, who adamantly believed in democracy, considered the courts an aristocratic embodiment that were democracy's arch foes. This was especially so because the justices, all appointed by the Federalist Party, were supporters of the previous regime.

On Jefferson's election the protection of the Constitution and the supremacy of popular representation instantly clashed. President Adams was defeated in the election and speedily appointed his supporters to various vacant jobs; among them, William Marbury was appointed a justice of the peace. Adams's term in office expired before Marbury's formal commissions had been delivered to James Madison. Jefferson immediately ordered the delivery of all of Adams's appointments halted, which, in his opinion "went beyond all good taste." Marbury turned to the court to have his appointment enforced and sought a court order (writ of mandamus) obliging the executive branch (the new secretary of state, James Madison) to go through with the appointment's delivery. The Judiciary Act of 1789 granted the Supreme Court the right to issue such writs.

Justice Marshall–President Adams's former secretary of state, the man who appointed Marbury, and the Federalist's Supreme Court land mine–held that the Supreme Court had the legal authority to try the case. By 1803, Republicans controlled Congress, and they were outraged by the Supreme Court's position. They were prepared to prevent judicial government at all cost. John Randolph of Virginia expressed a common fear among Republicans when he wrote that "[i]n their inquisitorial capacity, the Supreme Court...may easily direct the Executive by mandamus in what mode it is their pleasure that he should exercise his functions."[6] The congressional majority agreed that the Judiciary Act had to be revoked.

The Supreme Court faced a near unresolvable problem. It was clear that Secretary of State Madison and President Jefferson would not comply with the writ of mandamus, and the judiciary had no army to force them into submission. An unenforceable order would have meant the Court's end.[7]

[6] Quoted in Smith, 317.

[7] The Republican Congress threatened to repeal the Circuit Court Act of 1801, which would have been a great blow to the Supreme Court justices, because the act relieved them of having to ride around the country on horseback in order to sit on circuit courts. The revocation would have been a severe blow to the Supreme Court full of Federalist supporters who were the enemies of the people's will. (All courts consider traveling a delicate issue. See, for example, company cars.)

Marshall probably saw that the mandamus gave the courts too much power. Its use would amount to hubris, which could cause his fall because he lacked the power to enforce his authority. While the Supreme Court argued about the mandamus, Congress repealed the Circuit Court Act. But what if the Court declared the revocation itself unconstitutional? Simultaneously with the passing of the law, Congress canceled the Court's two subsequent sessions–certainly an unconstitutional move. After a fourteen-month delay, the Court could hear only Marbury's petition. The Republicans prepared for a final showdown: "The Judges of the Supreme Court must fall. They are denounced by the Executive, as well as the House. They must be removed; they are obnoxious, unyielding men..."[8]

When the Court finally convened, Marshall began by saying that Marbury's appointment was legal and irrevocable and that it was the executive's duty to carry it out. At the same time, the Supreme Court could not issue the mandamus because the authorization given by the Judiciary Act was found unconstitutional. According to the Constitution, the Court could issue a mandamus only when it acted as a court of appeal. Article 13 of the Judiciary Act was, therefore, null and void.

This is followed by Marshall's argument on the limitations of the legislature's power. The Constitution was written to remind us of these limitations. If it is possible to scale its barriers, then government's restriction comes to an end.

> It is a proposition too plain to be contested, that the Constitution controls any legislative act repugnant to it; or, that the legislature may alter the Constitution by an ordinary act.
>
> Between these alternatives there is no middle ground. The Constitution is either a superior, paramount law, unchangeable by ordinary means, or it is on a level with ordinary legislative acts, and, like other acts, is alterable when the legislature shall please to alter it.[9]

[8] Representative William Plumer, congressman from New Hampshire, in Smith, 319. Soon after, Jefferson had Justice Samuel Chase before the Senate for impeachment. Prior to Jefferson's move, Chase, who was a staunch supporter of the previous regime, leveled a charge to a grand jury against Maryland's Constitution for laying the country open to the mob and destroying the protection to property by granting universal suffrage. Though the two parties obviously represented wholly opposing views on the Constitution and constitutionalism, the rule of law prevailed and Chase was acquitted even though the Republicans held a two-thirds majority, a prerequisite for conviction.

[9] Smith, 321, quoting *Marbury v. Madison*, 5 U.S. (1 Cranch) 137 (1803) et al.

Politically the Supreme Court capitulated; the appointments were not carried through, and one of the sources of the Court's threatening power (mandamus) was done away with. A few weeks later, the revocation of the Circuit Court Act was also declared constitutional. The Supreme Court had to beat yet another retreat. But at the level of principles, the legislature, that is, the power base of the then-political enemies of the Court, suffered a humiliating defeat and was subjected to the Constitution's control and the Court's protection of it. The bitter and the sweet had to be taken together.

Attacks against the Court ceased, but only for the time being. Jefferson wanted to indict the justices, one by one. He then tried to amend the Constitution so that he could appoint new justices. He did not succeed, but two seats were vacated so he was able to appoint "his" people. But what is the power to appoint worth without the power to recall? Whom can we trust once we have given him independent power? The initial act of Jefferson's first appointee in his capacity as a circuit judge was to void Jefferson's decree that ordered all vessels carrying goods to countries at war as a violation of states' rights.

Conversely, a staunch Federalist judge–a supporter of the opposition in Congress–found the Embargo Acts (purportedly the basis of Jefferson's order) constitutional. The Embargo Acts restricted state powers and the Federalist-inclined justice, true to his party's views, found them constitutional, much to the president's satisfaction. (The president, before being elevated to this high office, fought for the rights of the states.)

With one decision going here and another going there, regardless of the justices' political affiliations, the Court proved its independence, and independence saved it. Nevertheless it continued to argue that it had the right to void unconstitutional acts. Several acts of the member states were invalidated during Justice Marshall's long term in office. But for generations after *Marbury* not a single federal law was pronounced invalid. The Court's self-restraint in *Marbury* (that is, they resigned a concrete right) proved to be politically prudent. It satisfied the executive's current demands and calmed those who sought the Court's ruin. The Court was probably aware that the judiciary's guarantee of the Constitution's supremacy was politically–and indeed constitutionally–rather risky.

Marshall and his colleagues–when hearing cases of primary political importance–did not venture off the narrow path that was still acceptable to the other branches of power, which were ruled by an antagonistic political majority. At the same time, the Court was allowed to play the role of the independent guardian of the Constitution. As the Court rarely fell into conflict with the legislature, it managed to preserve its right to supervise the legislature. To avoid conflict, the Court restricted its own power, too. It did not rely on the law to preserve its authority. By the 1820s the Court and the right of constitutional review were established, and with them, the victory of constitutionalism over pure popular republicanism became an undoubted principle.

The American model is based on the possibility that any judge can declare a law unconstitutional, if it is applied to the case currently before him. In federal cases the court ruling may be appealed up to the Supreme Court, which has the right to accept or refuse the case. Denial of *certiorari* can be interpreted as the upholding of the lower court's interpretation of the Constitution, but this implicit upholding does not constitute a precedent for the Supreme Court. If in the course of its hearings the Supreme Court finds a law unconstitutional, that law cannot be applied in the future. The U.S. model is based on the case or controversy requirement. Ordinary courts review the constitutionality of laws while hearing cases.[10]

With its happy ending, this complex story shows the dangers that new or even established constitutional courts face. When the much-respected U.S. Supreme Court opposed New Deal legislation, President Roosevelt pulled Jefferson's old idea out of the drawer and issued forth to change the composition of the Court. Fate again intervened; Congress was stubborn, and, as a result of deaths and that some of the justices changed their opinions, once confronted with the threat of court-packing, the need to amend the law evaporated.

Constitutional jurisdiction, which openly opposes the politics of the day, cannot, however, avoid its fate. When the South African Supreme Court, in the early 1950s, in the *Colored* case rejected the laws that institutionalized racial discrimination as unconstitutional, the government simply divested the Court of its authority via a series of constitutional

[10] The majority of South American countries let their supreme courts adjudicate issues of constitutionality. The Irish Supreme Court as a court of appeal may adjudicate upon such matters (Irish Constitution, Art. 34, sec. 3 (2)). In these states the ordinary (lower) courts, too, can decide on constitutional issues. For an overview, see Chester James Antieau, *Adjudicating Constitutional Issues* (London–New York: Oceana, 1985).

amendments. Similarly, the president of the Russian Constitutional Court was discharged, in 1993, because he intervened in a dispute between the parliament and the president.

7.1.2. The Victory of Judicial Review

The American model proved difficult to comprehend by Continental–more so by British–standards.[11] British constitutional precepts do not admit to doubts concerning the legislature's legislative right. What is more, until recently British courts have not even examined the constitutionality of ministerial orders, except in a very limited sense.

Out of fear of judicial legislation and government by judges, the French constitutional tradition rejected constitutional review for a long time. Judges had to accept applied laws as constitutional without question.[12] The protection of constitutionalism in the period between the world wars meant that French high courts attempted to put a constitutional interpretation to the laws, and the *Conseil d'État* (State Council) had the right to review–not with binding force–government bills for their constitutionality before submission to Parliament. But this form of review amounted to little, because the sections pertaining to rights were missing from the Third Republic's Constitution (from the fundamental laws that were considered to form the Constitution).

Despite the prevailing views on the supremacy and, therefore, unreviewability of the acts of Parliament, after World War I a constitutional court surfaced in the Austrian Constitution which was created to ensure that the Constitution was observed. This Constitutional Court satisfied

[11] The Norwegian practice, which corresponds to the American, is exceptional on the Continent, though in the past decades no laws were declared unconstitutional. In Greece it was the Constitution of 1927 that first authorized the courts to disregard unconstitutional laws–though such decisions were made already in the nineteenth century–and this practice has since then been observed with interruptions.

[12] At the end of the nineteenth century, Magnaud, a French judge, acquitted a woman who stole bread to feed her starving child. The judge ignored the unequivocal provisions of the law, not because he thought the law was perhaps unconstitutional but because he felt the applicable rules were unfair since they did not allow for an exemption in cases such as the one he was hearing. The sentence was voided on appeal, and Magnaud resigned not long after.

Hans Kelsen's "legal aesthetics," namely, his requirement of a closed legal system. He played an important role in drafting the Austrian Constitution.

Kelsen highlighted three arguments that supported constitutional review in terms of constitutionalism.

First, the precondition of a constitutional legal order is the logical unity ensured by correspondence to the constitution as the supreme law.[13] Article 1 (1), of the Czech Constitution, which preceded only by a few months the Austrian Constitution written under Kelsen's influence, reads: "all laws that contradict the Constitution, or parts of it, or the laws amending or modifying the Constitution are null and void."

Second, in Kelsen's opinion the various state organs may get into constitutional disputes with each other in the course of their work and their acts, including their legislation, and may violate the constitution. The state organ responsible for a given regulation will dispute the legality of the act of another state organ on the grounds of jurisdiction. (The Austrian Constitution discusses at great length the relationship of the central bodies with each other and the organs of the member states; however, it does not deal with basic rights.) The disputes among the constitutional organs are to be decided by the constitutional court. This body complements the legislature's constitutional function. It is, in Kelsen's opinion, a *negative* legislator because it *destroys* unconstitutional rules, while the legislature creates in a positive sense. Kelsen says that constitutional review, as a function of a state organ different from ordinary courts, is necessary if the constitution is to function.[14] In Ermacora's opinion–who purportedly follows Kelsen's views in part–constitutional review is the *efficient protection* of the constitution.[15] "Efficiency,"

[13] "A Constitution without guarantees against unconstitutional acts is not completely obligatory in its technical sense…A Constitution in which...unconstitutional laws remain valid because its unconstitutionality cannot lead to its annulment, is more or less, equivalent, from a juridical point of view, to desire without obligatory force." Hans Kelsen, "La Garantie jurisdictionelle de la Constitution (la justice constitutionelle)," Revue du Droit Public et de la Science Politique en France et à l'Étranger (1928): 250, quoted in Allan R. Brewier-Carías, *Judicial Review in Comparative Law* (New York–Cambridge: Cambridge University Press, 1989), 124.

[14] Hans Kelsen, "Wer soll der Hüter der Verfassung sein?" In *Die Wiener Rechtstheoretische Schule*, vol. 2, (Wien: Europa-Verlag, 1968), 1873.

[15] Felix Ermacora, *Grundriss der Menschenrechte in Österreich* (Wien: Manzsche Verlag, 1988), 30.

here, comes from meeting the conditions of applicability, legitimacy, and guaranteeability.

Third, the constitution's function–the protection of minorities–can be realized only if there is a forum restricting the parliamentary majority's dictatorship:

> If the essence of democracy is not seen in the all-powerful majority but in the constant arguments made in parliament between the social groups represented by the majority and minority, and in the ensuing social peace, constitutional review seems to be a particularly appropriate instrument with which to achieve this. When it is possible to threaten with a suit brought in the constitutional court, this can be an adequate instrument in the hands of the minority to prevent the majority from unconstitutionally violating the interests protected by law and it is an appropriate instrument with which to resist a majority dictatorship which is no less dangerous to social peace than is a minority dictatorship.[16]

The specific nature of the Austrian Constitution made constitutional review limited; only specific state organs could initiate proceedings,[17] and it was impossible to find anything unconstitutional in a violation of fundamental rights, because the Constitution was not taken as a document affirming human rights and natural law.[18]

Kelsen's model–despite all its limitations–sparked heated debates. Those familiar with the American practice argued that letting the courts review laws opened up a Pandora's box of judicial legislation and, indeed, of constitution writing. Another objection was that the necessary constitutional protection was not exercised by the appropriate organ. As Kelsen makes this the court's responsibility, the protection of the constitution is weak and incidental as the court, due to its nature, has to operate on motions and does not have the "physical" strength to enforce its decisions in the political arena.

Carl Schmitt saw the president of the republic (Reich) as the guardian of the constitution. The president, wrote Schmitt in 1929, should, in emergency situations, have direct powers to actively protect the consti-

[16] Kelsen, 253.

[17] As of 1975, one-third of the members of parliament–a sizable opposition–may begin proceedings.

[18] Since then, the Austrian view has immutably held that the given constitutional text can only be interpreted.

tution. Furthermore, by calling a referendum, he can always mobilize forces that will help him nullify any laws that violate it.[19]

After World War II, in response to the inhumanity of fascism, human rights were included in the constitutions. (This is a more definite restriction of majority rule as it is not a procedural but a content-based limit.) But the still-unresolved question was how these constitutional rights could be enforced and how the various other constitutional considerations regarding state organization could affect legislation. It seemed the creators of the new order lacked confidence in their judges. German judges, especially those who held positions in 1945, were at best indifferent to the Nazi's wanton violation of human rights. What is more, they were raised in a legal tradition where the revision of laws by judges was considered unacceptable. In Italy, between 1948 and 1956 (until the Constitutional Court was established) the ordinary courts had the right to examine whether laws were anticonstitutional, just like in the United States. But they had no difficulty applying the provisions of fascist legislation that remained in force, thereby violating the new Constitution.

Kelsen's centralized constitutional jurisdiction presented a solution; stronger protection for individual rights was added. The grounds for centralization were to be found in personnel policy considerations. Surely it would not present a problem to find a few dozen democratic judges who were ready to apply the new Constitution directly.

This was the principle on which the German and, later, Italian constitutional courts were established. The model was sure to find supporters in states where rule-of-law constitutions supplanted prolonged autocratic rule. This is what occurred in Spain and in the majority of post-communist countries. Where judges took no part in violating constitutionalism or where it was not necessary to heal the wounds inflicted by an anticonstitutional dictatorship, the procedure for the possible constitutional revision of laws was established only incidentally, or in parts, and often a separate court was not even established.

[19] Although the Weimar Constitution probably let the courts examine the constitutional nature of the laws applied, the antirepublican monarchist judges did not actually venture to do so. Only in one historically memorable case did the Imperial Court exercise this right. They reviewed the presidential order putting Prussian administration, including the Prussian police, under the central government's authority. The Court came close to declaring its review powers, yet the act was left in force. This move (the *Preußenschlag*) enabled the Nazis to take over the streets of Berlin.

German constitutional adjudication takes Kelsen's model a step further. Specified state organs (the government, the member states, one of parliament's houses, and, after a change in law, one-third of the delegates) can ask for a constitutional examination of a given law. This is an *abstract* review and has nothing to do with concrete cases. It goes far beyond adjudication in conflicts of competence because it makes a point of examining whether the law corresponds to the human (fundamental) rights in the Basic Law. Further, after exhausting all proper possibilities for legal redress, citizens may turn to the Constitutional Court, pleading that a state resolution used in the decision violated their fundamental rights. This also presents an opportunity to review the constitutional nature of applied laws.

On the Continent, the traditional view on the supremacy of the law and the impossibility of revising laws was, for historical reasons, strongest in France. Eventually, for political reasons, the Constitution of 1958 permitted constitutional review of legislation, but the reservations concerning the principle and the traditional fears put a rather strange stamp on the authority of the Constitutional Council.

By establishing the Constitutional Council, de Gaulle sought to restrict the power of the National Assembly. One of the Constitutional Court's responsibilities is to repress, at the government's request, Parliament's attempts at legislation in areas where original legislation is the government's constitutional prerogative. Further, the council's official duty is to examine organic laws before they are enacted–originally only at the request of the government, the president, or the speakers of the houses–and it controls the constitutional nature of laws already in force. The deadline is a rather tight thirty days from the day of the request.

Though originally the council was set up to be "a cannon directed at the legislature," and, while de Gaulle was president it always found his views and his governments constitutional, in a 1971 resolution it made the Declaration of the Rights of Man and Citizen of 1789 and the Preamble to the Constitution of 1946 part of the Constitution. Once human rights were incorporated into the Constitution, the council became increasingly active in voiding enactments. Their more active role was further increased because of a modification to the Constitution whereby sixty members (the parliamentary opposition) could begin proceedings.

In the past decades, some form of judicial constitutional review has become general practice throughout the Continent. (At times, like in

Belgium, the Court of Competences has begun to interpret the Constitution's provisions on equality in a broader sense, and the legislature has accepted this interpretation). An additional factor contributing to judicial constitutional review is that the European states have accepted the European Convention for the Protection of Human Rights, as interpreted by the Human Rights Court in Strasbourg, as the yardstick for all other rights. On event of complaint, the Strasbourg Court reviews the laws of individual states, too. This applies also to English law, which has rejected judicial review to this day. The practice adopted by U.K. courts is that the provision of law contradicting the convention is disregarded, and Parliament in due course generally revokes the law violating the convention, though its provisions are not considered directly applicable.

No matter how pervasive constitutional supervision of the legislature is, it is neither obvious nor self-explanatory to what extent the institution actually promotes traditional constitutional values. As the first decade of the French Constitutional Council demonstrates, it can turn out that the objective is only to strengthen the executive or the legislative branch. The most frequently cited arguments against constitutional adjudication emphasize the politicization of the constitutional court, which would mean the politicization of the administration of justice. Further, judges, who lack the legitimacy of popular representation and are democratically unaccountable, may go as far as writing laws and constitutions, which is irreconcilable with the function of the judiciary, indeed, it endangers it.

The objections partly concern the composition and procedure of the organizations engaged in constitutional adjudication and partly refer to the actual performance of constitutional courts. Although these courts are independent, the justices are, most often, purely political appointees (even though candidates must satisfy certain professional conditions). When appointing Supreme Court justices in the U.S., the partisan political views of the president prevail, while in Germany some of the constitutional justices are elected to correspond proportionally in number to the distribution of parties in the parliament. In France it is also the president's opinion, the majority's opinion in the Senate, or the National Assembly's opinion that prevails. The political determination of appointments, because of the rules of renewal, does not necessarily influence the body.

Contrary to the political bias of the legislature of the day, the political sympathies of the constitutional judicial body hark back to the views of the parties ruling before. So the body is not homogeneous, which does not prevent the justices from making mutual concessions, and unity requires compromise, which enhances legitimacy. The courts insist that earlier precedents guide their decisions. Dependence on current political trends is further reduced because, in theory, the justices and the court are independent of the other branches of government. This, of course, is not absolute; where reelection of the justices is possible (like in most East European systems), personal dependence cannot be excluded. Where reelection is prohibited (for example, in Italy), it can happen that the justices speculate on the benefits they might gain from the ruling party–after their term expires–since they, too, will have to make a living later on. Understandably, they grow accustomed to the respect shown to them and the lavish lifestyle. In the majority of cases, however, growing institutional independence from those who appoint is more characteristic. At least this is the conclusion to be drawn from the politicians' frequent objection to the courts' independent legislation.

7.1.3. Interpreting and Rewriting the Constitution

There is no doubt that where abstract–or indeed prior–norm control occurs, political issues have to be decided. When the parliamentary opposition or one of the member states in a federation requests the voiding of a law, it attempts to prolong the political struggle lost at the legislative level. But the political nature of the complaint does not necessitate a political answer, though it does transform the political fight into a constitutional and legal one, depoliticizing and legitimizing the laws kept in force. In this respect, constitutional adjudication strengthens the constitutionality of the legislature, and it may lend support to the system of checks and balances. The state's will, manifest in laws, is to be adhered to not only because the laws were passed by the authorized entity in the process prescribed by the constitution, but as much because it is directly proved that they correspond to the constitution.

The voiding of unconstitutional laws is part of the constitution's protective function, that is, Kelsen's negative legislation. In the process of constitutional adjudication, however, laws are not only voided or confirmed as constitutional. The courts may also determine how laws to be made should look, or they provide a self-executing solution to which no further legislative steps are to be added, thereby establishing what is the constitutional legal condition.

As noted above, justices may go as far as rewriting their constitution. All courts have a certain degree of freedom in handling the constitution because they need to interpret the text; but very often something else occurs. The French Constitutional Council, waking up from her initial Sleeping Beauty slumber, quickly made the French Constitution longer by adding some twenty percent more text. Some members of the U.S. Supreme Court discuss privacy–the right to an undisturbed private life–as a constitutional right, although the Constitution has nothing to say on the subject. The German Constitutional Court uses notions and concepts not found in the Basic Law to decide, for example, how the federation and the member states (*Länder*) should relate to each other when faced with regulatory issues. The very same Constitutional Court chooses the conditions of the abortion law that it finds acceptable. In 1982, the French Constitutional Council made a resolution on the modifications that it would require before accepting the nationalization of companies by the Socialists.[20]

The influence of constitutional courts is even stronger if one considers that the legislature (the government's bills) takes as its starting point the constitutional court's assumed interpretation of the constitution (and not the constitution, which as a text, is certainly ambiguous).[21]

The anxieties sparked by traditional constitutional considerations concerning constitutional adjudication (as seen above) seem justified. When Hamilton in *The Federalist Papers* no. 78 says that the decisions made by judges dealing with the Constitution have to be observed by the other branches, he accepts the judges' authority because they *interpret* the rules of the highest order, acting as mediators between the people and the legislature.

[20] The case shows that constitutional adjudication is not bound by day-to-day party politics. All members of the Constitutional Council holding positions in 1982 were appointed by previous governments. When the nationalizations occurred, the "appointers" attacked the nationalization from the opposition position. On the whole, the Constitutional Council did little to frustrate the work of the Socialist legislature, bar a few minor matters.

[21] During the French nationalization debate, on several occasions the National Assembly modified legislative proposals to coincide with the Constitutional Court's anticipated reaction.

But it never occurred to Hamilton that judges could *rewrite* the Constitution and actively participate in deciding what should go into the laws. To take away legislative power violates the system of checks and balances. What is more, this is done by an organ that is not legitimized democratically. The modification of the constitution–on the pretext of interpretation–questions the foundations of constitutionalism. It deprives the constitution of its legitimization by the constituent power, and it makes the legal system unpredictable and defenseless.

It could be true, however, that we are now up against a new form of constitutional legislation more adaptable to the complexities of our times. This new type of legislation does not affect–indeed, it may even help enhance–fundamental constitutional values, limited government, and the prevalence of fundamental rights. As far as the legislature is concerned, having two chambers in parliament is highly desirable; the second chamber provides for correspondence with constitutionalism and limits the arbitrariness of the legislature, although in terms of representative democracy this seems rather twisted. If this is so, would it be possible for a confirmed complementary part of the legislative process to be a body that is divorced from the parliamentary selection process and current partisan political considerations, different in composition, observing a logic that is distinct from parliamentary legislation, and primarily following constitutional arguments? Though the decisions of this body go beyond negative legislation, nevertheless, it is only a qualified participant in the legislative process, and it cannot assume an initiating role. This is almost unreservedly true of the French model's norm control. Where constitutional jurisdiction is linked to concrete cases, legislative freedom increases because the number of interventions are unlimited in real-life situations. So it is the randomly chosen situation itself that determines to what constitutional review refers and not the legislature's inclination as to what it thinks should be regulated. The American Supreme Court can choose from among several cases and may come upon a solution that (primarily, the solution thought constitutional by the Court), at the given time, had not even occurred to the legislature.

Justifications that fit into a broader constitutional precept can also be found for the (re)writing of the constitution, realized alongside constitutional adjudication (something courts mostly deny doing–save the proud Hungarians–saying they only interpret). Let us not forget that the constitutional foundation on which constitutional adjudication rests cannot be touched by ordinary legislation. After World War II, neither in France nor in Germany could the legislature easily adjust the constitution to the law, as it had before the war. Technically the supremacy of the fundamental law required by constitutionalism comes from the increased protection of the constitution, as opposed to laws from amendment.[22]

The development of the constitution and the resolution of disputes among the branches of power is obviously necessary for the constitutional system's operation. If instead of the authorized legislature, which can be influenced politically and has a more direct political or private interest, the responsibility for developing the constitution falls to the "least dangerous branch," the judiciary, the changes will be less likely to follow party lines and deviations from earlier concepts less radical, compared to the formal modifications of the constitution.[23] The U.S. Supreme Court–as the institution having the longest tradition in "constitution development"–does not really write a new constitution or law, nor does it deal with what would be advantageous or disadvantageous from the point of view of maintaining and enforcing the current power. The Court is not interested in who gets what as a result of its rulings. As Chief Justice Hughes said, "Behind the words of the constitutional provisions are postulates which limit and control."[24] The court rules in accordance with neutral and general principles that are current constitutional traditions. At times the German Constitutional Court assesses laws based on the fundamental law's objective values. Felix Ermacora is of the same opinion concerning centralized constitutional adjudication. In his view the protection of constitutional principles is legitimate when, and insofar as, it corresponds to preexisting constitutional principles; and if there is a discontinuous decision, the ensuing rule has

[22] It is perhaps no coincidence that the Norwegian Supreme Court, on the basis of the Norwegian Constitution, which can only be modified in two legislative cycles, found laws unconstitutional already in the last century. There was no danger of the Constitution being modified to fit the law; while such amendment was the first reaction of the last communist Parliament in Hungary, when in the first months of 1990 the newly established Constitutional Court nullified specific paragraphs of the law on voting rights.

[23] In the long-run, however, the changes will be radical. In the United States the right of the state to make rules adjusting the economy was first rejected (*Lochner*), and a generation later, under Roosevelt, it was endorsed. (*Lochner v. New York*, 198 U.S. 45 (1905).)

[24] Principality of *Monaco v. Mississippi*, 292 U.S. 313, 322 (1934). Quoted in Herbert Wechsler, "Toward Neutral Principles of Constitutional Law," *Harvard Law Review* 73 (1959): 15–17. Wechsler also gives a brief overview of the precepts of neutral principles.

to fit into the structure of the constitution. A reinterpreted constitution is merely the extension of the principles of the previous one, unfortunately, many a time to the detriment of the written text.

There are certain experts who regard constitutional adjudication and the ensuing development of the constitution as a legitimate political activity. In addition, they consider the court as a politically and democratically legitimized part of the democratic decision-making (legislative) process. According to John Hart Ely, this is quintessential for the (American) constitutional model. In his view, the majority carries out the plan of constitutionalism in the legislature, as the majority will neither endanger their own rights nor treat those not belonging to the majority in a systematically different way from how it would treat itself. The majority lets minority interests seep into decisions, and it does not permit the law's application to discriminate against individuals. The justices' role is to supervise this democratically justified process which, it should be added, is also borne out by the majority's self-interest. The judges are there to ensure that the elected representatives really represent. "[R]ather than dictate substantive results [the court] intervenes only when the 'market,' in our case the political market, is systematically malfunctioning."[25] The minority will need protection in the name of the constitution in the courts when the majority misunderstands its legislative mandate and fails to consider the interests of the minority and the ("universal") rights made for everyone. Ely's concept of democracy becomes meaningful if legislative representation is truly representative of the whole society and not just the majority.

This supervision by the courts, however, can be accepted by the other democratically more legitimized branches of power only if self-restraint is exercised. In democracies, social problems are usually resolved in election booths and not in courts. Contrary to all other reports, in the boom years between 1937 and 1967, the United States Supreme Court voided only twelve acts of Congress.[26] If the Court really protects mi-

[25] John Hart Ely, *Democracy and Distrust* (Cambridge, Mass.: Harvard University Press, 1980), 102–103.

[26] Charles L. Black, *Structure and Relationship in Constitutional Law* (Baton Rouge: Louisiana State University press, 1969), 67–76. Most of the laws nullified were made by the member states. By comparison, the most activist postcommunist constitutional court, the Hungarian one, voided forty acts (provisions) of the legislature in its first three years of existence (1990–92).

nority interests, it is expedient to exercise this protection when minority views do not have a chance or are not given the opportunity for consideration in the majority's legislation. This begs the following question: Would the separation of the branches of power continue to function if it were not backed by a powerful judicial authority when it comes to the constitution's modification? This question is especially valid in the case of the American model. The legislature, owing to separation, cannot effectively control the executive branch. For the executive to be truly controllable, the weight of the judiciary would have to be increased. In Europe, constitutional adjudication had to become independent to protect the constitution, because of the collusion of the branches of power and the greater dependency in their relationship compared with that in America.

Continental constitutional adjudication is strongly in favor of the increased protection of fundamental rights. In view of this fact, the majority of Italian, German, and Spanish cases grow out of actual legal disputes, and constitutional review there occurs mostly as appellate constitutional adjudication. Constitutional adjudication does not primarily affect the legislature but it does the ordinary administration of justice, and in practice, it extends constitutionalism (primarily through the protection of fundamental rights) to areas beyond public law, to criminal, administrative, and private law.

Constitutional adjudication would be unable to exercise the function of protecting minorities without creative activity, which is also part of constitutionalism as politics of antiexclusion. This form of minority protection means the protection of the parliamentary minority–and the groups backing it–(when the laws adopted are reviewed at the request of the minority). But it also implies the protection of social minority groups against the majority will. This is the conveyor of a new kind of constitutional culture. The emerging culture of constitutionalism is not reflected in the constitutions with their purportedly democratic assumptions on majority rule. When this culture prevails it can only be the result of an enduring procedure in a democratic system built on the principles of majority rule, based on the assumption that the winner in parliament takes all the fruits of victory.[27]

[27] See above Chapter 2.2 on majority rule.

In the parliamentary system of government, the governing political party or coalitions of parties, displacing both the legislative and executive powers, becomes omnipotent. The popular belief in judicial review establishes the courts, on the one hand, as the guarantors of the basic consensus on which democracy is founded, and, on the other hand, as the arbitrators that adjudge how far the reforms of regulations dictating the social, economic, and cultural life conform with this consensus, without reversing it.[28]

[28] Cited by Louis Favoreu, "Constitutional Review in Europe" in *Constitutionalism and Rights: The Influence of the United States Constitution Abroad*, eds. Louis Henkin and Albert J. Rosenthal (New York: Columbia University Press, 1992), 56; and E. Spiliotopoulos, "Judicial Review of Legislative Acts in Greece," *Temple Law Quarterly* 56. (1983): 501.

Chapter 8

FUNDAMENTAL RIGHTS

> But what do those want
> who would hear not of
> virtue or tyranny?
> *Saint-Just*

8.1. FREEDOM AND HUMAN RIGHTS

Constitutionalism's intention is not simply to complicate state decision making and the enforcement of decisions. It is not an end in itself. It enables people to live in freedom or at least free from governmental despotism. A constitution appropriate for constitutionalism differs in its attempt to guarantee freedom from a fundamental law that merely determines the structure of the state. All other state objectives–welfare, glory, and salvation, all self-imposed state responsibilities for providing services–can endanger liberty. Freedom (to be free from autocratic or despotic rule) is built upon the assumption that the desirable government is one under which the individual can make up his own mind about what he wants to do and what will be good for him.

There is no compelling reason why freedom should be the priority in determining state organization.[1] Some experts contend that freedom is not guaranteed by constitutionalism anyway but by other institutions, such as pure parliamentarism, the direct democracy of the people, or corporatist participation. According to others, the whole freedom-enhancing approach is mistaken; the state has to provide welfare services or fulfill other more sublime or higher missions. Benjamin Constant and his followers, however, insisted on a constitution that conforms with constitutional principles, because the alternatives soon lead to serfdom.

[1] There are societies that are indifferent to individual freedom; happiness or welfare are elevated here to the rank of "social objectives" instead. The nature of happiness and welfare is not determined by the individual but at best by shared misunderstandings.

The Age of Enlightenment in the eighteenth century strove to enthrone human reason.[2] To freely follow reason wherever it led was the coming-of-age program of mankind. Reason liberated from superstition and collecting knowledge from a variety of sources, enabled man to act independently. And, it followed, as reason could be found in anyone, all people were entitled to act independently, that is, to be free.[3] The liberties of individuals who can now act independently are not subject to recognition by the state; everyone is entitled to their freedoms at any time. The state has to observe and respect these most important rights. This natural-law-based approach serves as a starting point for regulation. The purpose of the constitution, by restricting the autocracy of the state, was to enable people to remain free. "*[The] end of Law* is not to abolish or restrain, *but to preserve and enlarge Freedom*..."[4]

The taming of human rights in the process of turning them into positive law preserved little of this radical starting point. The recognition of human (natural) rights as a basic constitution, as one can see in the workings of the French National Assembly–at Abbot de Sieyés's prompting–could not avoid restrictions and compromises. The prohibition of torture is perhaps the only natural-law prescription accepted unconditionally as an absolute prohibition by all constitutional states. But if an assassination is to be prevented, in practice even this prohibition is readily put aside.

The acceptance of the natural-law argument supporting rights is not self-evident. Even where people accept that the state has to serve freedom–human self-determination and the realization of hidden human potential–one cannot expect a consensus on what freedom actually means. In the believer's eyes, behavior violating his religious dogmas is

[2] In this discussion, the Americans and the French are unjustly favored because they were the first to include these rights in their constitutions, while all the other liberal constitutions were merely variations of these two models. However, the principle of "no punishment without law" can already be found in the Austrian Criminal Code, which came into force in 1787.

[3] Reason could be found in anyone, but it was not yet fully developed in everyone. Consequently, in the Age of Enlightenment, simultaneous to the recognition of individual liberty and self-determination, the rights of the "not completely reasonable," of the uneducated, and of those who could not make decisions because of their financial dependence were restricted. In other words, full (political) freedom was granted only to the wealthy.

[4] John Locke, "The Second Treatise of Government" in *Two Treatises of Government*, ed. Peter Laslett (Cambridge: Cambridge University Press, 1991), § 57.

unacceptable, and such declarations are untenable and have nothing to do with freedom, indeed, they should be punished. There are religions which proclaim that he who fails to use his "freedom" to help others convert and save them from living in sin, risks his own salvation. The believer's concept of freedom is different from that of a nonbeliever. Should people be allowed their "self-realization" through their self-destructive inclinations? J. S. Mill's classical liberal answer is that intervention is only justified if a person's self-destructive freedom poses a danger to someone else.[5]

A tolerant concept of freedom within the framework of constitutionalism helps resolve these dilemmas. The objective of the organizing principle of tolerance is to ensure the coexistence of liberties.

If we accept–and manage to convince others to accept–that we have rights which have to be observed by the state (and everyone else), we can in theory be free, at least in terms of not being forced to do things we do not want to do. The state will be "obliged" to honor these rights if an order *from above* obliges it to and if the rights constituting freedom are *above* the state. This is the image that corresponds to the hierarchical view of the world that is imprinted in our minds from childhood. Parents hover above us, protective and full of goodwill. We recognize commands because they come from above. The various "*natural-law*" concepts come up with a whole system of commandments that are above the state and guarantee citizens' freedom. But what happens if the state power does not believe in these prescriptions or if it interprets the messages coming from nature, divine order, and reason as restrictions of freedom? When children have grown up, their beliefs in prescriptions function mostly as routine.

Constitutionalism–realizing how unsatisfactory this vertical upward-looking image of the world is–wants to break up this linear subordination, consequently, it links the *safeguarding of freedom with the system of checks and balances.* This is not to say that constitutionalism in all its forms resigns the advantages of justification by natural law. But during the development of constitutionalism–owing to the chaos surrounding natural law and revolutionary destabilization–rights were often of secondary importance in constitutions as they focused on limiting the state's power through checks and balances.

[5] John Stuart Mill, *On Liberty* (London: Penguin Books, 1987).

The belief that people are entitled to certain rights irrespective of what the state may desire, restricts power in a way that is advantageous for the individual:

> The human person possesses rights because of the very fact that it is a person, a whole, master of itself and of its acts, and which consequently is not merely a means to an end, but an end, an end which must be treated as such. The dignity of the human person? The expression means nothing if it does not signify that by virtue of natural law, the human person has the right to be respected, is the subject of rights, possesses rights. There are things which are owed to man because of the very fact that he is man.[6]

The first sentence of modern constitutionalism written in the American Declaration of Independence of 1776 reads:

> We hold these truths to be self-evident, that all men are created equal, that they are endowed by their Creator with certain unalienable Rights, that among these are Life, Liberty and the pursuit of Happiness. That to secure these rights, Governments are instituted among men…

Why was it necessary to use natural law to lay the foundations of constitutions? The American revolutionaries had to struggle constantly with a crisis of self-justification. In 1789, their French followers had similar problems. In the Tennis Court Oath, the deputies of the future French National Assembly declared that they as representatives would draft France's constitution. As they were neither delegated nor summoned for that task, only natural law could justify the self-appointed representatives. If the deputies apply the fundamental principles of human rights, which are granted for, and clear to, everyone, their diligent efforts are justified and right, as their acts correspond to these precepts. All they need to do is find and follow the principles that offer justification. All revolutionary legislators inadvertently return to human rights because these are reasonable and legitimate to all human beings. This is why some people turned to human rights in postcommunist legislation, as this seemed "the way back to normal."

It is, of course, debatable to what extent human rights are "natural," that is, to what extent their existence is independent of the legal order.

[6] Jacques Maritain, *The Rights of Man and Natural Law* (London: G. Bles, Centenary Press, 1944), 37.

There are many sceptics. Jeremy Bentham denounced natural rights with hostility:

> Right is a child of law; from real laws come real rights, but from imaginary law, from "laws of nature," come imaginary rights ... Natural rights is simple nonsense; natural rights and imprescriptible rights (an American phrase) are rhetorical nonsense, nonsense upon stilts.[7]

During the early constitutionalizing of natural rights, only rights established as human or natural rights made it into the constitution. Rights had to be universal individual rights, or, more precisely, they were rules that could be made *universal*. The universality of a right does not mean it can be applied anywhere, though at a particular level of civilization it has to apply to everyone. Universality means it can be applied to anyone who is in the *particular situation* of applicability without the subject of laws having to have a personal capacity, position, or role in that situation. It is acceptable to beggars and princes, the innocent and the guilty: it serves the benefit of all. The freedom that is compatible with the freedom of others is obviously acceptable to everyone. Property rights do not simply mean that what I have cannot be taken by the state. The state has to prevent others from disturbing me in the possession of my property. This is a universal rule inasmuch as anyone can become the owner of some kind of property. Being the owner of some kind of property will have meaning only if the above condition is observed.

In connection with the safeguarding of fundamental property rights, when we assume "anyone can become the owner of property" we are thinking of human beings in the abstract. As real social beings are not abstract human beings, the acceptance of this precept presupposes a prior choice. If we foresee that we will never be owners, respect of a universal property right will obviously not be our constitutional starting point. We will not imagine ourselves as property owners but as persons who will never own anything. In this case, our starting point is the right to equal distribution of wealth. (Of course, the possession of that equal wealth still needs some property-like recognition; otherwise there is no end to perpetual theft.) Further, if freedom is considered the origin of

[7] Jeremy Bentham, *The Works of Jeremy Bentham: published under the superintendence of his executor John Bowring*, vol. 1, *Anarchical Fallacies* (Edinburgh, W. Tait; London, Simpkin Marshall, 1843), 501.

human errors, or if one desires to find salvation with the help of a special ritual, then freedom can not be the starting point for the organization of the state. Anyway, bourgeois societies and modern secular constitutions are in favor of universal freedom and private property. The argument supporting this choice is that the outcome is acceptable, even if one does not believe in the starting point. Even the person who expects salvation or prosperity from the functioning of society may benefit by the "bourgeois" order, because the *possibility* to prosper or find salvation is left unhindered. If a system mandates salvation, however, it will be acceptable only to those who believe in one or another (enforced) salvation. It is impossible to compare systems that are based on incompatible values; yet comparison remains possible based on results.

If constitutions are neutral, they include only those fundamental natural rights which allow actions that can be reconciled with the similar actions of any other person. Based on the universality principle, the possibilities of actions we wish for ourselves must be accepted, even if others wish to take advantage of them, too. Our maxim of action then, is the following: it is only possible to accept the freedom that is acceptable to everyone else, if viewed through the eyes of a neutral observer. It is up to the reader to decide when accepting some kind of an order whether it is satisfactory to him that this order is advantageous for him and not disadvantageous for others.

If the answer is *yes*, he needs to be assured that the inclusion of fundamental rights in the constitution is really justified by the above. For instance, that freedom–the condition wherein everyone is guaranteed to be able to live the life they want–is advantageous for everyone, including the reader (provided the way of life chosen does not harm anyone and does not endanger the security of the state). The believer in salvation will obviously not find this satisfactory because he thinks the proper way of life is not a matter of personal choice. He believes that everyone should live in a manner so as not to endanger salvation (yours, mine, or theirs). This person cannot be convinced of the universality of fundamental rights, and yet the salvation seeker may accept neutral constitutional protection of rights (for example, of free exercise) on the grounds that, by following his own logic, he himself might venture outside the sphere of constitutional protection, because other salvation seekers might find his way of life unacceptable. Thus tolerant coexistence is the most reasonable constitutional point of view. If one's salvation happens not to prevail, at least *he* will not be damned because no one will interfere with *his* way of life. At this stage we must again point out that the constitution is acceptable to *everyone*, at least as a minimum order, because it guarantees everyone's autonomous existence.

The person living the majority's way of life is naturally upset by any deviation from the majority opinion. Freedom of private life does not mean one cannot be outraged at this freedom. If it is a constitutional right, the *state* cannot interfere with these personal decisions, nevertheless, my outraged neighbor will not become completely defenseless vis-à-vis my provocative privacy. If one's neighbour's way of life violates one's own way of life, in theory one may ask for legal remedies (for example, an injunction for trespassing). If one suffers damages because of the neighbor's exercise of his freedom, there is a possibility for legal redress provided given conditions are met. One can still respect another person's freedom and not be violating constitutional rights if one does not greet a "deviant" person upon meeting him. But if an eccentric or "different" person is treated in a manner that causes him distress, injury, or degrades the core of his dignity, this may amount to crime or tort, not necessarily because of a human right to be different, but because living in security implies that the state has to make laws to safeguard security.

We consider fundamental rights to be general and universal, that is, everybody is entitled to them. It follows that the liberties and rights of a people living in a country should be guaranteed by law and the constitution as things to which the people are entitled. In a constitutional system, this requires us to then answer the following questions: What are the constitutionalized human rights (*fundamental rights*)? In other words, what kind of rights would one need to ensure freedom in a constitutional system? What follows if a right is claimed as a "fundamental right"? Who is bound by it? The state, or the citizens, too? And what does "being bound" mean? Simply to honor the claim, or nonintervention, or the unrestricted activity of the person who is entitled to the right? Or the protection and enhancement of the right and its holder, too? (Do we prevent anyone from obstructing an action that is based on a right? Do we call to account the person who violates a right? Do we provide the conditions of freedom and the organization of free action?)

Originally, freedom seemed an absolute right. Living in a state and operating the fundamental rights in a state bring about a situation where the exercise of freedom comes up against other freedoms and requirements concerning the functioning of the state. To what extent can fundamental rights be restricted?

These questions require a *legal definition*. All definitions are negations so it is important *who makes the definitions*, that is, who makes the negations and *exclusions*. It is at this stage that the checks-and-balances condition of constitutionalism becomes important. Determining the definitions is not the privilege of one person or institution; it is a divided process. In itself, even a democratically legitimized legal definition may be insufficient to guarantee freedom if the power to define falls under the exclusive authority of only one governmental organ.

The control of the legal-definition procedure was so important for constitutionalism–at least at the beginning of the constitutional era–that a more precise indication of the rights to be included in the constitution was not considered to be the task of a constitution. The homogeneous elite of the American settlers, victorious in the War of Independence, probably had good reason to assume that there was a consensus in the political community concerning which rights the people were "entitled" to automatically. This community of understanding is expressed in the opening phrases of the Declaration of Independence. The original assumption was that as far as constitutionalism is concerned, the procedure of the definition of the restriction of rights is what counts, namely, that none of the branches of government have an exclusive right in this procedure. Even the French Declaration of 1789 (Art. 16), which insisted on natural rights, states that in "any society in which the guarantee of the rights is not secured, the separation of powers not determined, has no constitution at all."

Although constitutionalism is intended to enforce liberties or–from a different aspect–human rights chosen by the state somewhat at random, the list of rights is missing or only parts of it are included in the constitutions of several constitutional states. Rights depend almost solely on the effective balance among the branches of power. This approach prevailed in the constitutions of the nineteenth century and until the Mexican and Weimar constitutions. Even after World War I, Kelsen envisioned the Austrian Constitution as a description of the state structure along these traditional lines.

Constitutional systems survive to this day where fundamental rights are mentioned only exceptionally (for example, the Belgian or the Austrian constitutions).[8] But the typical constitution in force today contains as a rule a list of these rights to which people (or perhaps citizens only) are entitled. The list of rights varies, of course, as does the weight given in each constitution to these rights, the extent to which they are considered unrestrictable, and the conditions of restriction.

Whether one believes that the enforcement of human rights is required by a natural divine order, one should approve (more or less unconditionally) of certain rights, either because of a love of freedom or because of a respect for other people's dignity, or out of pure self-interest. Rights and liberties have to be defined in a particular context so that they correspond to the conditions of coexistence in a given society. Even if the text of the constitution manages to convey what seemed important for the freedom of people at the particular moment of constitution making, freedom and fundamental rights will remain at the mercy of circumstances and history. Even the Human Rights Court in Strasbourg, which is the most advanced supranational enforcer of human rights, "cannot but be influenced by the developments and commonly accepted standards in the...policy of the member States of the Council of Europe."[9]

At this stage an attractive dream popular with international lawyers has to be mentioned, namely, the idea that "binding" human rights exist in international documents or are "recognized" by international law. No doubt these obscure and unenforceable international documents carry some weight because constitutions–especially as the role of real partici-

[8] Canada supplemented its constitution with fundamental rights only in 1967 and 1982. In Britain, from time to time, the need for a "bill of rights" arises, which would be given increased protection against the legislature; however, the time was not yet right as of 1998. Certain patterns of historical development result in a strong consensus among the political elite regarding fundamental rights, or the legal, social-control mechanisms (beliefs or traditions) facilitating the enforcement of these rights seem so strong that the constitutions need not concern themselves with fundamental rights. This may change, however. No fundamental rights can be found in the Australian Constitution, but to everyone's surprise, in 1992 the Supreme Court declared that it went without saying that Australia as a representative democracy safeguarded free speech. Likewise, the text of the French Constitution of 1958 is silent on fundamental (civil) rights. In 1971, the Constitutional Council incorporated these rights into the Constitution by declaring that the provisions of the 1789 Declaration and the Preamble of the Constitution of 1946 were applicable constitutional texts.

[9] *Tyrer v. U.K.*, Ser. A 26 (1978), par. 31.

patory confirmation is so small–use for their own legitimation the fact that they incorporate rights that are deemed *recognized internationally*.[10]

Besides actual domestic demands and the minimum ideological considerations, especially since World War II, international demands for the recognition of human rights as a minimum condition for participation in the international community have to be taken into consideration by all constitution makers, at least to the extent they wish to be recognized by other countries. Membership in international organizations may be attractive, but there are conditions attached to it, namely, the need to observe certain rights. The minimum requirements concerning international human rights are taken from the list of fundamental (human) rights prevailing in countries important in the international political context. The minimum requirements are laid down in universal catalogues of human rights, which, though a short list, are much contested by experts. International recognition gives constitutionalism a special kind of self-generating dynamic that is strengthened by international organizations and international courts. A state can hardly afford not to grant the rights granted by other countries with which it lives together in a cultural and economic community. If it resists, it shuts itself out of the club, becoming an international outcast.

Fundamental rights, similar to other parts of the legal system, have always to be reconciled with society's other–not clearly defined–political demands (motivated by public peace and sometimes by the public good and by public interest). The interpretation and meaning of freedom change with culture, too, and need flexible accommodation.

Differences may arise because of the changing technological conditions of societies and because the meaning of freedom may be interpreted to comply with current moral standards, which to a certain extent are determined by prevailing sociopolitical realities. Women's rights, for instance, have undergone a significant change, depending on what their role in the job market is perceived to be and what form and meaning biological reproduction in the given society takes. To put it in a rough materialistic manner, if social reproduction required women to bear and

[10] This recognition at times is extremely formal, for instance, when the United States stipulates that the condition for granting most-favored-nation status is the observance of human rights. (It is quite possible to turn a blind eye to this criteria on the grounds of national security or foreign policy interests and grant most-favored-nation status to friendly and allied dictatorships.)

rear children for twenty years, their "rights" will be different from the rights of women who are needed as independent bread winners–or it will not at all be acceptable to society that they have (political and property) rights. Pre-World-War-II feminists were opposed to abortion, while today most feminists believe in free choice.

8.2. DEFINING FUNDAMENTAL RIGHTS

8.2.1. SHOULD THE LEGISLATURE BE AUTHORIZED TO DEFINE FUNDAMENTAL RIGHTS?

Which human rights should be recognized by the constitution? The human-rights concept, by introducing democratic legislation into the process of "defining" rights, seems to have solved the uncertainty surrounding the content of human rights, while at the same time it cares for their protection. For who else would know better than we citizens what our inherent natural rights are? Our close relationship with the legislature enables us to express and protect these rights.

Accordingly, it seemed the best guarantee of human "natural" rights–at least in revolutionary America–that the people whose rights and freedom were at stake get to make their own decisions concerning rights and liberties.[11] It would follow that constitutions should have provisions in matters left to the administration of justice, that is, in a domain into which the legislature does not necessarily penetrate. Accordingly, the early constitutions go into detailed guarantees of freedom in matters of criminal proceedings. The "less important" practical reason for this "procedural interest" is that the French did not trust the judiciary, while

[11] This approach prevailed in the Pennsylvania Constitution of 1776, written under Tom Paine's influence. This was undoubtedly the most revolutionary declaration in the United States. The Preamble of the Pennsylvania Constitution sums up the principle as follows: "Whereas all government ought to be instituted and supported for the security and protection of the community as such, and to enable the individuals who compose it to enjoy their natural rights, and the other blessings which the Author of existence has bestowed upon man; and whenever these great ends of government are not obtained, the people have a right, by common consent to change it, and take such measures as to them may appear necessary to promote their safety and happiness."

in the eyes of contemporaries, the most serious manifestations of the autocracy of British and French kings occurred at trials. Throughout their lives, Voltaire and Rousseau felt persecuted by orders of detention, and they did not refrain from letting others know of this. In the nightmares of the bourgeois revolutionaries, dungeons and chains are omnipresent.

But even in the honeymoon period of unalienated popular legislation, there is some suspicion brewing in the legislators. The legislature embodies a whole population. The whole of the people (or at least those who are wealthy) is given the chance to express its will. The exact shaping of rights by the legislature has its dangers. What will happen when a majority group forces its will upon the others, if it restricts or enforces human rights as its interests or whims dictate? Pennsylvania's example shows that the more complete the popular democracy is, the less it can be expected that the definition of rights, as a result of the dictatorship of the majority, will not degenerate into an arbitrary restriction of rights.[12] This assumption was later proved correct by the bloody manipulation of fundamental rights by the Jacobin militants who tried to couple rights with obligations and virtue. If virtue and rights are the *sole* foundations of legislation, the result can only be anarchy.

The Virginia Constitution of 1776 offers an alternative to the Pennsylvania model. Virginians wanted to guarantee fundamental rights, to which the good people of Virginia and their descendants were entitled, based on a relative separation of the branches of government.[13] Pennsylvania tried to set up a model where centralized and omnipresent democracy was thought to be the safeguard of rights. Political reality and perhaps deeper reasons brought about the success of the Virginia model

[12] The domination by factions was from the beginning of modern constitutionalism a source of real danger. When human rights were guaranteed, in reality the existing political and religious groups had to be reconciled with each other. As Pennsylvania was the home of many sects, its constitution, besides guaranteeing freedom of religion, had to provide detailed rules so that no sect member be disadvantaged in civil life. Thus an official oath is made to a God not belonging to any of the denominations, and belief in any kind of God is enough to exercise civil and political rights.

[13] The Virginia Constitution of 1776 was based on the assumption that tyranny could be prevented by the separation of the branches of power. Thus it paid little attention to guaranteeing freedom of speech or the inclusion of the principle of habeas corpus in the constitution. These were contained in the nonenforceable Virginia Bill of Rights.

against radical democracy.[14] The direct and permanent exercise of popular sovereignty proved inadequate. Natural rights, although known in those days as self-evident, were left unprotected, among others, because radical democracy failed to provide stable government.[15]

If there is something constitutionalism adamantly abhors, it is direct popular sovereignty.[16] Constitutionalism is based on laws *not* directly determined by the people; this is especially true of the laws on fundamental rights.[17] Who then defines human rights? Or should we conclude that a definition is unnecessary–as is restriction–or will the legislature be authorized to define them based on the content of the constitution and the rules of separation of powers, including judicial review?

Other approaches are possible, too. The American Republican tradition claims that democratic legislation is necessary for the protection of fundamental rights, exactly because the content, validity, and consequences of these rights have not been clarified. The responsibility of the legislature is not so much the observance of these rights but the determination of their content, using the democratic expressions of human agreement. After all, human rights do not create concrete situations ("rights") for the people living in the country. They are merely a promise that these points will be taken into consideration when determining the legal status of citizenship.[18] This is exactly what the French Constitutional Assembly promised (bound itself) to do in 1789.[19]

[14] The Pennsylvania Constitution of 1776 established a unicameral system; the executive council and the judicial organs functioned in personal dependence on the assembly of representatives. All this–influenced by human-rights advocate Tom Paine–was based on remarkably extended franchise and popular control.

[15] Illusions of democracy are, nevertheless, stubborn and have a tendency to recur. The Estonian Constitution of 1920 made it possible for the people to decide nearly all legislative issues by referendum against enactments of Parliament. This permanent popular sovereignty (and the similar but constitutionally restricted Swiss system of referenda) puts human rights at the mercy of popular will.

[16] Even Rousseau rejected the people's direct legislative will, although he said of British representative legislation, that the people were free only on the day of the elections. In his view it is the people's duty to complain if the freedom-guaranteeing constitution is not observed. The complaint serves as a representation of the people, but whether the complaint is admissible is decided by a body elected by a narrow cross section of society.

[17] Some constitutions or acts on referenda contain special restrictions concerning this issue.

[18] Jeremy Waldron, "Rights and Majorities: Rousseau Revisited in Majorities and Minorities," in *Majorities and Minorities*, eds. John W. Chapman and Alan Wertheimer,

That the safeguard of human rights was left to the legislature is understandable from the point of view of democratic republicanism. It makes sense in every place where the revolution was directed against the executive power and where the victors took over parliament seeking to restrict the executive power–the source of all dismissal of rights–from there. The Belgian Constitution of 1831 was, for instance, a response to the Dutch monarch's autocratic and aggressive religious and language policies. The constituents' starting assumption was that the monarch (the most powerful power) would still be the source of violations of the people's rights, so it seemed to be satisfactory for restoring freedom to turn to law to be the sole ground and form for the inevitable restrictions of civil rights, as laws were made by the bourgeois victors.

This guarantee came to nothing because the relationship of the executive power and the legislature grew closer and the legislature was drawn under the influence of the modern executive branch. The situation whereby the legislative power was entrusted with safeguarding human rights was turning into something like leaving the fox to mind the chickens. What is more, the awe-like respect for human rights petered out by the middle and of the nineteenth century. In the Age of Positivism, the belief in the normative force of the supernatural had vanished. Bentham's radical skepticism seemed to triumph. From the end of the nineteenth century, legal positivism prevailed. It was commonly held that entitlement was a restriction on the authorities ordered by law, or, as German legal dogmatics proclaimed, a reflex of judicial redress. In England, Victorian self-confidence outlived Queen Victoria by fifty years. History and tradition supported British parliamentarism as a safeguard of liberties instead of a constitutional arrangement centered around enforceable rights. British parliamentary democracy was made powerful not because rights were only seldom violated but due to its powerful cabinet system and a devoted and independent army of civil servants not bound by fundamental rights or complex power-restricting machinery guaranteeing fundamental rights.

Nomos XXXII (New York: New York University Press, 1990), 52.

[19] The Declaration was to have provided guidance for the constitution, which was to be drafted at a later stage, and for the legislation of the Constituent Assembly. The solutions presented in the Declaration are fundamental decisions regarding modern (liberal) fundamental rights, though they were made very much on the spur of the moment, dictated by practical political considerations and the power relations in the Assembly.

But in other countries, after inhuman forms of oppression, revolutionary flare-ups, or tragic national collapses, it was again deemed necessary that human rights be protected in a manner that was not so much at the mercy of the legislature. It was thought this could be achieved by incorporating the details of rights *into* the constitution and by protecting fundamental rights *against* the legislature. After World War II, following organic developments in the U.S., this protection was offered primarily through constitutional adjudication.

8.2.2. Which Fundamental Rights Should be Protected by The Constitution?

(a) The classical list

Human rights are as many as their drafters, the ages and social conditions. There is no agreement even on the most fundamental human rights among the "prophets" of constitutionalism. Locke not only recognized the right to property but also that this right was restricted by the right of those in need to get a share of the surplus value acquired through property.[20] Grotius, Hobbes, and Montesquieu were of the same opinion, though for different reasons.[21] Blackstone, on the other hand–to protect the owners–says property does not derive from natural law. Property rights are created by the laws of states.[22]

At the dawn of constitutionalism, the list of human or natural rights included only Locke's triad of rights (life, liberty, and property). On the other hand, the more detailed way a minor German prince prescribed a subordinate's conduct and the privileges of the various estates, the more

[20] John Locke, "Second Treatise of Government," in *Two Treatises of Government*, (Cambridge: Cambridge University Press, 1980), § 37.

[21] Hayek also recognizes the community's responsibility to care for the needy and use public funds for this purpose. But there is no mention of the *rights* of the needy. Friedrich August von Hayek, *The Constitution of Liberty* (Chicago: Chicago University Press, 1960), 285–286.

[22] The rights of the needy cannot be interpreted because it is not clear who is obliged. Personal safety, namely, the uninterrupted enjoyment of property and immunity from arbitrary arrest, seem simple cases: on the basis of these rights, the person entitled to them has to be left alone. But is it the state's responsibility to care for the needy? Is this then something the public must pay for to the degree that it can?

detailed was the human-rights catalogue of the current local freedom-fighter (for example, the dismissed pastor). The plethora of human rights brought with it the ridiculous, such as the case of having the right to cut one's nails. Even the Virginia Constitution of 1776 includes several concrete human rights that can hardly be listed under the heading of negative freedoms of "let live."

Natural law, with its unrestricted, unlimited, and absolute rights, is unable to give a viable and predictable solution for rights legislation. For this it is necessary to determine which human rights require protection.

The constitution–if it wishes to avoid the unproductive and incidental legal definitions of fundamental rights–is forced to make conscious and somewhat arbitrary choices. It has to prepare a list of fundamental rights in the hope that this will bind the legislature. Constitutions have to define the inner circle of the liberties they want to observe and have others observe. In theory, the stronger the popular legitimacy of a constitution, the more probable that the values chosen will be acceptable to most of the members of society, or at least these will turn out to be less disputed. Despite the somewhat elitist and imposed nature of the actual constitution-making processes, the catalogue of rights represents the conditions of social coexistence and the demands of existing institutions.[23] The list of fundamental rights in some revolutionary constitutions reflects the values of the constitution-drafting elite. Revolutionary elites expect that their values will change society. On the other hand, the basic assumption of the neutral-individualistic (liberal) concepts of fundamental rights is that the liberties of the abstract person who dwells in the minds of the legislators has to live together with other human beings of similar rights, and, in the long run, they have to be acceptable to eve-

[23] Freedom of religion, for example, promotes the peaceful coexistence of various religions groups. The American Constitution (the First Amendment) prohibits Congress from establishing a religion. The reason behind this principle is to prevent any division of the state by any dispute arising among the denominations. Conversely, in other countries, where one denomination undoubtedly predominates, it is traditionally recognized in the constitution as the "established church." This is what happened in Great Britain, the Scandinavian countries, Greece, and until 1972, in Ireland. The constitutions of some of the fiercely Moslem countries declare their countries Islamic states. France, on the other hand, defines itself as a secular republic. India, which faces a problem of sectarianism somewhat similar to that of eighteenth-century United States, would commit suicide if it had to identify itself with any kind of religion or ideology.

ryone, at least in principle. Being acceptable, according to John Rawls, means that anyone who is put in a position created by the guaranteed rights should not be better or worse off than others in the same situation.[24]

What can then be found on the list of fundamental rights?

In its original articles of 1787, the Constitution of the United States only mentions the institutionalized elements (for example, habeas corpus) of certain rights in connection with the allocation of federal legislative competences. In 1789, particular fundamental rights were added as amendments to the Constitution. The amendments adopted in 1791 refer to the following rights: freedom of speech and religion; the freedom to bear arms (as a member of the militia); the right to just compensation if private property is taken for public use i.e., the protection of property; immunity from quartering soldiers; and guarantees of personal liberties in criminal procedure, for example, the conditions of a search warrant, trial by jury, and guarantees of procedure for the defendant, for example, the prohibition of being a witness against himself, the right to defense, and due process.[25]

After the Civil War, more rights were added, namely, the right to personal freedom (abolition of slavery), equality before the law, and general *due process*, to safeguard life, liberty, and property. General voting rights were also recognized in the Fifteenth Amendment and (for women) in the Nineteenth Amendment (1920). The list is rather short, containing issues mostly arising out of the needs of a particular time in history (for example, quartering).

Originally the list was made so short because it was thought these rights would be included in the member-states' constitutions, which were considered at that time to be more important than the federal Constitution. The brevity of the list later forced the Supreme Court to read many other rights into these few and to recognize constitutional rights outside the text of the Constitution (for example, the right to *pri-*

[24] John Rawls, *A Theory of Justice* (Cambridge, Mass.: Harvard University Press, 1970).

[25] The English Bill of Rights of 1689 confirmed the right of trial by jury and of bail and prohibited cruel and unusual punishment. The American settlers demanded these rights as a birthright because of their British citizenship and not as the unalienable and natural right of human beings. Most of these institutions were already guaranteed by English common law.

vacy). As a consequence of this "forced incorporation," such issues as the right of assembly (although expressly guaranteed) and elements of other political rights (campaign financing) have been incorporated into the freedom of speech.

The French Declaration of 1789 gives a short list of human rights, and in most articles it mentions the form and basis of the restriction of rights rather drastically–in other words, it is less absolutist than the U.S. Bill of Rights.[26] The Declaration states that the right to freedom, property, security, and resistance to oppression are imprescriptible natural rights (rights from birth).[27] The free exercise of the same rights of others, as determined by law, is the limit to liberty (human rights). Law may also prohibit acts injurious to society, even if no one is actually harmed by these acts. The imprescriptible rights are followed on the list by the rights of *political* participation; these rights are necessary to determine the constitutional content of laws in a liberty-enhancing manner. After references to a few criminal laws and procedural guarantees of liberty, the freedom of religion and speech–both abounding in restrictions–appear on the list. Freedom of religion and expression of opinions cannot be punished if their expression does not disturb public order (Art. 10), whatever the law means by public order. Men are responsible for the abuse of freedom of expression in the cases determined by law.

The French Constitution of 1791 provides a more complete list of civil and political rights and takes a more determined stand on legal equality than does the U.S. Constitution. Equality in contributing to public burdens is proportionate to one's means; however, there is full equality before the law. Political rights are equal, though in keeping with Sieyés's idea, active and passive voting rights were differentiated. The legislature is based on indirect representation, which is far from the republican democracy that was so popular among some American revolutionaries and French Rousseauians and which, in the end, had to be restricted here and there, too.

Liberties, as constitutional rights, mean *security* and *immunity*. Personal freedom as security means that no one can be *arbitrarily* arrested

[26] There has been a century-long debate about whether the Declaration was simply a copy of the American Bill of Rights, written two years earlier.

[27] "Imprescriptible" does not mean that the rights cannot be restricted; it means that people cannot resign these rights. For example, a man cannot become a slave of his own accord.

and convicted and that people cannot be restricted in their movements.[28] Up until the end of the French Revolution, security also meant that people's existence should not be uncertain, that is, people have the right "not to starve."[29] Liberties may only be restricted as stipulated in the Constitution.[30] Freedom of speech and expression is guaranteed, and censorship is expressly prohibited. Censorship was singled out as it was considered to be a most dangerous earlier practice. The right to petition and to peaceful assembly without arms is a novelty compared with the earlier Declaration of 1789. These rights are to be interpreted within the boundaries of police regulations and with a content stipulated by law. The law, on the other hand, cannot obstruct the exercise of natural and civil rights, but the abuse of these rights may be punished.[31]

[28] The guarantees of personal freedom can be found in Title III, Chapter V on judicial power in the Constitution of 1791. These rights were defined as individual rights and general prohibitions, however, and not as special procedural rights related to the administration of justice. The conditions restricting criminal procedures appear as individual rights guaranteeing individual freedom. For instance, among these conditions are that no man can be put under arrest or detained, except by virtue of a warrant from police officers (sec. 10), and shall be examined at the latest within twenty-four hours (sec. 11). The place of confinement may only be a place legally and publicly designated to serve as a jail, court house, or prison (sec. 13). Basic criminal procedural rights were written into the Constitution, including rules on indictment (sec. 9), the right to assistance by council (sec. 9), and the right to be released on bail (sec. 12). The defendant has the right to be heard by the judge assigned by law (sec. 4), to a trial by jury (sec. 9), including the right to reject up to twenty members of the jury without giving reasons (sec. 9), and to a public hearing (sec. 9).

[29] The French Constitution of 1791 stipulates the state's obligations, which do not generate rights as we see them today, that is, they cannot be enforced; but as constitutional obligations they can, to be sure, influence the position of individuals and their rights (though they do not necessarily enlarge freedom). The obligations involve the establishment of free public instruction (Tit. I, par 3. 13 of the French Constitution of 1791; included also in Sect. 44 of the Pennsylvania Constitution of 1776).

[30] Professional literature, which is influenced by the French model, often distinguishes three lawful methods to restrict rights: preventive, regulatory, and retributive. The Belgian Constitution states that assembly in a closed place is completely permissible and free, while assembling in open places is subject to regulation. This qualification was then extended to the exercise of all rights in all open places.

[31] The exercise of free speech may be punished only if it is abused in ways stipulated in the Constitution, namely, if it incites one to purposefully disobey the law, oppose the constitutional authorities, or commit a crime, or if it abuses a public officer. In keeping with these traditions, the current Greek Constitution discusses at length the possibilities

The French list of rights was not broadened in merit in the liberal era but was made more explicit. The Belgian Constitution, later on used as a yardstick, included in briefer form the essence of all the 1791 French rights (except "social security," like job opportunities for the unemployed).[32] Equality means equality before the law, that is, *the law has to apply to everyone equally*. The right of association is added to the list, something that was emphatically forbidden and rejected in France during the revolution, the reason being that all associations would "mediate" and, therefore, distort the relation between individuals and the general legislature (the general political will).[33] The private domicile and correspondence are inviolable. This prohibition is absolute, and explains why it is impossible to tap conversations legally in Belgium even today. The search warrant that meets all legal conditions is exempt from the absolute protection granted to the home. The Belgian Constitution of 1831 included freedom of opinion in teaching in its list of constitutional rights. Press freedom is supplemented with the prohibition on deposit.[34] Finally, as in all revolutionary constitutions, there are a few rules that prohibit the most injurious violations of rights that were committed by the tyrant of the prerevolutionary era. Thus the state cannot intervene in church appointments; the civilian death sentence has been abolished (civil death being a penalty that divests the individual of all civil rights). This is why freedom to use one's language is granted, but the law may prescribe the language in which official matters are to be conducted.

(b) Positive rights: economic and social rights and the protection of institutions

Most of the civil rights are directed against *the state as prohibitions requiring nonintervention*, sometimes highlighting and listing the interventions

---

of restricting freedom of the press. If the exemptions restricting constitutional rights are enumerated in the constitution, this is unobjectionable, at least in the formal sense.

[32] By 1831 the list of civil–formally, political–liberties was practically complete. Later extensions were mostly technical, for instance, when the inviolability of correspondence was extended to include modern telecommunications and press freedom came to cover all the media.

[33] See Le Chapelier's Act (1791), which is decidedly against the workers' attempts to self-organize.

[34] Art. 18 of the Belgian Constitution provides that "no caution money shall be exacted of writers, publishers or printers."

that have typically violated freedom in the past (for example, censorship or denial of the Church's right of investiture). In the liberal era, the state had little to do with fundamental rights other than to provide for the administration of justice and free education.

The Declaration of 1789 is silent on social rights.[35] Liberal constitutionalism did not observe the social traditions of the French Constitution of 1791 but "verified" the original 1789 "omission" as a matter of principle, that is, it endorsed it.

By the end of the French Revolution, with the apparently complete victory of private property, human rights were interpreted according to the canons of possessive individualism. The narrowly tailored public duties of citizens were based on the concept of an almost night-watchman-like state. Public burdens (taxation) affected only a small group of property owners.

Apart from a few exceptions, until 1917 the constitutional, individual fundamental rights simply prohibited the state and its organs from doing certain things. All that the state was expected to do was enact specific laws so that these prohibitions could effectively protect freedom from the state. Further, if the state's responsibility is believed to protect society from the abuse of freedom–from the violation of the individual's rights by others exercising their freedom–it is obvious that the state must make laws that protect from and remedy abuse, including their incorporation into criminal and civil law.

At the end of the nineteenth century, earlier negative constitutional rights that required the state to restrain itself were reinterpreted, and attempts were made to make laws that satisfied the demands of the poor and the "workers." The Mexican (1917) and the Weimar (1919) constitutions were among the first at the beginning of the twentieth century to provide express constitutional grounds for social interventionism. Attempts to redefine the state were at times thwarted by the courts (like until 1935 in the United States) and formal amendments to traditional constitutions often proved too difficult.

Thermidor and liberalism wiped away the poor laws and turned the state apparently neutral. After 1917 a new era began, heralding the evo-

[35] In the summer of 1789 the committee proposals of the Constituent Assembly were full of ideas about how to provide for the poor, but as the Declaration was proclaimed when it was only half ready (because it suddenly became urgent to write a detailed constitution), the disputed social rights were not included.

lution of antiliberal constitutional arrangements. Social engineering, social democracy, and corporatism highlight objectives for the state in the hope of ensuring social peace. This is a high-risk venture for constitutionalism: one of the cornerstones of constitutionalism is endangered by noninterference into liberties. The increased role of government has upset the balance of power in favor of the executive, which was traditionally disinterested in civil-rights matters.

Hayek, the Nobel Prize laureate free-market advocate, summarizes these dangers.

> A government which cannot use coercion except in the enforcement of general rules has no power to achieve particular aims that require means other than those explicitly entrusted to its care and, in particular, cannot determine the material position of particular people or enforce distributive or "social" justice...If the government is to determine how particular people ought to be situated, it must be in a position to determine also the direction of individual efforts...Distributive justice requires an allocation of all resources by a central authority; it requires that people be told what to do and what ends to serve...[W]hen the opinion of the community decides what different people shall receive, the same authority must also decide what they shall do.[36]

The endangering of negative liberties through constitutionally provided services originates in attempts to buy social peace at times of social unrest. Political rights were extended first without satisfying the needs of the emerging social movements.

As the enlargement of political rights was not enough to guarantee social peace and democracy, the drafters of the Mexican Constitution of 1917, to put an end to the long years of revolutionary chaos, included in the Constitution an entire chapter concerning workers' rights. The chapter guaranteed an eight-hour workday, minimum wages, equal pay irrespective of gender and nationality, and the right to strike. Employers had to guarantee safe working conditions and one day off from work per week. The Constitution made it the legislature's responsibility to draw up the employment regulations that granted the implementation of these rights. It also voided a number of employment agreements repugnant to the Constitution.

[36] Hayek, 231–232. The nature of coercion is not changed by the fact that it is used for what the majority demands.

Sanctioned in the turmoil of the defeat in war, the Weimar Constitution introduced more innovations, further undermining the traditional constructs of rights protection. Institutions and groups, and not only individuals, were now granted constitutional protection. The former practice resulted in constitutionally *protected institutions*, while the latter raised the issue of *group rights*.

Article 119 serves as an example of the protection of institutions.

> Marriage, as the foundation of family life and of the preservation and growth of the nation, is under the special protection of the constitution. It rests upon the equal rights of both sexes.
>
> The preservation of the purity and health of the family and its social advancement is the task both of the State and of the local authorities. Families with a large number of children have a right to corresponding provision.
>
> Motherhood has a claim upon the protection and care of the State.

A doctrine like that of Art. 119, especially in the chapter on rights, cannot remain idle, particularly if the constitution is otherwise taken seriously. It is not surprising that in the 1920s, the Germans invented the doctrine of institution protection, replacing or coupling actually exercised civil liberties with a kind of governmental and judicial paternalism. The doctrine holds that the constitution does not so much protect the liberties of concrete individuals but supports freedom as a social value or institution, or perhaps it supports social values and institutions independent of freedom. It is not the individual who has the right to determine his marital status, that is, to marry or divorce; it is the family, the stability of marriage that is protected. Similarly, it is not the expression of individual opinions that is surrounded by a protective wall but freedom of the press. The institutional protection of press freedom often occurs at the expense of the expression of individual opinions. For example, to ensure continued circulation (an institutional value), the right of citizens to reply to the press is curtailed or the press is exempted to pay punitive damages for libel.

The furtherance of social rights can be taken as the accommodation of state-socialist criticism with the tradition of negative fundamental rights. These critics asked: What can one do with the right to education and self-realization if one has no money to pay the school fees? What is freedom of the press worth if only the wealthy have money to print papers? What of the freedom of speech if television only broadcasts what can be advertised?

The Soviet–Russian Constitution of 1918 and the decrees realizing the Soviet concept of social justice–in the name of actual implementation and "the real exercise of rights"–restricted freedom of the press. Supplying and subsidizing paper for printing became a state monopoly so that workers could indeed buy newspapers but only these serving communist propaganda purposes. The papers were fully subsidized, making *Pravda* (Truth) accessible to all and Pravda *only*. Once the publishing companies were all nationalized, the state could decide what could be published and what had to be left out. Under such circumstances there was no need for formal censorship. No doubt in a capitalist society, too, the proprietor or the editor representing the proprietor's wishes may influence what is to be aired or what is to go into print. In state socialism, however, the "furtherance" of rights by the state ensured that purely political views dominated internal censorship. Private proprietory self-censorship extends to only a few papers or television channels, but opinions can compete even in media oligopolies. In state socialism one central will prevailed over the whole of the press, printed and electronic.

The welfare states–partly to answer the challenge of socialist economic rights–accepted the challenge presented by welfare rights. They undertook the provision of services furthering rights and, in some cases, "constitutionalized" them. In the absence of appropriate countermeasures, this brings with it the dangers presented by the socialist concept of law. If it is the state's responsibility to further the "genuine exercise" of rights–together with material services–it has to impose new public burdens. Further, the government's desire to be the one who determines how to exercise individual rights grows. Fortunately, this is not the only open road. Enhancing press freedom does not only mean state-supported programs of subvention. It can be furthered by a negative regulatory approach, namely, by the dismantling of media monopolies. The implementation of the concept of impartial editing and the fairness doctrine, or fair access rights in political election campaigns, may also contribute to satisfying the public function of a free press.

Requirements of contemporary equality further increase the state's social responsibilities. The liberal views of the last century and even in the Weimar Constitution gave a narrow interpretation of the equality clause in constitutions. Legislatures and courts considered equality to mean "equality before the law" only, that is, equality in the administration of justice and the formal application of the law. Nineteenth-century constitutional texts and their later copies–probably because of the increased importance of democratic legitimization of government–are interpreted today as meaning that the legislature cannot differentiate between individuals or citizens with respect to most of the fundamental rights.[37]

The "tradition" of social rights was carried on after World War II in the Italian Constitution, written with the participation of the Socialist and Communist parties, and in the Preamble of the French Constitution of 1946 (now part of the current Constitution). The Universal Declaration of Human Rights of 1948 was written in a similar spirit. Article 22 proclaims that everyone has the right to social security, to exercise economic, social, and cultural rights; for the free development of their human dignity and personality; to employment; to just and favorable remuneration; and a paid holiday.[38] What is more, it holds that everyone has a right to a standard of living "adequate for the health and well-being of himself and of his family," to social and unemployment benefits, to health care, and to a pension. All these socioeconomic and welfare rights significantly differ from traditional human or fundamental rights. On the other hand, their universality is questionable because some of them expressly refer to special status (employees) or because they are conditional upon the resources of one's respective State. Besides being relative, vagueness is also a characteristic of socioeconomic rights. For instance, who are recipients and who are the obliged? Or, what is the legal nature of these rights?

With some of the employment rights we can safely assume the employer will be the obliged party. But it is unclear whether social security funds are to be maintained solely from the employers' contributions,

[37] See the new interpretation of the Belgian Constitution. The German concept of constitutional rights comes to the same conclusion, though the starting point is different. As everyone is entitled to human dignity and people are entitled to fundamental rights *because* of human dignity, any discrimination with regard to fundamental rights is unconstitutional.

[38] "Everyone, as a member of society, has the right to social security and is entitled to realization through national effort and international co-operation and in accordance with the organization and resources of each State, of the economic, social and cultural rights indispensable for his dignity and the free development of his personality." Art. 22 of the Universal Declaration of Human Rights.

whether the employees should pay, or whether the state should be contributing from tax revenues. And should it be doing this as a state service, or is it enough to decree by law what kind of institutions should function? Further, while with other rights the individual rights-holder–the subject of the law–was known and the individual could turn to the court if his right was violated, with minimum welfare standards it all becomes rather uncertain.

In welfare-state constitutions (other than those of the state-socialists), in most cases social rights, as opposed to classical civil and political rights, are recognized at a lower level. Besides the theoretical and historical reasons, there is also a practical reason as to why this is so. Some welfare rights are very expensive while not being universal, that is, they are more biased and do not necessarily favor the political winners. Prevailing doctrines do not place these rights in the same class with classical rights enforceable in court; they are more like state objectives and responsibilities. The careful language used, from the Weimar Constitution to the current Spanish one, follows this categorization. Social rights correspond to the state's undoubted constitutional responsibilities, but its activist duties are nonjusticiable. The individual cannot sue if his or her social rights are not fully realized. At most it is a constitutional omission if no legislation whatsoever is written to enforce a state task, but the legislature's efficiency cannot be examined once the government implements the state task. From a different point of view, the state's activity is constitutionally justified if it passes laws with regard to social rights and if it spends money to satisfy social needs.

Rather boggy ground. The cult of social and cultural rights strengthened all over the world, not only courtesy of socialist propaganda but for inherent reasons of capitalism, too. The changes in internal power relationships and the pressure from social-democratic solidarity resulted in concessions in market economies worldwide. However, it is of dubious intellectual value to treat these rights as fundamental constitutional rights. At least partly for this reason, the social and cultural fundamental rights are missing from the German Basic Law, although it declares Germany to be a "social state." The text of the Basic Law–but not the legal practice around it–protects property only partially and expressly permits the socialization of branches of industry. Even the Netherlands and Sweden–model welfare states–omitted the constitutionalization of welfare services. Naturally, the greater the threat that these benefits will cease, the more important the constitutional declaration of these rights is to those who are in danger of losing them.

8.3. WHAT DO FUNDAMENTAL RIGHTS IMPLY?

8.3.1. State Power Bound

Once revolutionary constitution making turned to the foundations of natural law, the readers and users of constitutions faced these questions: What follows from individuals having constitutional rights? And what does this imply? In the case of classical negative rights, constitutional protection does not mean so much that individuals have the right to do this or that. After all, if freedom is the starting point, if liberty is of primary importance, the state simply has no grounds to do certain things that would destroy the opportunities for action that constitute freedom.

If the starting point of a constitutional government is the citizens' freedom, they should preserve their freedom in the state. As some of the constitutions of the states liberated from paternalistic oppression declare, *everything is allowed that is not prohibited.* The state can only regulate, restrict, or prohibit what in itself does not harm anyone and only if it is specifically authorized.

In connection with the French Declaration of 1789, following Siéyes's suggestions, it was accepted that political community under a constitutional state did not mean the restriction of freedom under a social contract; rather, natural liberties were *retained* and were indeed thought to become complete in legal relationships.

The objective of constitutional rights is to restrict government power. The First Amendment does not say that the individual is entitled to freedom of speech and religion. Most Americans took this for granted. What was left in need of clarification is what this freedom meant for government. The First Amendment gave clear instructions: Congress cannot pass laws abridging the freedom of speech or of the press; prohibiting the free exercise of religion; neither can it establish religion.

The lists of rights keep changing, and the consequences of being listed keep changing, too. But by accepting that the constitution is a provision of law from which obligations are derived, that is, it is a document of normative force, rights incorporated in the constitution become *normative* in character in a rule-of-law system.

Fundamental rights bind the state, but what does the state's obligation mean? All this brings us to the core of the *direct protection* of the rights incorporated into the constitution and to the question of direct legal effect. The incorporation of fundamental rights or human rights into the constitution means at least that the state is bound by it. It is bound not to violate these rights. But is the state also bound to enforce these rights against other rights and interests, too? To a certain extent the state has to guarantee the enforcement of the rights connected with freedom. In this respect, fundamental rights are more than mere constitutionally recognized liberties giving one the chance to act. But what does this state guarantee mean? Does the individual have a right to compensation if his or her constitutional rights are violated but no further law specified these rights? Is there further compensation if these rights were violated by an organ or individual acting in the name of the state? And what if it is infringed by a private individual? Even in the United States where ordinary judges read the Constitution with perseverance, it took a long time for the Constitution to become the legal basis for damages for constitutional torts. The interpretation of Continental constitutions, for example, the Hungarian one, does not allow direct compensation or redress in civil cases (torts) on the basis of the constitution if someone else's fundamental right is violated by an activity that is not otherwise prohibited.[39]

8.3.2. The Effect of Fundamental Rights on Nongovernmental Relationships

The constitution prohibits the state from involving itself in certain relations protected by fundamental rights and liberties. Further, when the

[39] As an exceptional ruling, the German Constitutional Court institutionalized a form of monetary compensation not found in the Civil Code for the protection of personal rights–indeed it was excluded by the code. The ex-wife of the Shah of Iran, Princess Soraya, was granted compensation for nonpecuniary damages in relation to a defamatory article. The principle of direct applicability of the constitution (for damages) has not been invoked ever since (34 BVerfGE 269 (1973)).

state attempts to restrict rights–if the restriction of a fundamental right is permitted by the constitution–it can only follow prescribed procedures.

It is hard to imagine certain rights without state involvement. Though constitutions usually refrain from mentioning that the state has police powers–going back to preconstitutional times–democratic legitimization could make these powers recognized by referring to the principle that the legislature expresses the sovereign will of the people. But is the state *obliged* to go as far as prescribing or creating such social circumstances that help to really enforce rights and liberties? Is it a violation of the constitution if an individual deprives another individual of his liberty by holding him in captivity and it is *not* punished? Does the state have to provide a service, the expectation of which was created by a fundamental right? And is it the state's *constitutional* obligation to guarantee legal redress when fundamental rights are violated by citizens, or to prevent the violation of rights? If this is so, an article violating a person's honor, or the whole newspaper, would have to be confiscated before it ever hit the streets.

The answers to these depend on the perception of the constitutional mandate of the government and, also, on the role of the state in providing services for the society and the economy. At the beginning of the nineteenth century, in the formative decades of market economies in the more advanced countries, it was necessary to restrict the powers of government that handed out and strove to maintain privileges and monopolies. Constitutions written in this period clearly opposed excessive state interference, especially by the defeated executive power, in economic affairs and private life.

Today the U.S. Supreme Court maintains that government has no obligations pertaining to active protection of rights. "[N]othing in the language of the Due Process Clause itself requires the State to protect the life, liberty and property of its citizens against invasion by private actors."[40]

[40] *DeShaney v. Winnebag County Department of Social Services*, 489 U.S. 189, 195 (1989). In this case, the Department of Social Services took certain measures when it learned that a father was brutally abusing his child, but it did not initiate proceedings to divest the father of his parental rights. The child suffered brain damage because of the abuse. The mother filed charges against the state for failing to protect the child's life. The issue here was not the existence or validity of the legislation but the sufficiency of these measures and whether the state had a constitutional *obligation*.

There are, however, different patterns of development. In countries where the state historically did take a more active economic role than in the United States, society is a lame duck without the state's services. This will determine the state's constitutional role. The state will have an active role in protecting and furthering rights. It is obliged to protect rights irrespective of who is threatening their infringement. This precept is not satisfied if governmental bodies fail to provide protection against violations of rights.[41] In an effort to protect the right to life of the fetus, he German Constitutional Court went as far as to declare that the state must protect the right to life by criminal measures. In the abortion case of 1975, even the dissenting justices argued merely on the appropriateness of criminal law protection. They agreed, however, that the legislature and governmental social services should take measures to protect the fundamental right to life.

After 1989, the Eastern European countries did not wish to eliminate the state's influential role–in the short run there was no source that could have provided a substitute for state services. As a typical case, Article 8 (1) of the Hungarian Constitution declares that the protection of fundamental rights is the primary obligation of the state. The state's rights-protection "services" were preserved as constitutional requirements in most cases.

The rights protective role of the state is a matter of degree. How far reaching is the impact of fundamental rights on government and, in particular, is the state obliged to guarantee fundamental rights in private relationships? Does the constitution penetrate private (civil law) relationships?

Classical liberal constitutions were based on the assumption that the constitution should be enforced against the state, that is, the constitution should be observed by the state only, and the constitution was irrelevant in *private relations*. This concept of a Chinese wall between the public and the private was supported by the traditional, Continental separation of the branches of law. The Continental doctrine held that the world of private autonomy was characterized by the fact that only specific civil-

[41] In Germany, the state's obligation to protect rights (to protect the right to life and dignity) was declared, for instance, in connection with the safety of nuclear power stations and chemical weapons, but up till now, the Constitutional Court has found appropriate whatever level of protection the German legislature grants.

law rules could apply to it; otherwise it was in the area of free individual choice. Due, among others, to the growing influence of the German Constitutional Court, which considers the Basic Law as an expression of objective values, by today it has been increasingly recognized that to extend the impact of the supremacy of the constitution in the legal system, constitutional values have to be enforced in civil relations, too.

If we acknowledge that the legislature and the state have constitutional obligations in fundamental-rights protection, fundamental rights and constitutional values have to be enforced in civil relations, too. This implies direct effects through the appropriate civil law legislation channels (for example, voiding unconstitutional, private discriminatory agreements) and the appropriate judicial application of the constitution in private matters.

All this results in a new set of difficulties that at a certain point may endanger the constitutionally protected liberties as shown in the example below. Does the employer who refuses to hire an individual because of his political beliefs violate the right to equality in (nondiscrimination for) political beliefs as a fundamental right of the constitution? And is the government justified in not employing an individual on the grounds of his political beliefs? Is it constitutional to refuse to employ a teacher who criticizes the political system or the legislature or who belongs to a group that disputes the principles of the constitution? [42] Can a citizen be excluded from public employment on the grounds of belonging to a formerly legal association–as the laws on political screening (*lustration*) would require?[43] Let us now return to the private employer who refuses

[42] In the 1970s, Ms. Glasenapp, a secondary school teacher and a West German civil servant, was dismissed because she supported the local Communist Party's plan to build a nursery. The Strasbourg Court found–opposing the Committee's 10-to-9 vote–that the dismissal was not discrimination on the grounds of opinion because no one restricted Glasenapp from expressing her views. Public employment was a different matter and not an area for the free expression of one's opinion. *Glasenapp*, Ser. A 104 (1986).

[43] The law on *lustration* in the Czech Republic limited access to public positions and offices of those who collaborated with the organs of oppression of the "previous regime."

In Germany, after 1945 the rights of Nazi Party members were collectively restricted. The Basic Law excluded these restrictions from the scope of judicial review. It declares that the constitutionality of the rules passed by the Military Administration before the enactment of the Constitution cannot be reviewed. The exclusion of former *Stasi* agents from public employment after the unification of Germany, in 1990, was not to hire an individual because of the applicant's opinions and beliefs. The grounds for nonemployment may be that the employee's extreme opinions will frighten away prospective customers. On a slightly different ground: Why should the employer have to look at a person all day whose face he does not like? The proprietor may think it is part of his property right to enjoy his property as he wishes.

Today, in many rule-of-law states individuals cannot be discriminated against because of their natural characteristic features (race, gender, sexual orientation, age, or disability). Discrimination on the grounds of a lack of ability to carry out a task is not considered unconstitutional discrimination. If the grounds for discrimination are personal views or private membership, the case is not so straightforward, as constitutional protection in this regard keeps changing. In the most intimate relationships, however, there is an undeniable "freedom" to discriminate. At home anyone can be a racist and keep from their home whomever they despise; when setting up a family it is not discrimination to pick and choose from among the lovely candidates or to follow a race bias, though revolutionary equality perhaps strives for justice in this area, too.[44]

The Hungarian Constitution elevates equality to the rank of a superlaw or a major principle penetrating all laws. [45] According to Article 70/A, it is the state's constitutional responsibility to enforce nondiscrimination.

> (1) The Republic of Hungary guarantees for all persons in its territory human and civil rights without discrimination on account of race, color, sex, language,

---

characterized as imposing punishment for membership in a political group but for the act of "denouncing" people to the police.

[44] "Man was born to live in independence. All men should have good wives, healthy and strong offspring: there is no need for the rich and the poor." Saint-Just, *L'Esprit de la Révolution suivi de Fragments sur les Institutions Républicaines* (Paris: Union Générale d'Éditions, 1963), 12.

For a modern example of radical egalitarianism resulting, at least potentially, in constitutional scrutiny of private relations, see Art. 70/A of the Hungarian postcommunist Constitution.

[45] The result–if anyone takes the provision seriously–is a system of equality outbidding all fundamental rights, a kind of Jacobin tyranny of antidiscrimination. The major offense in all walks of life, including private life, too, turns out to be discrimination against others on the basis of their protected qualities through the exercise of our rights.

religion, political or other views, national or social origins, ownership of assets, birth or on any other grounds.
(2) Any discrimination falling within paragraph (1) against persons is strictly punishable by law.

How is the differentiation in employment to be assessed in terms of the Hungarian Constitution? The abundance of human and citizen's rights makes it difficult to find an area in private life where there are no fundamental rights. Can a woman divorce her husband if he becomes disabled? Isn't this discrimination on grounds of personal capacity related to the exercise of a fundamental right (the right to free choice in family matters)?

8.4. WHEN FUNDAMENTAL RIGHTS MAY BE RESTRICTED: RECONCILING THE STATE WITH FREEDOM IN CONSTITUTIONALISM

8.4.1. Limiting Fundamental Rights

Blackstone held that civil liberties were the same as natural freedom, but only to the extent they are restricted by human laws and are necessary and useful for the general advantage of the community.[46] Freedom, then, is subject to limits–though only to the extent necessary for the sake of the community. The standpoint explained in the language of natural law expresses the characteristically positivist approach of the practicing lawyer. Legal regulation does not guarantee preexisting rights but is concerned with stipulating obligations and, eventually, with restricting certain human actions. Rights, at best, are created by the grace of state regulation. This is quite understandable in the Blackstonian world where all institutions (including property rights) are created by the state or humans and are formed by tradition and judges.

The possibility that rights can be restricted was not refuted by the revolutionary human-rights declarations that advocated the primacy of rights. Classical constitutionalism attempts to reconcile the need to live

[46] Sir William Blackstone, *Commentaries on the Laws of England*, vol. 1 (Chicago: Chicago University Press, 1979), 125.

under government so as to achieve social peace with freedom. During the positive enactment in the late eighteenth century of revolutionary natural law, that is, its recognition and incorporation into the constitutions, the requirements for social order and peace were not considered with the same weight as in Blackstone's positivist theory. It was only admitted with reluctance that it is possible to disregard the enforcement of fundamental human rights on the grounds of some public interest. This reluctance is surprising. After all, the possibility of such recognition, at least in a Rousseauian democracy, is preestablished: here participation in the political process enabled everyone to enforce their will to let the "real" advantage of the community dominate.[47] If it is in the public will, human rights do not make a difference. But isn't there a happy constitutional middle ground between the absolutism of human rights and the demands of state and community regulations?

Article 2 of the French Declaration of 1789 declares liberty, property, security, and resistance to oppression as imprescriptible and natural human rights. To be "imprescriptible and natural," however, does not mean to be "exempt of restriction." Characteristically the Declaration discusses in some details how these rights can be limited.[48]

According to Sieyés, the exercise of natural rights can be restricted only if we want to guarantee the exercise of the same rights for others and not because of some internal or inherent obligation. Further, restrictions should be prescribed by law.

This–similarly to the American approach–captures the essence of the relationship of constitutionalism and fundamental rights (though it does not by far give the only possible solution). Constitutionalism tells us the extent to which rights recognized as fundamental may be restricted. Conversely, this indicates the extent to which these rights restrict the powers comprising the state. In this formula there are two variables that

[47] Although, admittedly, people's decisions are not egotistic most of the time, and they may be guided by charity, solidarity, and moral demands, and indeed from time to time they are ready to make personal sacrifices, it is quite right to ask: Why should people (who make decisions by voting) be concerned with the public good if it holds nothing positive for them?

[48] The regulatory problem is this: What should we do with the rights that are taken for granted? Constitutions–as starting points–recognize fundamental rights, but if they are so supreme–trumps, as Dworkin would say–then it is necessary to decide when it is allowed to play a trump and whether bigger trumps are played at all.

on their face depend on the state and the constituent power. (1) There are fundamental rights limiting government, but it depends to a large extent on the constituent's decision which rights have this capacity. (2) The extent to which the legislature is limited in restricting a right is also a matter of governmental choice.

In reality, social values and claims in a constitutional system (both during the constitution-making process and later when the constitution is interpreted and implemented) significantly determine the extent of rights. The principles of constitutionalism also delimit to what extent it is possible to disregard those restrictions on state action that would follow from the logic of rights.

The constitutional state inherited one of the functions of its absolutist legal predecessor, namely, the *regulatory power of the government to serve the public interest and maintin public peace*, that is, the police powers, which enable the law to penetrate the realm of freedom. At most, there might be content-based restrictions to prevent penetration, if freedom is to be protected as a fundamental right. Once regulation is extended in the welfare state, the content of negative rights becomes insufficient to check police powers. Once there are no limits to criminalization, using freedom as an argument does not help if somebody is criminally prosecuted. At this stage it is necessary to determine the concrete boundaries of increasing state intervention that no longer has to respect private spheres of action.

But determining such limits is never finished. While it is possible to agree on the fundamental rights, fundamental liberties and values, and on the principle that everyone is equally entitled to them, the statutory consequences are often rejected by the majority. Freedom of speech is little disputed in societies supporting rational cognition; but that pornography should be permissible on this basis is unacceptable to many.

The constitution, when determining the content of rights, keeps in mind that its primary responsibility is to maintain the state's ability to function. The state's activities are dictated by the need to ensure social peace.[49] The state has to provide services in the course of which it has to meet certain conditions of efficiency. For similar reasons, fundamental rights cannot receive absolute protection, even though the logic of human rights would dictate such. Social peace, including international se-

[49] As noted in Chapter 1, constitutionalism and state institutions presuppose a prior homogeneity and provide a minimum certainty of existence for everyone.

curity, which strongly supports the *raison d'État*, has to be enforced by the constitutional order to the detriment of freedom.

Even if freedom is protected to the furthest possible extent, there is a constant tension between freedom and the public order as produced by government. Excessive human-rights obligations and their inclusion in the constitution may in the end endanger the stability of the entire political system. Constitutionalism searches for ways to protect rights that do not endanger the preconditions of their own existence. Classically this is demonstrated in the dilemma of how much tolerance the government will exercise in front of intolerant enemies of the constitutional order using their fundamental rights to threaten the state. It is much too simple an answer to say that the tolerance protecting the rights of the individuals attacking the regime goes far beyond what would be necessary. The restrictions of rights introduced to protect the regime may undermine constitutionalism just like the "democratic successes" of the enemies of the constitutional system do.

8.4.2. The Limits to Limiting Rights

It would follow from the supremacy of the legislature that the legislator may do anything. But constitutional systems, with regard to the rules connected to fundamental rights, impose limits on the legislator's freedom. These limits derive mostly from the conditions of the rule of law (state organs act in keeping with legal prescriptions). However, while in a rule-of-law state these principles were primarily applied in connection with governmental activity (mostly for specific acts and not in the making of laws), the constitutional system enforces these principles against the legislature, too.

Only some of these restrictions can be found in constitutions, and the ones that are not included have been introduced in the course of judicial practice. The advantage of the judicial limitation of rights restrictions is that judges can better adapt to current social demands, needs, and difficulties when settling the boundaries of restrictions than the framers of a constitution. Naturally, judicial participation is also the reason for certain disadvantages. The French Declaration of 1789 already included the principle which held that rights could only be restricted by law. This means it is considered the legislature's exclusive privilege, and for good reasons (generality, expertise, professional knowledge, and responsibility).

Modern constitutions often distinguish between recognized fundamental rights on the basis of their restrictability. In particular cases the constitution subjects the restriction or even the legislative regulation of the right to a special procedure (qualified majority or organic law). In theory, certain fundamental rights may be limited only if it is necessary for the exercise of other rights and only if, without setting limits, another individual's rights would be violated.

Sometimes the constitution indicates general interests or values that have to be protected against fundamental rights, too. The seemingly absolute American fundamental right to freedom of speech may also be restricted, if the speech evokes direct threat of a crime or clearly endangers public order. The German Basic Law considers the protection of young people or personal honor as good enough reasons for restricting freedom of speech.

Below is a list of reasons from the German Basic Law (and in other constitutions, too), providing grounds for the restriction of fundamental rights: if the fundamental right is abused or used to help commit a crime; the right to peaceful assembly may be restricted if the assembly is a violation of criminal law or if it is injurious to the constitutional order. (There are constitutional limits to what can be included in the criminal code.) Fundamental rights may be restricted for reasons of state security (for example, the freedom of movement may be restricted to prevent any direct danger threatening the democratic constitutional order). The right to the inviolability of the home may be restricted, among others, to avert danger to the public or an acute threat to public safety, or to protect young persons at risk. Property may be taken in the public interest. Sometimes the restriction of rights has no attached condition, for example, when people assemble in public places.[50]

In Germany, the grounds for rights restriction differed from the usual European practice only in their complexity. The yardstick is the European Human Rights Convention of 1950, which made almost all protected human rights subject to restrictions on the basis of national security, public safety, public health, the protection of morals, the protection of public order, and the prevention of disorder or crime. In cases of emergency, further restrictions were permitted. The right to privacy

[50] The need for the protection of public order led to the introduction of such measures in the Belgian Constitution as early as 1831.

could be restricted in the interest of the economic well-being of the country–this is better left without any comments. To be sure, this *is* the international document that considerably furthered the protection of constitutional rights in European states.

Enforcement without the effective restriction of state and public interests would mean there are no real limits to government, and the fundamental rights would lose their significance. The situation where rights are restricted in the interest of the state, or following the dictates of the *Staatsraison*, is, in theory, not much better than the socialist concept of law, which permitted the exercise of rights only in the interest of workers.

In reality, however, enabling rights restrictions in the name of super-flexible concepts did not become a source of regular abuse of rights in post-World War II Europe. The essential content of fundamental rights and human dignity cannot be restricted, according to the Hungarian and German constitutions.[51]

The democratic exercise of power and the antiauthoritarian social culture, which also influences politicians, encourage society to respect fundamental rights. Because of the judicial control of the constitutionality of laws, the legislature is forced to attribute realistic, nonarbitrary meaning to the limits to which constitutionalism binds the restriction of rights.

The courts may examine the social necessity of rights restrictions. On the grounds of societal necessity they can closely examine whether restrictions are necessary for the *functioning* of a *democratic state*.[52]

A further limit to restrictions of fundamental rights is evoked by the principles of the rule of law delimiting discretionary powers. The restriction of a right has to be *reasonable* and *proportionate*. A particular restriction meets these conditions if the regulation is appropriate for the legislative objective and if the restriction is necessary or essential for the

[51] Most modern constitutions permit further restrictions in cases of emergency and war. The Basic Law contains very few further restrictions in this respect: the time spent in custody without judicial approval increases to four days. In all other respects, in the interest of public peace there are an ample number of rights restrictions allowed as per the generally applicable rules of the Basic Law.

[52] This uncertain approach, though appropriate for control purposes, characterizes the European Court of Human Rights, which, applying the text of the 1950 Convention as a point of departure, examines whether the restriction of rights is necessary in a democratic state. The Canadian Charter of Rights and Freedoms of 1982 contains a similar principle.

realization of this objective (the objective cannot be realized otherwise). In current constitutional legislation it is unclear *which* legislative objectives provide legitimate grounds for restriction.

Acceptability of restrictions may differ in scope. Different levels of restrictions are probably legitimate for the sake of another individual's similar right; another fundamental right; a constitutional obligation; a constitutional aim; the protection of state and public order; or legitimate legislative aims.

On whatever grounds restrictions are introduced, the burden cannot be "excessive." Often the legislator has to prove that the chosen means of restriction are the least dangerous to the protected fundamental right.

8.5. WHAT PURPOSE DO FUNDAMENTAL RIGHTS SERVE IF ABUSED?

Freedom often seems frightening, especially if it is exercised by others. Our own freedom makes us uncertain because of the responsibility it entails. It deprives us of being told what to do. Freedom and the fundamental rights supporting it give rise to aversion, especially in two respects: the freedom of speech and the rights of the accused. Public opinion demonstrates great intolerance, or at least impatience, in these two areas.

The question that often arises is this: Why do *defendants* need so many and such expensive rights? These are what make criminal proceedings so long and costly. Why the numerous formalities? Why should a defendant be let off because of procedural mistakes? Just because he confessed under pressure or because he did not have a lawyer? Why is it necessary to get a court order for every minor thing, like a search warrant or tapping a telephone conversation? This could mean "fatal" delays for the investigation. Why can police inspectors not be trusted? After all, what harm would come to the person whose telephone is tapped? Honest people have nothing to hide. Why should suspects be released, especially when they are suspected of involvement in a serious crime? The worst that can happen is that the suspect did not commit the crime. If proved innocent, he will be released. (Never mind he will have been kept in custody until then.)

People's indifference toward criminal defendants and individuals involved in legal proceedings stems from the belief that nothing like this could ever happen to them; such things happen only to those who are guilty. The individual rights and dignity of the guilty do not inspire sympathy. And there is little difference in the public eye between the accused and the convicted. Of course, this is shortsighted. Historical experience shows that power becomes dangerous and the police may run amok without procedural restrictions. Criminal-investigation authorities enjoy a huge advantage during criminal proceedings. Without obstacles, the investigating authorities may completely change the course of criminal proceedings. If there are no bars to the pressure that can be put on the detainee, he will even admit crimes he has never committed. It is not mere caprice but real psychological experience that requires the person in custody to be brought before a judge within a short period of time following arrest and to see his lawyer or to learn of what he is accused. Without these, the detainee may collapse.[53]

The main objection against freedom of speech and of the press is that these rights protect something that those exercising the right mostly abuse. The papers besmirch people's character, they lie, and distort or conceal the truth. Protecting free speech allows people to shamefully incite others, destroys public morals, shows a bad example to youth, and outrages normal people with immorality. Why should television be allowed to show suffering, arguments, and dissension? Governments–beginning with the makers of the Alien and Sedition Act of 1798 in the United States to the Jacobin censorship institutionalized to protect the French nation–usually argue that "deceitful" announcements undermine their standing and the respect and loyalty they are due, which are badly needed "in these difficult days." They are "subversive" and only show the negative side of events.[54]

[53] Anyone who has seen the film "In the Name of the Father" may remember that the British police managed to get confessions from the detainees because the time they spent in custody was extended to exceed the generally accepted time for human resistance to interrogation. The authorities proceeded on the basis of an antiterrorist law that was later found to be repugnant to the European Human Rights Convention.

[54] The Alien and Sedition Act prohibited false, scandalous, or malicious criticism that would incite dissatisfaction with the government. Congress under President Jefferson did not renew the law (originally directed against Jefferson's party) when it was about to expire and had compensation paid to those who were found guilty of violating the act.

These views are perhaps less compelling when we realize that once the restriction on free speech was enabled, to a certain extent everyone came under pressure because it is impossible to know *which* opinion will be prohibited. If we cannot say what we think, we deprive ourselves of self-expression and self-realization. If we cannot express our mistakes, there will be no possibility for others to correct them, and we will continue to live stubbornly with our misconceptions as will others. Whether there is such a thing as absolute truth, one thing is certain: there is no era in history or a single scientist who possesses all the wisdom on earth, so we can only hope to come nearer to the truth in a free debate. But what does getting nearer the truth count for in political arguments? In politics the truth might be useful, but the most important thing is not the revelation of new, truer rules of policy. But there is simply no democracy without free debate, and the whole constitutional system will collapse without the right to one's opinions and free expression.[55] If there is no debate, the press cannot report opinions–be they ever so offensive–and people cannot make informed political choices. If this be the case, those outside political power will not get the chance to replace those in power by persuading voters. If there is no freedom of speech, there is no public opinion, which acts as a watchdog, controlling and restricting those in power. There would also be no information from which the leaders of the state could glean their knowledge. "[F]reedom of the press…[is] that freedom which is as necessary to governments as it is to people; that freedom, the violation of which, in this respect, is a crime against the state."[56]

[55] In various democracies there are divers degrees of recognition regarding the importance of free speech. Often the protection of public order or the reputation of individuals is given precedence over the protection of free speech. However, political announcements are given increased protection everywhere because of their importance in the functioning of the political system. Even the German Constitutional Court, which considers human dignity as the most important value, is of the opinion that politicians are entitled to less protection than the average citizen when engaged in political discourse.

[56] Benjamin Constant, *Political Writings*, trans and ed. Biancamaria Fontana (Cambridge: Cambridge University Press, 1988), 150. The Supreme Court of the United States stated the role of the press in democracies is so important, as it the driving force of other rights and freedoms, that it has to be protected even from self-censorship. If a newspaper has to pay excessive damages for defamatory falsehood, it will think twice about what it prints the next time, and this leads to self-censorship. Consequently, the court awards compensation for incorrect and offensive reports about political and public personalities only in cases of malice or recklessness.

8.6. HOW PRECISE SHOULD THE DEFINITION BE?

Fundamental rights tend to be declarations of principles rather than legal prescriptions (norms). As they are vague, they need fine-tuning. They are not absolute, partly because they conflict with each other and with other people's similar rights, and partly because they have to be enforced in the government's sphere of operations. Besides the freedom given by rights, we must keep in mind the need to preserve the state and social peace.

As mentioned, the American Constitution and its amendments are narrowly tailored; they simply name the rights without giving them precise content. This may be the consequence of the implied, shared, common legal and political assumptions of the framers and their contemporaries; but it is more likely that this imprecision was necessary so that everyone would accept the text. A general statement can be interpreted in any way one may wish, and with time, one of the interpretations will prevail.

Fundamental rights–for historical reasons, too–are there to restrict government despotism. It is possible to restrict the state if its organs are divided and, following constitutional prescriptions, if they counteract each other to protect rights. One condition is that the right to be protected be adequately defined; another being that the given administration of justice allows an injured party to enforce his rights.

Constitutional rights are specified, refined, and implemented by the legislature. The legislative definition guarantees that the executive power (the public administration), subordinated to the law through binding constitutional prescriptions, observes the constitutional rights. If this does not occur, the courts can force the executive power to do so. In order to bind the state organs, it is best to include in the constitution the prohibition of the most frequent violations and abuses of rights. Also, the most important procedural and content-based conditions that the state must observe may be enumerated.

The clarification of the protection and content of the rights, including the identification of the necessary restrictions, makes the legislature the master of the situation. We have seen the dangers present in such a case: rights are put at parliament's mercy. It is not enough to know only that a specific fundamental right is regulated by the law and can be exercised within its confines. It is possible to say that the meaning of these standards indicates that freedom can only be restricted in a legal procedure; however, this does not offer much security. It needs to be explained what makes these procedures "legal" (for example, by a hearing in court). The manner in which the details are given is also important. Many constitutions refer to a reasonable deadline for a hearing. Whose reason are we talking about here? What a police inspector or the police do within an inconveniently short time frame and with rationally allocated scarce resources might be an irrationally long period of time for a person waiting in custody under humiliating circumstances. It is the rights of the person in custody that are at stake here, so rationality should be discussed from his point of view. A time frame for detention may be unreasonable for the detainee and, at the same time, be irrational for the purposes of the institution as well, because after this period it can be expected that the person in custody will make a false confession implicating himself. The deadline then should at least be determined by using the latter argument as a starting point.

It is a mistake to believe that it would be in the legislature's interest to disregard the basis of its legitimacy, the constitution. The legislature does not function in a vacuum; in view of the moral justification–general acceptability of fundamental rights–government cannot ignore public opinion, which is instrumental in the reelection of politicians.

> [P]olice powers are always restrictions on the liberties of individuals, and the starting-point of our public law is the body of liberties of citizens. The Declaration of the Rights of Man is explicitly or implicitly the frontispiece of republican constitutions, and any controversy of public law must, in order to base itself on general principles, start from the point of view that freedom is the rule, and restriction by police is the exception.[57]

All the legislature has to do (according to the French interpretation) is adequately clarify the application of the law. Beyond this the legislature has some scope for movement, which can be scaled down by the constituent if he finds it too risky. Fundamental rights may be restricted by the legislature on the grounds of *public order*. The extent to which the

[57] Corneille, commissaire du gouvernement, *1917 Conseil d'État*, 10 August 1917, Baldy, Leb. 637.

standards need to be restricted is determined by the condition of the public order and the dangers threatening it.[58]

With room for movement, constitutional values and liberties are constantly in touch with the prevailing social concepts and activities of the day. When constitutions repudiate cruel and unusual, or disproportionate, punishments, they obviously follow the current–changing–social values. The degree of the severity of punishment was different at the beginning of the nineteenth century from the degree considered acceptable today. In 1972, the U.S. Supreme Court concluded that the death penalty was cruel and unusual. Four years later (after some amendments to the pertinent laws regarding enforcement) the Supreme Court succumbed to the prevailing social opinion.[59]

It would follow that rights in the constitution are only words at the mercy of interpretation. The traditions behind the words adapt to the

[58] In 1981, French legislators were of the opinion that the need to protect individuals, given escalating terrorist activity, required the police to step up a campaign against these criminals, and as a result, the police needed to be granted the right to keep anyone in custody for six hours to verify his or her identity. The Constitutional Council accepted this argument, but it added that the phrase of the act "custody until identity is established" means–in view of liberty being the main rule and police restraint being the exception–that all proofs of identity have to be accepted and that the public prosecutor could be notified at any time during the period the person is in custody. When the socialists came to power, in 1983, the legislature reinterpreted the right of personal freedom in the following way: custody may be applied only if persons or property are directly endangered. Since then, every time the political Right and the Left have changed places, the custody powers of the police are enlarged or narrowed. In other words, the purview of the right keeps changing. But never has the individual's personal freedom been threatened. Fundamental freedom, then, is not absolute, yet it delimits an area of movement within which the current majority will is prevalent.

The boundaries of this area depend partly on the text of the constitution and partly on prevailing public opinion. In 1981, it did not even occur to the staunch right-wing supporters of the "law and order" movement that a person could be kept in custody, for example, for identification purposes, and for twenty-four hours.

[59] As there is "room for movement," various concepts on the prevalence of individual liberties can exist side-by-side, and people can live in worlds with different value systems not necessarily communicating with one another. When the German Constitutional Court ruled that abortion was criminal, it also acknowledged a woman's rights over her body, and the possibility of abortion on the grounds of social conditions was recognized. So if a doctor decided on a pregnant woman's request that the said social conditions existed, there would be nothing preventing the abortion. It is a completely different matter if the legislature specifies objective social indicators.

circumstances in a thousand ingenious ways. We should hold no illusions: constitutions are enforced by men and not machines programmed following the algorithm of the inscrutable will of the legislature. Perhaps this is the only way to ensure that the constitution does not descend upon the public as an alien power. Although constitutional values and concepts are subject to changing and flexible interpretations, they do have a core meaning that we need to insist on if we want the words and the law to convey some sort of meaning. Maybe all orders and all concepts are like Peer Gynt's onion; we can keep peeling off the layers until we reach the center and find nothing there. Constitutionalism, however, requires us to believe that there is a core. This belief does not ban peeling off the layers and does not demand us to proclaim human rights absolute and immutable.

Fundamental rights are the most efficient where they are expressed as specific commands, binding all governmental entities, like the one that prescribes within how many hours a person arrested should be taken before a judge. While it is hard to dispute what amounts to twenty-four hours, it is a matter of judgment (sometimes hysterical) what can be considered a "fair" criminal trial and, from the point of view of "public safety," to what extent this can be restricted. The right in this case will be protected primarily by procedural provisions in the constitution (qualified majority, multiple readings of bills, and the like) and dogmatic judicial control. If the constitution proclaims that torture is prohibited and adds that this means the causing of any bodily pain, the position is clearer and the level of protection is increased. But whether the constitution says this outright or not, "fairness" in criminal proceedings would dictate the same interpretation as, for instance, concluding that depriving a diabetic of insulin is unacceptable and falls under torture.

The definition of fundamental rights has far-reaching consequences. Is it enough to name the right and recognize it? ("Freedom of religion and speech are recognized.") Or can the person only feel safe if the definition is more precise? Are there any disadvantages to being specific?

Let us consider, for example, the rights regarding religion. The simplest definition would say "all persuasions of faith are free." Strictly speaking this means that the state cannot persecute anybody because of their religious beliefs or lack thereof. The sanctioning of cult activities is not, however, clear. The Russian socialist constitution of 1918 recognized freedom of religion. But this principle strove to ensure for the workers the "true" freedom of conscience. To accomplish this, it separated the state from the Church and guaranteed every individual the right of religious and antireligious propaganda. There was no mention of the freedom of *worship* (free exercise). This, of course, was no mere coincidence.

Even in nonsocialist states there is a lot of confusion surrounding statements like "freedom of religion" and the "separation-of-Church-and-state" model was pronounced to be a "vague" precept at best by Justice Burger.[60] The combination of "freedom of religion" and the separation doctrine cause endless intellectual conflicts. May a congregation build a church on the basis of the freedom of belief? More precisely, can the law prohibit this? How are construction and engineering related to belief? If the freedom of exercise is absolute, on what terms do urban planning regulations apply to churches? And what does "exercise" mean beyond religious services being conducted according to the prescriptions of faith and the establishment of conditions of worship? Is the maintenance of denominational schools part of "exercise"? And the maintenance of hospitals? To what extent should general professional rules and controls be enforced in denominational institutions such as these? And if denominations in general are not entitled to the right of maintaining hospitals, is the denomination that regards healing or support to the needy as part of its religious life entitled to this right? And if the state functions separately from the Church, should the state undertake by law, or in its absence, to pay the social-security contributions of all ecclesiastical employees (the current Hungarian practice) and perhaps their remuneration, too (which puts the Church at the mercy of the state)? In both cases atheists pay for the free exercise of religion of others in the form of public contributions.

Speaking of employees, what constitutes ecclesiastical employment? Is an employment matter relating to an ecclesiastical employee an internal affair of the Church? Can the janitor at Desert Gymnasium, which is open to the public but operated by the Mormon Church, be dismissed if he is not a member of the Church?[61] Isn't this discrimination on religions grounds? And if, as the Hungarian Constitution says, an individual cannot be discriminated against because of his sexual inclination, can a priest be dis-

[60] *Lemon v. Kurtzman*, 403 U.S. 602 (1971).

[61] *Corporation of the Presiding Bishop of the Church of Jesus Christ of Latter-Day Saints v. Amos*, 483 U.S. 327 (1986). The Supreme Court found the position of the Mormon Church constitutional.

missed if his sexual inclination–contradicting an article of faith or a canonical rule–renders him unfit for his office? (Not being able to exercise his clerical function is not the same as the termination of employment, and the violation of a Church rule does not mean the violation of a statutory law.) If the Church's regulations correspond to the organizational rules of a private employer, this would be a violation of the constitutional "background agreement" of the legal relationship. As long as the constitution's antidiscriminatory prescriptions apply to "private" organizational schemes, the constitutional examination of the beliefs and tenets of a church are inevitable. Such review, however, is hardly compatible with the concept of freedom of religion and with the prevailing interpretations of the separation of the state and the Church, because it requires the review of internal Church doctrine by secular authorities. Further, can the legislature interfere in issues of Church organization required by worship, just as the government has the right to subject all human organizations to general rules?

To what extent is "exercise" admissible in civilian life and in government activities? Should citizens be barred from state office because they refuse to take a specific oath? Is it at all possible to specify membership or nonmembership in a denomination as a condition of employment in a state (or other) office? May anyone be barred from taking a state office on the grounds that the responsibilities and duties of the office are contrary to the prescriptions of a specific religion? (For example, in the U.S., to comply with the prescriptions on military uniforms, it was held constitutional to prohibit Orthodox Jews from wearing their skull *yarmulke* caps. In Canada, however, Sikhs may wear their turbans.)

These are not merely theoretical questions. There have been and there are currently serious ongoing debates concerning the relationship of the state and the Church. The Belgian Constitution–which mentions the freedom of opinion in the same sentence with the freedom of religion–devoted a separate paragraph (Art. 15) to the principle that no one can be compelled to take part in any religious ceremony. Article 16, on the other hand, protects the autonomy of churches against the Belgian state, prohibiting the state from intervening in the appointment of priests.[62] If such

[62] The Belgian Constitution of 1831 also declared that priests could not be prohibited from corresponding with their higher authorities or publishing their reports. This special rule was obviously made in deference to Catholics. Normally this right would have followed naturally from the paragraph on freedom of the press and correspondence. Bad previous experiences prompted detailed and redundant rules.

specific provisions were thought necessary, this means they obviously did not follow from the principle of freedom of religion. But rights may lead, or allow to be led, to opposite conclusions. The Mexican Constitution of 1917 also guaranteed the freedom to choose one's religion and the freedom to worship (in public places of worship or at home, Art. 24). It prohibited the Mexican Congress from passing any law establishing or banning a religion. But the freedom of religion coupled with "separation" incorporated a long list (Art. 130), enumerating the rights of the state as *opposed* to the Church and what the Church *could not* do.[63]

Meaning is not trivial. Rights lack and do not offer guidance. Constitutionalizing rights cures these shortcomings.

[63] On this basis it is the federal states that decide how many priests each church can have in a specific area, depending on the demand. The restrictions on churches have been eased in the past decade.

The Weimar Constitution, like the Mexican one, discussed in detail the meaning of freedom of conscience and belief and found it necessary to declare the opposite of all that was included in its contemporary, the Mexican Constitution.